EARLY CHINESE CIVILIZATION:
ANTHROPOLOGICAL PERSPECTIVES

Harvard-Yenching Institute Monograph Series Volume 23

Early Chinese Civilization: Anthropological Perspectives

K. C. Chang

HARVARD UNIVERSITY PRESS
Cambridge, Massachusetts, and London, England

Printed in the United States of America
Second printing 1978

Library of Congress Cataloging in Publication Data

Chang, Kwang-chih.
Early Chinese civilization.

(Harvard-Yenching Institute monograph series; v. 23)
Bibliography: p.
Includes index.
CONTENTS: The beginnings of agriculture in the Far East.—China toward urban life.—Urbanism and the king in ancient China. [etc.]
1. China—Civilization. I. Title. II. Series: Harvard-Yenching Institute. Monograph series; v. 23.
DS723.C38 931 75-14094
ISBN O-674-21999-6

Preface

That the conquest of the last contending state by the Ch'in Dynasty in the year 221 BC is used to mark the close of the "ancient" period of Chinese history should provoke few protestations. After all, words such as "ancient" and "modern" can only be used arbitrarily and flexibly to designate the differently demarcated segments of Chinese history under different schemes of periodization. But the Chinese history prior to Ch'in forms a prefatory unit to the rest of the Chinese history in a very real sense. By "ancient history of China" one may refer to one of two things: the history of Chinese civilization during the ancient period (assuming an essential continuity from a precedent, formative foundation to the traditional China as epitomized by Ch'in and Han), and the history of the Chinese geographic space, including the various local and regional cultural traditions that came to be unified politically under the banner of Ch'in Shih Huang. Realistically the Ch'in unification marks the end of "ancient" China by ending the historical bifurcation discussed above. Before, the ancient Chinese were but one of the local peoples of China. After, the Chinese were to become the people of China.

The papers collected here have to do only with the Chinese component of ancient China. This includes the Shang and Chou civilizations and the various prehistoric cultures that, in our best judgment, provided the foundation of Shang and Chou. There are a number of reasons for singling out the Chinese from among all other peoples of the Far East for study. They were the only literate people in the Far East in the ancient period, and for many of the studies literary texts are indispensable. Also, it is a fact that ancient Chinese history is at the base of all Far Eastern history, so that in order to understand the roots of events in any period one ought to be acquainted with what happened in ancient China.

As an anthropologist (or an anthropological archaeologist) by profession, my studies may be regarded as being somewhat offbeat. I remember after I proposed some new interpretations of the Shang genealogy in a Chinese paper in 1963, a Chinese scholar (and a former teacher of mine!) wrote a bitter piece denouncing it, and one of the things that apparently aroused his ire was the fact that I encroached upon the *yen-chiu fan-wei,* or "research sphere," of ancient historians and other more appropriate specialists. Whose "research sphere" is the study of ancient China? Allow me to quote myself:

The object of scholarly research and the scholarly discipline devoted to its study should, in theory, be at one in scope and fit, but, in actuality, they are often in conflict. The reason is that their relative positions of predominance and subordination are, in the world of scholarship, often the reverse of what they are in reality. The object of research should have predominance, whereas the scholarly discipline devoted to its study should be subordinate in regard to the scope, methodology, and emphasis of study. But when scholars have engaged in scholarly work for a long time, they sometimes mistake their own work for the center of things and perhaps unknowingly ask that the real world conform to the traditions and the habits of their own disciplines. . . .

Ancient Chinese history is the history of the ancient Chinese. Its object of study is the ancient people themselves; its techniques are the collection of the relevant data in all aspects—antiquities, writings, legends, myths, and so forth—and the analysis, interpretation, and synthesis of that data. But the actual situation often is not like this at all. Historians discuss Yao, Shun, the Three Dynasties, and the classical texts. Archaeologists talk about Peking Man, Yang-shao, Lung-shan, the Yin Ruins. Among palaeographers there are those who specialize in oracle bone inscriptions, and those who concentrate on bronze inscriptions. It is the same *Book of Poetry*, but the language aspect is given to the philologist, the artistic part to the literary historian, and the institutions to the cultural and social historian. Deep troughs often exist between different disciplines, and ancient Chinese history consequently is cut into fragments. It is as though the history of the ancient Chinese should serve the various scholars who study it, instead of having the scholars serve the history. . . . A basic remedial approach must be made during the training of future scholars. It is important that to them, unlike to us, the ancient history of China be the Master, and the scholarly disciplines that study it, the servants. (K. C. Chang et al. 1973:i; liberally translated)

From this point of view, my own training ill-equipped me for my task. My immediate task may be regarded as an attempt to discover aspects of the historical reality of ancient China to the end of the Chou period, but my training in college and graduate school did not include some of the most crucial theoretical apparatus and empirical knowledge necessary to complete the task. A little autobiographical digression should not be out of place here.

I was born in Peking in 1931, the year the Japanese invaded Manchuria, and in Peking I lived and studied until the end of 1946. This bit of personal history is relevant in two ways. First, I was brought up at the time of China's major cultural transformations, when the Chinese Classics nonetheless still retained a degree of prestige and substance in the modernized schools. Second, the Japanese knew very well the value of the classical Confucian code of behavior to those in the role of ruler, and during 1937-1945 the Chinese Classics were quite actively promoted in the schools of occupied Peking. For these reasons I received, as a child, a rudimentary but significant education in traditional Chinese scholarship.

This education was not received gratefully. As youngsters we instinctively and correctly associated the Classics with The Enemy and The Collaborators and hated all the courses installed by them. It was they who promoted the Classics, primarily and notoriously through the Hsin Min Huei, or the New People Society, a collaborative front deriving its name from *Shu Ching* and thus recalling the renovative efforts of the Chou to transform the conquered Shang people. We were also forced to study Japanese, and that is probably why I have never truly mastered the language, much to my later regret. In addition, my father was a leading member of the Taiwan New Literature Movement (a May Fourth-inspired, but short-lived and not very consequential effort in Japan-occupied Taiwan of the early twenties), and I was myself an ardent reader of practically every May Fourth and subsequent anti-Confucian and anti-traditional novel and essay writer. Consequently my learning of the Chinese Classics was anything but ardent, yet I am now glad that I was brought up at a time, and in an environment, where I was given some solid classical training—a kind of training no longer available to Chinese students without specialized college and postgraduate education.

I am not about to advocate that Chinese Classics be a part of every Chinese student's primary education. The trouble lies rather in the nature of the specialization in college and graduate school during studies pertaining to ancient China. In Republican China (including post-1949 Taiwan), universities are organized around academic departments, and academic departments follow the traditional disciplinary lines. Under the College of Arts at National Taiwan University, for example, the departments of Chinese Literature, History, Philosophy, and Archaeology and Anthropology all have curricula pertaining to ancient China. Theoretically, students majoring in any of these disciplines may easily take courses in the other departments. In practice, they seldom do. Students must handle a large number of required courses within each discipline, and the faculty as a whole do not usually encourage interdepartmental programs.

I enrolled in National Taiwan University from 1950 through 1954, majoring in the Department of Archaeology and Anthropology. In the early fifties, when the Academia Sinica and its Institute of History and Philology had just moved from Nanking to Taiwan, some of the most outstanding scholars of ancient China, mostly in their fifties and at the peak of their careers, were also professors in the College of Arts at the National Taiwan University. These included Li Chi, Tung Tso-pin, Shih Chang-ju, Kao Ch'ü-hsün, Ling Shun-sheng, and Ruey Yih-fu, in the Department of Archaeology and Anthropology; Fu Ssu-nien, Li Tsung-t'ung, and Lao Kan, in the Department of History; and Tung T'ung-ho, in the Department of Chinese Literature. I was extremely fortunate in having had all of these distinguished scholars for my teachers, save Fu Ssu-nien, who died very soon after my matriculation. The program in which I was enrolled was intended to be well-rounded and included all branches of anthropology (physical anthropology, archaeology, linguistics, and cultural anthropology) and many courses relating to ancient China (such as Chinese Ancient History, Oracle Bone Studies, and many courses in Chinese Archaeology and Chinese Ethnology). Its major deficiency lay in the lack of any formal work in textual materials as primary sources and, also, in the absence of any contact with natural and physical sciences relating to the study of the human past. Courses in some of these disciplines were offered in other departments, but there was neither time nor incentive for a student in my position to actively seek them out.

My postgraduate education at Harvard (1955-60) strongly molded my thoughts in anthropology and archaeology, and some of my theoretical perspectives in the study of ancient China were formed during this period. It was also during this period that I began to apply many anthropological models to the study of ancient Chinese culture and society, and in so doing my lack of formal training in the Chinese Classics was painfully exposed. I did more reading in ancient Chinese texts during these five years than I had ever done before. For this I was most grateful to the Harvard-Yenching Institute, whose library is the best sinological library I know. Only in these efforts did I realize the tremendous help given me by my early contact with the traditional Chinese scholarship in Peking.

My experiences are not atypical of Chinese scholars my age, and

I believe that for younger scholars and today's students the problem of specialization and fragmentation is even worse, not better. In the mid-sixties I taught for a year at my alma mater in Taipei, where I found the only difference from my student days is that many of the older teachers were replaced by younger ones, whose anthropology was of course more modern but whose traditional scholarship was much weaker. As for the students, they were not fortunate enough to have had even a brushing acquaintance with the books of the Old China. I have no firsthand information about the situation in the People's Republic of China but I would be most surprised if it were any better in this particular regard.

In the United States, the pedagogical tradition is of course entirely different, and no students of ancient China can count on any contact with Chinese scholarship out of and prior to the college and postgraduate contexts. But the department structure based on the traditional disciplines is identical. The difficulty is compounded greatly by the tight squeeze experienced by today's graduate students between the lengthy education imperative to acquire the basic research tools (some of which a Chinese student would bring to the graduate school), on the one hand, and the financial desirability or necessity for a short graduate career, on the other. A competent and productive career in ancient Chinese studies is, in this country at this time, only for the extremely gifted or the very rich. Motivation and hard work alone are no longer always sufficient.

Scholarly disciplines carry traditional burdens and entrenched interests with them, and I am not naive enough to think, or hope, that the irrational and the illogical can be replaced by the rational and the logical by any kind of scholars' agreement. I do feel very strongly that those scholars, like myself, who place history first in their order of priorities rather than disciplines can and should train their students with that conviction in mind. At least in this country the graduate programs at many places are flexible enough so that students can devise their programs to suit their particular interests. I believe that these programs must be designed in accordance with the needs of the object of study rather than with the traditions and habits of the scholarly disciplines that are in some way involved. Students of Chinese prehistory, for example, need to acquire all the essential research tools and knowledge pertaining to their object of study: prehistoric man, his culture and society, and his environment. Such tools and knowledge may be obtained in the departments of Chinese, anthropology, geology, geography, and biology. On the other hand, students interested in Shang and Chou China would need a drastically different program to prepare themselves to handle the data and the issues in their field—a program which must include not only anthropology and Chinese language but also a thorough training in the Chinese Classics and in Chinese palaeography. In other words, in the study of the Chinese past, one does not assume the role of historians, anthropologists, art historians, classicists, and the like. Instead, one becomes a specialist of a period and equips himself with everything necessary for the study of the data and issues of that period.

I was born decades too early for that kind of training, and my own work, as represented by the papers collected here, is far from the kind of object-oriented research that I advocate. You recall that Chinese women used to have their feet bound. When the custom was first abolished in the early part of the twentieth century many women who had their feet bound for a while as young girls had what were then called the "liberated feet"—feet not quite natural but not exactly bound either. My papers on ancient China are sort of liberated feet. But anthropologists think they employ a holistic approach, and it is possible that these papers are more "liberated"—that is, object- instead of discipline-oriented—than many other works on ancient China. That, of course, is for others to judge.

These papers cover a ten-year period, a time when my own thinking had evolved somewhat. Since these studies are meant to be still current, minor editorial and other changes were made where such changes appeared highly desirable. I wish to thank the publishers for their permission to reprint these papers in this book.

For style of citation I follow the usual anthropological convention throughout. Where a different style was used in the original publication, it has been changed completely to conform with the rest. For romanization, the Wade-Giles system is used. All Chinese characters are romanized according to their modern, Mandarin pronunciation. A few scholars of ancient China would romanize Shang and Chou characters according to the reconstructed Archaic Chinese phonology. Except where the pronunciation is relevant, such as in philological discussions, I am opposed to this practice. Writings about ancient China are difficult enough to read as they are, and there is no reason whatever to make them more so unless the quality of the writing is involved. After all, it is the Chinese characters that count, and their romanized versions serve merely to make them more easily read by the Western audience. The Wade-Giles versions of the Chinese characters in this book are merely meant to serve as temporary substitutes for the real thing, which may be found in the Glossary.

K.C.C.

Contents

1 The Beginnings of Agriculture in the Far East *1*

2 China toward Urban Life *22*

Addendum: Radiocarbon Dates from China, Some Initial Interpretations *38*

3 Urbanism and the King in Ancient China *47*

4 Towns and Cities in Ancient China *61*

5 The Lineage System of the Shang and Chou Chinese and Its Political Implications *72*

6 Some Dualistic Phenomena in Shang Society *93*

7 Food and Food Vessels in Ancient China *115*

8 A Classification of Shang and Chou Myths *149*

9 Changing Relationships of Man and Animal in Shang and Chou Myths and Art *174*

Bibliography *199*

Glossary *217*

Index *221*

Figures

1. Ancient Culture Chronologies of North China (from K. C. Chang 1968, Table 15). *36*
2. Ancient Culture Chronologies of South China (from K. C. Chang 1968, Table 16). *37*
3. The character of *yi* in the oracle bone (upper row) and bronze (lower row) scripts (after H. P. Sun 1934; K. Jung 1959). *62*
4. Locations of Shang and Chou City Ruins. *66*
5. Ruins of the City of Hsia-tu, State of Yen. Note the layout of the various functional parts (after K. C. Chang 1968, Fig. 106). *69*
6. The Royal Genealogy of the Shang Dynasty. *81*
7. A Reconstruction of the Rules of Marriage and Succession of the Shang Royal Lineages. *85*
8. The Royal Genealogy of the "Hsia" Dynasty. *86*
9. Marriage Relations between the Lu and Ch'i Dukes. *91*
10. Characters Relating to Cooking, Eating, and Ritual Use of Food. 1: Butchering; 2-9: Cooking; 10-23: Serving in various contexts; 24-32: Ritual use (1, 11, 21, 22, 25, 28 from K. Jung 1959; the remainder from H. P. Sun 1934). *117*
11. Major Food and Drink Vessels and Utensils of Shang and Chou. 1-4: Cooking vessels; 5: Storage jar; 6-13: Serving instruments and vessels; 14-19: Drink vessels. *127*
12. Scenes of Ritual Feasts from Bronze Vessel Decorations, Eastern Chou Period (from Weber 1968, Fig. 76). *130*
13. Rubbing of a Han Tile, Offerings of Food and Drink. Collection of Szechwan Provincial Museum (after Fairbank 1972). *131*
14. Food and Water Bowls Decorated with Fish Designs. Did they serve fish in them? (*Lower,* Yang-shao Culture at Pan-p'o, Sian, *ca.* 4000 BC; *Middle,* a bronze *p'an* of Shang or early Western Chou, in the Freer Gallery collection; *Upper,* a Ch'u pottery *tou* from Ch'ang-sha, Hunan.) *145*
15. Different Social Classes Had Different Foods and Food Vessels (*Upper,* a *Life* magazine reconstruction of a Shang feast, by Alden S. Tobey; *Lower,* two pit-house floors with remains of food vessels, Shang period, at Anyang, Honan, from C. Li 1956). The contrast between the two ways of life is obvious. *147*

16. Some Common Decorative Motifs of Shang and Chou Bronzes (reproduced from *An Outline of World Archaeology,* vol. 6, 1958, Tokyo: Heibonshya). *177*
17. Animals and Men in Archaic Bronze Art (*Upper,* from C. Li 1957a; *Lower,* from *Sen-Oku Sei-shō,* Kyoto, 1934). *178*
18. Animals and Men in Archaic Bronze Art. Collection of the Freer Gallery of Art. *179*
19. Scenes of Men Fighting Fantastic Animals in the Huai Style Art (reproduced from P. C. Kuo 1959). *181*
20. Scenes of Men Fighting Fantastic Animals in the Huai Style Art (*Upper,* from S. Umehara 1944; *Lower,* from S. Umehara, *Studies of the Bronzes of the Warring-States Style,* Kyoto, 1936). *182*
21. Men Riding Fantastic Animals in the Huai Style Art (from C. H. Ch'en, in *K'ao-ku* 1959 [12]: 657). *183*

Tables

1. Principal Cultivated Plants of the Four Belts in the Far East (after H. L. Li 1966). *17*
2. Neolithic-Bronze Age Continuities and Discontinuities in North China. *35*
3. Twenty-eight Radiocarbon Dates from Ancient China. *40*
4. Radiocarbon Dates of Cultivated Plants. *45*

Early Chinese Civilization: Anthropological Perspectives

1 The Beginnings of Agriculture in the Far East

Recent archaeological and botanical studies of a number of major food plants throughout the world have clearly shown that the initial domestication of each of them was a slow and laborious process, carried out by generations of experimentalists familiar with the total ecosystem of which the plant was a part (Darlington 1963; Harris 1967, 1969; Ucko and Dimbleby 1969b). Therefore, any pronouncement about the who, where, how, and when of the domestication of a food plant must be based not on general preconceptions but on local facts. One sees a paradox in many otherwise sophisticated recent writings about the beginnings of agriculture (a term used here simply to refer to the cultivation of any useful plant by whatever means): that the authors of excellent data derived from the Near East, Europe, and to some extent Africa make the explicit or implicit claim that their conclusions are applicable to the Far East as well, and generalize about origins and histories of peoples and plants accordingly (e.g. Ucko and Dimbleby 1969a; Brothwell and Brothwell 1969). They fail to extend the rigorous scientific standards they apply to Western materials either to the Far Eastern data they use or to the conclusions they draw.

I make this complaint only to justify my attempt to summarize some pertinent facts, even though the facts are still meager, their articulation remains essentially interpretative, and definite conclusions are therefore remote. But for scholars investigating new frontiers these facts suggest that the results of archaeological exploration of agricultural beginnings in the Far East may alter our entire understanding of a significant portion of Old World prehistory. Such research opportunities should not be foreclosed by default. Those seeking an understanding of, or writing about, Old World prehistory would also do well to avail themselves of the available evidence.

The name Far East, now often avoided by scholars because of its occidental bias, is used here as a convenient term that includes both east Asia and southeast Asia. In this area we recognize two inter-

---

Note: This essay was originally published in *Antiquity* 44 (1970): 175-185. Reprinted with permission of *Antiquity*.

related primary belts or zones in which the earliest activities of plant domestication were concentrated—north China and southeast Asia. Studies in these regions have been pursued during the last three decades by archaeologists, botanists, ethnobotanists, and historians; some of the results are factual, others are new material still needing corroboration, and still others are frankly speculative.

To place events in proper chronological perspective, identify the cultures responsible, and attempt to explain how and why they took place, we must first outline the prehistoric cultures of the Far East during the period in which the first major plants of the area were being domesticated. This is in itself no slight undertaking, for Far Eastern prehistory is now being drastically reworked and any outline of it must represent an interim judgment. My reservation, however, pertains only to how the data are put together, not to the data *per se.*

Remains of the last glaciers have been located in the whole Tibetan plateau and in scattered highlands in the rest of the Far East. The last glacial maximum, according to a recent pollen study in central Formosa (Tsukada 1966, 1967), was reached between 48,000 and 60,000 years ago, when the mean annual temperature was perhaps 8°-11° below that of the present. The mainland was connected by land with Japan in the north and with the Malay archipelago in the south. Remains of Palaeolithic cultures dating from this interval and its adjacent periods are found throughout the Far East, from Siberia and Japan to Palawan, Borneo, Celebes, and Java (K. C. Chang 1962: 4-6; Solheim 1969: 127-8). Almost everywhere they indicate an advanced lithic industry, characterized by flake, blade, and microlithic technologies. Although glaciers were by no means extensive, the climate in many areas must have been adversely affected, and clusters of populations probably found shelter and livelihood in widely separated enclaves providing distinctive assemblages of wild animals, fish, and plants; their cultural equipment often exhibits correspondingly differing features. In some places—mainly southeast Asia—small but characteristic assemblages of pebble choppers and chopping tools, reminiscent of the more ancient lithic tradition of the area, have been found. This looks like and has been called a retardation, but it may actually be an actively adaptive manifestation.

The last glacial advance took place around 30,000 years ago when the mean annual temperature was probably only 4°-6° C below that of the present. The cold climate continued until about 14,000-12,000 BP, when an ameliorating trend began to set in, according to the Taiwan pollen profile. A hypsithermal was reached between 8000 and 4000 BP; at its height the temperature in central Formosa was probably 2°-3° C higher than the present (Tsukada 1966). This warming interval is also shown in several other pollen profiles as far north as Manchuria and the Soviet Far East (K. C. Chang 1968: 34).[1] The ameliorating trend between 14,000 and 4,000 BP in the Far East was presumably felt to varying extents in different parts of the area, but generally speaking a more moist environment with a thicker vegetation obtained over much of the area during this crucial interval, with rising temperature and increased water distribution from periglacial and marine transgressive sources. For the inhabitants this meant diminished natural barriers on land, submergence of many land bridges in the sea, and, in regionally relative terms, a greater abundance and an increasingly greater diversity of faunal and floral resources that gradually but decisively altered the ecological equilibria of the preceding glacial and periglacial conditions.

Changes in early cultures that may be related to this changing ecological context manifest themselves in the wide appearance of ground or edge-ground stone implements and, concurrently or after a yet undetermined interval, of cord-marked pottery. Some of the earliest facies of the new culture occurred in southwestern and southern coastal China, Indochina, Malaya, and a few islands to the south, where it has been referred to as Late Hoabinhian (Solheim 1969). Early Hoabinhian refers to the same culture of pebble tools without edgegrinding and pottery (Matthews 1968). The absolute dating of the Hoabinhian culture is uncertain; carbon-14 dates in the order of 8,000 to 11,000 years BP are known from Thailand from a nonceramic Hoabinhian assemblage (Gorman 1969a, 1969b), but the occurrence of cord-marked pottery could be about as early in Formosa (Chang and Stuiver 1966). I am doubtful that in the whole area of its distribution the Hoabinhian can be divided into preceramic and ceramic stages or levels that are manifest in the archaeological sequence everywhere at the same points in time. The Hoabinhian as a whole may be considered as a culture type that had already appeared locally during the glacial maxima, and subsequently proved to be suited to the ameliorated environment of a wider area in the southeast Asian tropics. It be-

1. Not to burden the reader of this paper with numerous references to publications, I cite here and elsewhere my 1968 book as a convenient place where interested readers may find some of the original sources listed.

gan to expand perhaps 14,000 years ago and persisted thereafter for almost ten millennia with only gradual and regionally diverse changes, tool grinding and/or pottery manufacture being two of its spreading but by no means universal components. The pottery was in the beginning exclusively of the cord-marked kind (and its related varieties of basket and mat-marked wares), but during the Hoabinhian's later millennia other kinds of pottery (including painted pottery) may have emerged in various regions. The subsistence base of the Hoabinhian in general consisted of shellfish gathering, fishing, small-game hunting, plant gathering, and a certain amount of cultivating. The last item will be discussed later.

Another postglacial manifestation in the Far East is the Jomon Culture of Japan (Kamaki 1965), now firmly dated by the radiocarbon method to some 10,000 years ago (Kotani 1969: 153). Also lasting for eight or more millennia with only gradual changes, the Jomon shares with the Hoabinhian its cord-marked pottery, but in the Jomon there was a direct continuation of stone types from an Upper Palaeolithic flake and blade base. The subsistence pattern of the Jomon is not much different from that of the Hoabinhian but, presumably because of the latitude, tropical agriculture did not make its way into Japan.

A third, and in the long run the most important, region of postglacial cultural change in the Far East is the so-called nuclear area of north China (K. C. Chang 1968: 85). Here both the process and the dating of the beginning of the new culture are highly uncertain, but, as in the Hoabinhian and Jomon, the earliest remains are characterized by coarse cord-marked pottery. These remains have thus far been found only in the lower Weishui River and on the banks of the Yellow River in western Honan, but stratigraphically they represent the earliest ceramic culture of north China. Typology and geographic proximity both indicate that the earliest cord-marked pottery of north China and of the Hoabinhian are probably akin, although the distinctive stone inventories of these two cultures argue against the view that the Chinese culture was simply a northern Hoabinhian branch. There are as yet no absolute dates for the northern Chinese culture, but I should not at all be surprised if future evidence were to place its beginnings in the neighborhood of the 10th millennium BP, or roughly contemporary with the earliest phases of both the Hoabinhian and the Jomon.

It can hardly be a coincidence that these three cultures—Hoabinhian, Jomon, and northern Chinese—emerged at about the same time in the postglacial period of the Far East and, further, that despite their distinctive stone inventories they are all characterized by coarse cord-marked pottery. The point about the stones makes it likely that the three cultures reflect separate and largely independent developments in three widely divergent ecological situations from local Upper Palaeolithic bases as an active response to the postglacial environmental changes, but one is tempted to ask several questions. Was stimulus diffusion involved in their nearly simultaneous occurrence? Do the common features of pottery wares suggest such diffusion? Where is the center of any such diffusing influence? What is the relationship of this cord-marked pottery tradition with the earliest pottery centers in the Near East and the New World? Before the ascription of very early carbon-14 dates to the Jomon, and the new excavations in north China, Formosa, and Thailand, these questions could not have been thought of, and even now they cannot be answered on the basis of hard evidence. The new information mentioned above, however, must be taken into account by any scholar who generalizes about Old World prehistory, so as to avoid making such sweeping statements as Darlington's (1969: 68) that:

> What we see today is the decisive evidence (of Braidwood, Mellaart, Helbaek, and others) that agriculture in the Old World arose in a single connected region, a Nuclear Zone of Anatolia, Iran and Syria before 7000 BC. And that it arose here at a time when no other region of the Old World shows evidence of any similar settled life.

The subsequent development of the three earliest new cultures of the postglacial Far East is better known. As far as the agricultural aspect is concerned, the Jomon of Japan continued with only gradual changes until the first millennium BC (when the Yayoi Culture made a dramatic appearance on the islands), and for present purposes further consideration of it is not necessary. The northern Chinese culture, on the other hand, underwent profound changes from a cord-marked pottery base to the Yang-shao Culture of painted pottery, then on to the Lungshanoid cultures, to a series of local Lung-shan cultures, and finally to the Shang civilization, which began in the early second millennium BC. The Yang-shao Culture was largely confined to the northern Chinese nuclear area, but the large series of post-Yang-shao cultures constitutes a widespread Lungshanoid horizon that indicates the eastward and southward expansion of the Chinese tradition from a Yang-shao base. These cultures include the Miao-ti-kou of Honan, the Ta-wen-k'ou of Shantung, the Ch'ü-chia-ling of Hupei, the Ch'ing-lien-kang of Kiangsu, the early Liang-chu of Chekiang, and the Feng-pi-t'ou of Formosa. The Feng-pi-t'ou Culture (Chang et al. 1969) is carbon-14 dated to begin around 2500 BC, which suggests a late fourth-millennium BC date for the related cultures of north China and a fifth, or sixth millennium BC date for the Yang-shao. I have discussed in detail elsewhere the process of the Lungshanoid spread in northern, eastern, and southeastern China (K. C. Chang 1968: 144-50).

In many places in south China, such as the southeastern coast, Formosa, and possibly the Upper Yangtze, the southern fronts of the Lungshanoid spread, in various degrees, intruded into or touched upon the native Hoabinhian, during the last three or four millennia before Christ. Up to this time, changes in Hoabinhian had not been archaeologically conspicuous, although the known Hoabinhian sites in general offer poor chronological evidence for a detailed history of their development. At this time, however, possibly with the impetus of Lungshanoid contacts, several ceramic complexes, all bearing unmistakable resemblance to the Lungshanoid, appeared in the archaeological record. These include the Sa-Huynh of south Vietnam and Laos, the Ban Kao—Gua Cha of central Thailand and northern Malaya, and the Kalanay of Borneo and the Philippines (Solheim 1964: 1969). Some of these complexes contain a much more substantial component of cord-marked pottery than is the case with any of the Lungshanoid cultures, and despite Lungshanoid similarities they are highly distinctive. If we must speculate about their ancestry at this time, I believe they could all be called outgrowth from a Hoabinhian substratum.

This outline of the earliest postglacial cultures in the Far East, necessarily brief and highly generalized, differs quite drastically from some older beliefs and in a few significant details from other current reconstructions. It should nevertheless suffice as a working hypothesis for the arrangement and understanding of the current, still inadequate, data pertaining to the cultivation of plants in East Asia.

Earliest Cultivators of Southeast Asia

Since the 19th century southeast Asia has been recognized as the source of many tropical Asian cultivated plants (Candolle 1883). N. I. Vavilov, in his classic 1936 study of cultivated plants, listed them under India (including Assam and Burma) and Indo-Malay (Vavilov 1949/51). Vavilov's area lists for the rest of the world have been substantially modified by subsequent writers (see Harris 1967), but for the Far East his treatise is still the most comprehensive and systematic. In a recent paper Li Hui-lin (1966) re-examined the grouping of cultivated plants in the entire Far East and proposed to subdivide them according to four 'belts': (i) north China: the Yellow river valley, from southern Manchuria and the southern fringes of the Gobi in the north to the Tsinling mountains in the south; (ii) south China: south of Tsinling; (iii) southern Asia: Burma, Thailand, and Indochina; and (iv) southern islands: Malay peninsula and the Malay archipelago. Table 1 lists the major plants Li considers to have been first or long cultivated in the various belts (Li 1966: 26).

Although this list for the Far East is much more comprehensive and more carefully assembled than any other I have seen it can be supplemented by additional archaeological and ethnobotanical material. To mention only the most important: bamboos, a widely used group of industrial and food plants, undoubtedly originated in the Far East; probably the small bamboo (*Phyllostachy* spp.) was first cultivated in Li's south China belt and the great bamboo (*Dendrocalamus asper*) in his southern Asia or southern islands belt. Such major food plants as buckwheat (*Fagopyrum esculentum*), velvet bean (*Stizolobium hassjoo*), radish (*Raphanus sativus*), water caltrop (*Trapa natans*), and ginkgo (*Ginkgo biloba*) are commonly regarded as having been cultivated in China for a long time. The bottle gourd (*Lagenaria vulgaris*) figures prominently in the creation myths throughout southeast Asia and must have been in use in the region since antiquity. From a Lungshanoid site in Chekiang (K. C. Chang 1968: 157) came remains of broad beans (*Vicia faba*) and groundnut (*Arachis hypogaea*), generally thought to be native to central Asia and south America respectively.

Li's list may not be judged valid in its entirety by botanists, since many of the plants have still to be studied rigorously and definitively; but if the general trend is acceptable, a few significant points can be made about the problem of agricultural origins in the Far East. Comparing the plants of the northern and the southern parts of the area, Li sees important differences between them:

> In the north cereals and other seeded plants are emphasized, but in the south roots, tubers and other vegetatively propagated plants are more important. Legumes and edible oil crops are more important in the north than in the south. In the north a fairly large

variety of vegetables has been cultivated, and their changes through history have been marked. The number of vegetables first cultivated decreases as one moves south; a few if any leaf vegetables were first domesticated in the extreme south. Some plants for special industrial uses (e.g. the varnish tree and the mulberry) were first domesticated in the north (none in the south). There is nothing in the north that is comparable with such special food plants of the south as the banana and the sugarcane. Many fruit trees are cultivated in both the north and the south, but each area has distinctive species that it first domesticated: the northern fruit trees are temperate species and most belong to the family *Rosaceae,* but the southern fruit trees are tropical and do not show a comparable taxonomic concentration (Li 1966: 20-1, translated).

The north in the quotation above refers to Li's north China belt and the south to his southern Asia and southern islands belts. Li regards his south China belt as a 'buffer zone' between the north and the south. In short, modern historical botanists such as Li see two separate areas of cultivated plant origins in the Far East: north China and southeast Asia. South China is situated in this respect between the two, and from the viewpoint of prehistory this is a crucial area that ties the two centers together—a point that will be discussed again.

Even the limited enumeration above shows clearly that many cultivated plants of significance to man and to culture-history are considered to have been first domesticated in southeast Asia. The following questions become immediately relevant: Who first domesticated these plants? What was their culture like; when did they begin to domesticate plants; and what was their relationship with near and far neighbors? What was the process and sequence of the domestication of individual plants? Because the archaeological and palaeoenvironmental investigations necessary to reconstruct the ancient ecosystems in southeast Asia are far from completion, many of these questions cannot yet be answered. Several scholars, nevertheless, have made reasonable and interesting speculations from the ethnological, ethnobotanical, and botanical material (Barrau 1970; Sauer 1952; Burkill 1953). Some of these are listed below.

(1) Most of earliest cultivators of tropical and subtropical southeast Asia inhabited estuarial plains and low terraces and engaged for subsistence mainly in fishing. In their habitat were abundant wild plants, which because of the topographical complexity were highly diversified. These fishermen led a settled, stable life and

were familiar with their plant resources and the nature and uses of many plants. Utilization of select plants gradually gave way to their control and cultivation as a perhaps minor but essential means of subsistence.

(2) Wild and initially domesticated plants in the fishing-hunting cultures of southeast Asia were probably first used mainly for containers (e.g. bamboo trunks and bottle gourds) or for cordage for use in fishing (nets, fishlines, and canoe-caulking material); or were herbs with various uses, or poisons. Man's dependence upon plants for these and other uses, plus the obvious food value of many aquatic plants, wild fruits, berries, roots, and tubers, were among the strong reasons for their continued and growing use and eventual cultivation.

(3) Under these circumstances the first wild but utilized plants that became the cultigens in southeast Asia probably included bamboos, the bottle gourd, fruit trees, some aquatic plants, and such roots and tubers as the taro and the yam. There is almost general agreement that in southeast Asia root, tuber, and fruit plants were cultivated much earlier then cereal plants. Among the cereals millet, sorghum, and Job's-tears are thought to have been used before rice.

(4) The initially cultivated crops probably played a minor role in the total subsistence system of the inhabitants, supplementing a diet derived mainly from fish, wild animals, and shell-fish. Food cultivation was at first probably a small-scale undertaking in little patches near the individual homes. Only small peripheral forest clearings were necessary, and no tool more elaborate than a digging-stick was used.

These speculations have neither been vehemently opposed nor warmly embraced by interested scholars. Many details may never be proved, since preservation of the plants in question is thought unlikely; and without intensive palaeoecological research of great depth throughout the area the postulated ecosystems that are crucial to the hypothesis can hardly be assumed. Moreover, granted that many distinctive local plants were first cultivated there, the exact position in Old World culture prehistory in general of the supposed early cultivators in the Asian tropics cannot be ascertained without an areal chronology of prehistoric cultures. Carl Sauer's ideas (1952) about their being the earliest horticulturalists of the world, however interesting or logical, could not be seriously accepted without solid archaeological support.

Such support is not now at hand, but current archaeological

results indicate that conditions suited to this general hypothesis actually existed in parts of southeast Asia and south China at the right time, and that contemporary prehistoric cultures did possess at least some of the appropriate characteristics (K. C. Chang, ms). The most important of these results came from Formosa in 1964-5 and Thailand in 1967-8.

The Thailand work of 1967-8 produced important plant remains, associated with a Hoabinhian stone assemblage, from a limestone cave on the bank of the Salween about 60 km. north of the town of Mae Hong Son in the extreme northwest part of the country. In the cave, Chester Gorman (1969a) of the University of Hawaii excavated five deposit levels, which he grouped into two cultural strata: Hoabinhian, below, and advanced Hoabinhian with intrusive new elements, above. The Hoabinhian stratum is dated by a series of radiocarbon determinations to the interval of 12,000 to 8000 years BP (Gorman 1969a). From various levels of this stratum were found numbers of botanical macrofossils that have been identified by Douglas Yen and P. van Royen as including almond (*Prunus*), kotamba (*Terminalia*), betel nut (*Areca*), broad beans (*Vicia* or *Phaseolus*), pea (*Pisum* or *Raphia*), bottle gourd (*Lagenaria*), water caltrop or Chinese water-chestnut (*Trapa*), pepper (*Piper*), butternut (*Madhuca*), Chinese olive (*Canarium*), candlenut (*Aleurites*) and cucumber (*Cucumis*). These, Gorman (1969a) pointed out, include not only nuts, edible oil seeds, spices, and stimulants but also a group of food plants (bottle gourd, cucumber, water-chestnut, beans, and peas) that suggest 'economic development beyond simple food-gathering'. Despite the caution exerted by the botanists in the identification (in using only genus names), the surprisingly early date of these plants upsets some current conceptions of agricultural and plant origins such as Darlington's and it will not surprise me if this information is received by many scholars with scepticism, as were the first early Jomon radiocarbon dates that upset entrenched ideas about pottery origins.

To be sure, the unique Thailand cave discovery must be corroborated many times before any wide-ranging generalization can be made. But one can safely draw the following conclusions from Gorman's find: some plants which are thought to have a long history of cultivation in the southeast Asian tropics have now been archaeologically verified to be of great antiquity there and the Hoabinhian culture as this paper defines it is an archaeological entity in which evidence of the early cultivators of this area should be sought. The second of these points had become clear, before the Thailand find, with the new Formosan excavations.

Cord-marked potsherds with comb incisions were found in the advanced Hoabinhian stratum in Gorman's cave. This kind of pottery, occurring widely in Indochina and on the southern Chinese coasts, but little known, has long been found in Formosa, but in 1964-5 the excavations carried out on the island jointly by the National Taiwan University and Yale University established for the first time an early cord-marked pottery culture in its prehistoric period, which is undoubtedly related to the broadly defined Hoabinhian on the mainland (K. C. Chang, 1967; K. C. Chang et al. 1969). This culture exhibits the following characteristics: (i) in its three regions of distribution within Formosa, the sites of this culture invariably occurred on low costal terraces near river estuaries; (ii) the stone implements include chipped axes, polished adzes and chisels, hammerstones of pebble, pebbles with chipped ends probably used as netsinkers, perforated triangular slate arrowheads, and grooved stones resembling modern tapa beaters; (iii) shell-fish remains are lacking and animal and bone artifacts are rare; (iv) the coarse pottery has distinctive features of paste, form, and surface treatment, the most immediately relevant being the elaborate impressions produced with cord-wrapped sticks and paddles. The plainly indicated wide use of cordage tells not only of the utilization of fibrous plants (the probable bark-beater) but also of fishing-related uses (netsinkers and carpenters' tools). All of these coincide with the cultural conditions postulated earlier, without benefit of archaeological evidence, for the ancient cultivators.

The dating of the cord-marked pottery culture in Formosa is inconclusive except that it is known to be considerably earlier than the subsequent cultures dated to the third millennium BC. The pollen profile from central Taiwan mentioned above, however, gives some interesting indications in this and other connections. This was worked out in late 1964 by Matsuo Tsukada (1966, 1967) from a -12.79 m. core taken at the bottom of Lake Jih-yueh T'an that goes back about 60,000 years. Significant changes registered around 12,000 years ago began a trend of gradual but decisive growth of secondary forests near the lake and a steady accumulation at the lake bottom of charred fragments of trees. These are interpreted by Tsukada as signs of human activities that persistently disturbed the primary vegetation of the area. If this interpretation is valid, the human groups at that early date can only be those represented by the cord-marked pottery culture, and the deforesting activities may have to do with their cultivation. Similar but much more intensive changes are again registered in the pollen profile at 4200 BP, and there is no doubt that this was due to the activities of the Lungshanoid cereal growers, which will be described later.

The Beginnings of Agriculture in North China

The interrelationship of the earliest farming cultures of southeast Asia and north China is one of the most crucial topics in the prehistoric archaeology of the Far East for study in the next decade. If plant cultivation began in southeast Asia as early as it now appears, there is a strong possibility that the beginning of cultivation in north China was due to a southern stimulus—unless a comparable date can be shown for its beginning in the north (which is of course quite likely). A Western derivation of Chinese agriculture, once widely discussed, is no longer a serious probability, although contacts between China and the West since an early age are shown by wheat in ancient China and the *Setaria* and *Panicum* millets in Neolithic Europe.

There is a strong indication that the earliest ceramic culture in north China was part of a widespread cord-marked pottery horizon covering not only north and south China and southeast Asia but also the Japanese islands. Since there was north-south contact in pottery techniques and style, there could have been no effective barrier against the transmission of ideas for the cultivation and uses of plants. However, the Neolithic culture of north China had a very distinctive style from the beginning of the archaeological evidence, and the northern ecosytems were drastically different from those in tropical southeast Asia. The northern people must have carried out their own experiments in plant cultivation and developed a wholly original assemblage of cultivated plants, whatever the nature of their contact with the south across the Tsinling mountains and the Huai river.

There is general agreement on the essential make-up of this assemblage as shown by Li Hui-lin's list, but, because of the nearly complete absence of palaeoecological investigations at the crucial time interval, few plants are actually known and the process of the actual domestication is totally without evidence. The natural and cultural contexts of the north China farmers are not known until the Yang-shao period, but the Yang-shao sites are sufficiently numerous to outline a settlement pattern characterized by nucleation and location on the lower terraces of the tributaries of the Yellow river or on isolated low hills near the small rivers (Ho Ping-ti 1969: 108-17). The pattern of settlement distribution and the nature of cultural deposition suggest a generally slash-and-burn type of cultivation in fields, with small rivers on one side and wooded hills and mountain slopes on the other side (K. C. Chang 1968: 92-6). This indicates to Ho Ping-ti (1969: 117) a cultivation system with little extensive irrigation work.

In its broad outline this cultivation system is one adaptive to an ecosystem drastically different in climate and vegetation from the southeast Asian, and the assemblage of cultivated plants reflects this fact. These plants are mostly known from historical sources that cannot be pushed back in time beyond the middle of the second millennium BC, and here the dominating importance of millets (*Setaria italica* and *Panicum miliaceum*) above all other crops is plain (Ho Ping-ti 1969: 121-33). Archaeological finds of such plants as kaoliang, wheat, rice, soybean, and hemp have been reported from various late prehistoric and early historic sites, but for the earlier Yang-shao level the only definite evidence concerns the foxtail millet (*Setaria italica*) which is widely found and was undoubtedly the staple at the time, Chinese cabbage (*Brassica* spp.), and the mulberry, attested to by the remains of silkworms (K. C. Chang 1968: 89-92). Although the palaeobotanical history of the foxtail millet is not clear, its wide use and great antiquity in Neolithic north China confirms the botanical hypothesis attributing its first domestication to this area. Ho Ping-ti (1969: 130) also argues against the hypothesis of an Indian domestication of the broomcorn millet by citing the Indian words for it that suggest Chinese derivation (*cīnaka* or *cinna* in Sanskrit, *chena* and *cheen* in Hindi, *cheena* in Bengali, and *chino* in Gujarati; compare *cīnani* for peach and *cīnarājaputra* for sand pear, two fruits known to have been introduced into India from China).

The north China agricultural system exhibits its principal contrast to the southeast Asian in its emphasis on cereals and other seeded plants. It has been mentioned above that in southeast Asia cereals followed (after a long time-lag) roots, tubers, and fruits as major food plants. The increased importance of cereals in the south probably resulted from intensified contact with the northern Chinese culture, as indicated by the fact that both millet and rice first appeared in the archaeological record in the south at the Lungshanoid level. Millets of the genera *Setaria* and *Panicum* were probably introduced directly from the north, but rice probably came in by a more complex route.

Most scholars now regard the ancestor of the cultivated rice (*Oryza sativa*) as a perennial that grew wild throughout the swampy lowlands of southeast Asia from Bengal to south China and the South Seas. Haudricourt (1962: 41; 1964: 95) and others (Grist 1955: 130) believe that rice was initially encountered as a weed in taro gardens, and some early rice-planting techniques (such as transplantation and harvesting by knife-cutting the stem) were perhaps directly borrowed from taro-cultivating techniques. In other words, the early root- and tuber-growers of southeast Asia were responsible also for the domestication of rice. The only problem is that if the modern Pacific situation is any guide, the taro and yam would not only have yielded a much greater harvest than rice within identical acreage but must have also played important roles in the social and religious life of their growers. If indeed some taro and yam growers adopted rice as their staple food early in their history, the changeover could not have taken place without the strongest possible stimulus.

According to Jacques Barrau (1970) the only possible stimulus that could have accomplished this feat was a strong influence from the north or even the immigration of northern farmers.

> [In the swampy lowlands of the Western Indo-Pacific area] vegetatively propagated root crops were staple and it is difficult to imagine that the primitive gardeners growing them were those who domesticated this cereal. However, this part of the Indo-Pacific area received migrants from Inner Asia moving southward, through Yunnan, into the Indo-Chinese and the Malayan peninsulae. These migrants may have been used to a cereal-diet and they may have brought with them the foxtail millet for example, which probably originated in Central Asia. They may have found rice in the western Indo-Pacific area and begun its domestication. From there the cereal moved north-westward to India and north-eastward to China to segregated centres of domestication where it was greatly improved. This could partly explain some of the morphological and genetical differences between groups of rice varieties which developed separately far from the original habitat of the wild perennial relatives. . . . It seems therefore that the spread of cereals such as rice or millet in the western part of the Indo-Pacific area must have been due to some foreign influence. Rice by contrast with the old root-crops is a dry and mobile commodity, easily divided and measured, in a word suitable for trade economy.

In principle but not in detail this interpretation is strongly supported by the archaeological facts. The earliest remains of rice in south China occurred at the time level of the Lungshanoid cultures, spreading to the south along the seacoast, rather than from inner Asia as Barrau speculates. Three kinds of rice remains are known: carbonized husks and straws, binding materials in wattle-and-daub constructions, and imprints of paddy husks on pottery. Archaeological sites with such remains belong to various cultures: Ch'ü-chia-ling of Hupei, Hu-shu of the lower Yangtze, Liang-chu of the lower Chikiang, and the Ying-p'u of central coastal Formosa (K. C. Chang 1968). Despite their distinctive features, which are not insignificant, these cultures, all members of the Lungshanoid horizon, exhibit a number of important common characteristics. The most conspicuous are the rice remains and the rectangular and semilunar slate knives that are generally regarded as tools for rice harvesting. The Lungshanoid by definition signifies a rapidly spreading culture, which was unquestionably related to rice cultivation. The emergence of the Ying-pu' Culture in central Taiwan coincides precisely in time with the drastic changes registered in the Jih-yüeh T'an pollen profile in the late third millennium BC that saw secondary forest growths, charcoal fragments of leaves and twigs, and the fossils of cultivated and wild grains. This profile, as well as other Lungshanoid finds dated to the mid-third millennium BC by radiocarbon samples from Formosa, suggests a date in the fourth millennium BC for the earliest Lungshanoid on the mainland, making the Lunshanoid rice remains the earliest known (compared with the late second millennium BC rice remains in India; see Allchin 1969: 325).

If the Lungshanoid expansion of the northern Chinese Neolithic tradition marks in essence a migration of northerners into the subtropical south the immigrants would be ideally suited to the role in rice domestication assigned to them by Barrau. These would be the migrants used to a cereal diet who brought the foxtail millet with them into southeast Asia—from north China rather than central Asia, however. The finds of rice in north China at the same cultural level (K. C. Chang 1968: 138) would then be the northeastward feedback of rice postulated by Barrau.

I hesitate, however, to overemphasize the role played by actual migrations in both Lungshanoid expansion and rice domestication. The earlier cord-marked pottery remains are known in south China as far north as Szechwan, western Hupei, southern Shensi, and central Kiangsi as well as from its southern coastal fringes, and in these regions there could have been considerable cultural continuity from this substratum to the Lungshanoid. In pottery, stone, bone, and other artifactual inventories and in house construction, marked differences are observed not only between the north and the south but also among the southern cultures themselves. From a Lungshanoid level in the Ch'ien-shan-yang site came remains of rice as well as peach, melon (*Cucumis melo*), water caltrop, broad bean, sesame, and groundnut (K. C. Chang 1968: 157). Of these, water caltrop and broad bean had a long history in southeast Asia, as shown by the Thailand find; sesame is usually thought to have been domesticated in India, and groundnut in South America. This Lungshanoid abundance in non-north China crops supports Li Hui-lin's observation that in his south China belt the cultivated plant assemblage reflects a mixture of northern and southern elements.

These generalizations represent an interpretation in bare outline of the current material on the subject; the small amount of solid data available could hardly have been put together here into a systematic picture without much speculation. But the entire Far East is not an area where scientists can at the moment (or within the foreseeable future) carry out intensive research freely. The urgency with which research must be undertaken and the limited area in which it can be carried out permit only a carefully planned series of highly select spot investigations. Such a strategy cannot be productive without the guidance of successive working hypotheses. Here I present one such (compare: Dunn 1970; Solheim 1969)—an outline based on enough solid facts to warrant calling this Far Eastern area to the close attention of students of the early cultures of the Old World. An occidentocentric model of prehistory, in general or with regard to plant cultivation, surely should not prejudice prehistoric interpretations elsewhere. But, without empirical demonstration this logical slogan carries little force. The New World prehistory has long provided such a demonstration, and the Far Eastern model is beginning to do likewise within the Old World.

Table 1. Principal Cultivated Plants of the Four Belts in the Far East

Plant	North China	South China	Southern Asia	Southern islands
Cereals	Broom-corn millet (*Panicum miliaceum*) Fox-tail millet (*Setaria italica*)		Rice (*Oryza sativa*) Job's-tears (*Coix lachryma-jobi*) Japanese millet (*Echinochloa frumentacea*)	
Root and tuber crops	Chinese artichoke (*Stachys sieboldii*)	Chinese yam (*Dioscorea batatas*) Arrowhead (*Sagittaria sinensis*)	*Taro (*Colocasia antiquorum*) *Ape (*Alocasia macrorrhiza*) Greater yam (*Dioscorea alata*) Yam (*Dioscorea esculenta*) Yam bean (*Pachyrrhizus erosus*) Water-chestnut (*Eleocharis tuberosa*)	*Taro *Ape
Legumes	Soybean (*Glycine max*)	Adsuki bean (*Phaseolus angularis*)		

*Of uncertain origin or origins.
**Ancient crops no longer in cultivation.
†Introduced from neighboring areas in antiquity.

(continued)

Table 1. Principal Cultivated Plants of the Four Belts in the Far East (continued)

Plant	North China	South China	Southern Asia	Southern islands
Edible oil crops	Soybean	Oil cabbage (*Brassica chinensis* var. *oleifera*)		
Vegetables	*Bulb:* Garlic (*Allium sativum* f. *pekinense*) *Leaf:* **Mallow (*Malva verticillata*) **(*Angelica kiusiana*) **(*Lactuca denticulata*) **(*Nasturtium indicum*) **Knotweed (*Polygonum hydropiper*) **Violet (*Viola verucunda*) **Cocklebur (*Xanthium strumarium*)	*Bulb:* Lily (*Lilium tigrinum*) *Stem:* Manchurian water-rice (*Zizania latifolia*) *Leaf:* Chinese kale (*Brassica alboglabra*) Water mustard (*B. japonica*) Water dropwort (*Oenanthe stolonifera*) Water-shield (*Brasenia schreberi*) Water spinach (*Ipomoea aquatica*) Garland chrysanthemum	*Leaf:* *Amaranth (*Amaranthus mangostanus*) *Fruit:* *Balsam pear (*Memordica charantia*) *White gourd (*Benincasa cerifera*) *Serpent gourd (*Trichosanthes anguina*) *Luffa (*Luffa acutangula*)	

	Welsh onion (*Allium fistulosum*) Leek (*A. ramosum*) Chinese cabbage (*Brassica chinensis*) Celery cabbage (*B. pekinensis*)	(*Chrysanthemum coronarium*) Scallion (*Allium bakeri*) *Flower:* Daylily (*Hemerocallis fulva*)		
Fruit trees	Peach (*Prunus persica*) Chinese plum (*P. salicina*) Apricot (*P. armeniaca*) Japanese apricot (*P. mume*) Chinese cherry (*P. pseudocerasus*) Sand pear (*Pyrus pyrifolia*) (*Malus prunifolia*) Chinese hawthorn (*Crataegus pinnatifida*)	Sour orange (*Citrus aurantium*) Sweet orange (*C. sinensis*) Mandarin orange (*C. reticulata*) Kumquat (*Fortunella japonica*) Wampi (*Clausanea lansium*) Loquat (*Eriobotrya japonica*) (*Myrica rubra*) Litchi (*Litchi chinensis*)	Pummelo (*Citrus grandis*) Lemon (*C. lemon*)	Breadfruit (*Artocarpus incisa*) Jack-fruit (*A. integrifolia*) Carambola (*Averrhoa carambola*) Camias (*A. bilimbi*) *Coconut (*Cocos nucifera*) Lime (*Citrus aurantifolia*) Manogosteen (*Garcinia mangostana*) Rambutan (*Nephelium lappaceum*)

*Of uncertain origin or origins.
**Ancient crops no longer in cultivation.
†Introduced from neighboring areas in antiquity.

(continued)

Table 1. Principal Cultivated Plants of the Four Belts in the Far East (continued)

Plant	North China	South China	Southern Asia	Southern islands
	Persimmon (*Diospyros kaki*) Chinese jujube (*Zizyphus vulgaris*)	Longan (*Euphoria longana*) Chinese olive (*Canarium pimela*)		Lansoné (*Lansium domesticum*) Durian (*Durio zibethinus*) Kotamba (*Terminalia catappa*) Jambu (*Eugenia javanica*)
Other special food crops				Banana (*Musa paradisiaca, M. sapientum*) Sugarcane (*Saccharum offininarum*)
Beverage and masticatories		Tea (*Thea sinensis*)	Betel nut (*Areca catechu*) Betel leaf (*Piper betle*)	
Spices and condiments			Cassia (*Cinnomomum cassia*)	*Ginger (*Zingibera officinale*)

			*Pepper (*Piper nigrum*)	*Turmeric (*Curcuma domestica*) *Pepper Nutmeg (*Myristica fragrans*) Clove (*Eugenia caryophylla*)
Fibre crops	†Hemp (*Canabis sativa*)	Ramie (*Boehmeria nivea*) Chinese jute (*Abutilon avicinnae*) Kudzu vine (*Pueraria thungbergiana*)	†Cotton (*Gossypium arboreum, G. herbaceum*) †Jute (*Corchorus capsularis*)	
Other industrial crops	Mulberry (*Morus alba*) Varnish tree (*Rhus verniciflua*)	Tea oil (*Camellia oleifera*) Chinese tallow tree (*Sapium sebiferum*) Tung oil tree (*Aleurites cordata, A. fordii*)		

*Of uncertain origin or origins.
**Ancient crops no longer in cultivation.
†Introduced from neighboring areas in antiquity.

2 China toward Urban Life

In China, prehistoric archaeology is only just beginning. It may be said to have started in 1920 with the discovery of a Neolithic site at Yang-shao-ts'un, in Mien-ch'ih Hsien, Honan Province, by J. G. Andersson, and a Palaeolithic implement near Chao-chia-chai, in Ch'ing-yang Hsien, Kansu, by Père Emile Licent. During the subsequent decade and a half, through the efforts of Chinese and Western scientists, information concerning the stone ages and the initial bronze age began to accumulate at a moderate rate, until 1937, when the outbreak of the Sino-Japanese War put a stop to the scientific field researches in China. Systematic archaeological field work in this part of the world was not resumed until 1949, when Communist archaeologists began to unearth materials with bewildering rapidity. Thus, what scientific information we have on the formative stage of Chinese civilization was gathered during a mere twenty-seven years (1920-37, 1949-59). The brevity of this period of work, the shifting personal, national, and ideological biases of the Chinese and Western workers during its various stages, and the complete absence (with a handful of exceptions) of collaboration with natural scientists, all help to explain the tentativeness of the interpretation of the formation of the Chinese civilization that is to follow.

It is apparent that a complete areal coverage of China, as large in area as the whole of Europe or most of either of the Americas, with ecological zones no less varying, is next to impossible to achieve in a short essay. We shall therefore focus our attention here upon the area where Chinese cultural tradition emerged and developed, the area of the middle and lower Huangho (or the Yellow River). The northern peripheries of the area in Mongolia and Manchuria and, to the south, the part of the Huaiho, the Yangtze, and the Pearl River valleys into which the Chinese civilization and its formative phases radiated will also be briefly treated.

The temporal coverage of our subject matter is, on the other hand, not difficult to define. Since our interest, in this symposium, lies mainly in the process and mechanism of cultural and social development, suffice it here to delineate our time range, simply on

---

Note: This chapter was originally published in *Courses toward Urban Life*, eds. Robert J. Braidwood and Gordon R. Willey. Viking Fund Publications in *Anthropology* 32 (1962): 177-192. Reprinted with permission of the Wenner-Gren Foundation for Anthropology, New York.

the basis of developmental concepts, as stretching from the terminal stage of the Palaeolithic food-gathering cultures to the emergence of urban life in China. This time span, furthermore, can be pinned down in absolute dates. In spite of the fact that in China none of the modern techniques of dating have so far been utilized, we can date the termination of our developmental sequence in the nuclear area of Chinese culture to the middle part of the second millennium BC, when historic records began with the emergence of urban life, and place its commencement at the late glacial period, which probably is synchronous with the Würm glacial in Europe in geological terms.

The Terminal Food-Gatherers

After the stage of Choukoutien sedimentation, on the eroded surface of the reddish clay (*terra rossa*) in north China (Chingshui erosion of Barbour), a variety of zonal loessic facies accumulated during the climatic interval that has been correlated with the fourth glaciation of the Himalayas (Movius 1944) and the Würm glacial in Europe (W. C. Pei 1939). The climate over north China during the loessic stage was cool and dry—continental—with a prevailing wind from the northwest, though neither cooling nor desiccation is regarded as having then reached a higher peak than now exists in northeastern Asia (Teilhard de Chardin 1941: 35-36). The various regional facies of the loess in north China have been grouped by Père Teilhard de Chardin into two distinct subcycles: A, the true Malan loess with slope deposits dominant; and B, the Mongolian-Manchurian Sands with lake or *nor* deposits dominant (Teilhard de Chardin 1941: 37).

The human industry of subcycle A is represented by the Palaeolithic assemblage at the site of *Shui-tung-kou* in northwest Ordos in the province of Ninghsia, and that of subcycle B by the finds at *Sjara-osso-gol* in the southernmost part of Suiyuan (Boule et al. 1928). "The geological and palaeontological evidence shows that broadly speaking the two sites are contemporary, although Shui-tung-kou may be slightly older than Sjara-osso-gol" (Movius 1955: 279). Both assemblages are characterized by a blade-and-flake tradition and were presumably hunting cultures, as judged from the associated fauna (wild ass, rhinoceros, bison, ostrich, elephants, antelope, horse) and the presence of projectile points. But unlike Shui-tung-kou, which is a blade industry par excellence (blade cores, blades, burins, end scrapers) with a high percentage of "Mousterian" flakes (perforators, points, side scrapers), the Sjara-osso-gol assemblage is, above all, characterized by the predominance of a microblade tradition,[1] which, together with the abundance of bone and antler implements and the apparent increase of the microfauna (insect-eaters, rodents, birds), seems to indicate that, on the one hand, in addition to the hunting of big game the small-game collecting pattern also played an important role and, on the other, the importance of the composite tools apparently increased.

Subsequent to the loessic facies in north China began the recent period, which started with a land movement (and *Panchiao* erosion) and a climatic amelioration that intensified the lacustrine-riverine facies of the loessic stage and extended it to all north China. In other words, the post-Pleistocene started off there with the extinction of the Pleistocene fauna, a rise in temperature and precipitation, an increase of vegetation cover, and a gradual continental uplift and stage of general erosion. This was a moist and warm period, well covered by forests in the loessic highlands in western north China and Manchuria ("the Black Earth stratum") and by *nors*, swamps, marshes, and lakes in the eastern alluvial plains. The woods were inhabited by a variety of animals (including many southern and warm-climate species), but deer were the predominant inhabitants.

If the beginning of the Recent period intensified the lacustrine-riverine facies of the loessic landscape and witnessed its distribution all over north China, it did the same thing with the culture of this interval—the mesolithic stage of north China in general witnessed a general spread and upsurge of the microblade tradition[2] and of composite tool manufacture. But the stage did not spread all over north China. Remains of the early post-Pleistocene hunter-fishers are found only in Mongolia (along the oases where they primarily fished) and in Manchuria and the eastern fringes of the western north China highlands (in the woods and by the water where they hunted and fished; e.g. the Upper Cave of Choukoutien and the Sha-yüan assemblages in central Shensi and northern Shansi). Such remains are not noted in the eastern plains, which may possibly have been too wet to be habitable at that time.

1. This, however, may in part be due to the paucity of raw materials for stone manufacture (see Movius 1955: 279).

2. The microblade tradition in China, also known as the Chinese microlithic culture, is characterized, above all, by small blade cores; retouched or unretouched small bladelets; and the technique of pressure-flaking. It lacks the geometric forms of the microliths, made by the so-called microburin technique, which characterize many microlithic assemblages in western and northern Europe.

Emergence of Food Production in the Huangho Basin

We have little evidence on which to base a conclusion about the earliest dates of food production in China. Speculation is rife in the matter, but the paucity of reliable data forces us to refrain from commenting on the origin of food production in this part of the Old World in any positive manner. We do not even know whether it was spontaneously invented or introduced from the outside as the result of stimulus diffusion. The available archaeological record, furthermore, is regrettably lacking in evidence on the transitional stage from food-gathering to food-producing, and as yet we are substantially ignorant of the when, the where, and the how of this important event in China.

We can, however, legitimately make some well-grounded guesses. If the important event that Gordon Childe has termed the "neolithic revolution" took place in China at all, it probably did so in the region that I have tentatively called the "north China nuclear area," that is, the region around the confluences of the three great rivers, Huangho, Fenho, and Weishui, or the joining place of the three provinces Honan, Shansi, and Shensi (K. C. Chang 1959a). The north China nuclear area is in fact a small basin encircled on the north, west, and south by the Shansi plateau, the Shensi-Kansu loessic plateau, and the Tsinling Mountains, but open to the eastern plains. The speculative role of this region as a cradle for the food-producing cultures of north China has been based on a number of considerations. In the first place, as described above, during the "climatic optimum," the nuclear area was located on the border between the western highlands and the eastern lowlands, and thus it had both the "hilly flanks" and the habitat for the sedentary waterside fishermen that Robert Braidwood (1952) and Carl Sauer (1948) consider, respectively, as the birthplace of farmers and herders. It had, first, rain and warmth enough to be comfortably off and herds of game and fish shoals enough to sustain its inhabitants. It was also conveniently located at the intersection of natural avenues of communication. Second, it is in the nuclear area that the only Huangho basin Mesolithic assemblage was found in the Sha-yuan (sand-dune) region in Chao-i and Ta-li Counties in eastern Shensi of the lower Wei-shui valley (K. C. Chang 1958: 51-55). Third, the only stratigraphically suggested pre-Yang-shao Neolithic evidence was found in Pao-chi Hsien in the middle Wei-shui valley, peripheral to the nuclear area (T. K. Cheng 1959: 68). In the fourth place, the importance of fishing, as shown during the subsequent Yang-shao stage in this area, is highly suggestive (N. Hsia 1957). In the fifth place, archaeological evidence is ample to demonstrate that the nuclear area played a leading role in the transition from the Yang-shao to the Lung-shan (K. C. Chang 1959a; C. M. An 1959). Finally, during most of the four thousand years of historic China, the nuclear area had always been one of the strategically vital regions that have controlled the destiny of the entire Empire to a considerable extent (see Lattimore 1951: 27-33).

It is thus conceivable that at a few millennia BC the terminal food-gatherers in the nuclear area, having possibly already settled down and having a well-developed culture, switched to food production by inventing or adopting plant cultivation and animal domestication. Although in the subsequent Neolithic stages there were still a handful of items of a Mesolithic woodland heritage (e.g. pressure-flaked projectile points and arrowheads, chipped-stone discs, microblades, prismatic arrowheads, semisubterranean dwellings, and semilunar and rectangular stone knives), and the possibility cannot yet be entirely ruled out that the first idea of food production was introduced rather than invented, yet—from what we know of it—Chinese Neolithic culture assumed a distinctive pattern from the very beginning that shows independence and originality. The following traits, considered either singly or totally, have been enumerated as being characteristic of the Chinese Neolithic culture tradition (K. C. Chang 1959a).

1. The cultivation of millet, rice, and kaoliang (and possibly the soybean)
2. The domestication of pig, cattle, sheep, dog, chicken, and possibly horse
3. The *hang-t'u* (stamped earth) structures and the lime-plastered house floors
4. The domestication of silkworms and the loom (?)-weaving of silk and hemp
5. Possible use of tailored garments
6. Pottery with cord-mat-basket designs
7. Pottery tripods (especially *ting* and *li*) and pottery steamers (*tseng* and *yen*) and the possible use of chopsticks
8. Semilunar and rectangular stone knives
9. The great development of ceremonial vessels
10. The elaborate complex of jade artifacts; a possible wood-carving complex
11. Scapulimancy

In addition to these, the Chinese language presumably had a Neolithic basis. Such a cultural tradition was not accumulated overnight, but of its initial stages there is as yet scarcely any evidence in the archaeological record. That the earliest ceramic phases in north China were probably characterized by the cord-mat-basket-marked wares (Shengwen horizon; see K. C. Chang 1959a) has been speculated upon, on the ground of geographic distribution (Ward 1954), and is meagerly substantiated by some stratigraphical evidence (T. K. Cheng 1959: 68). But of the general cultural configuration of the earliest ceramic phases we know next to nothing. An era of incipient cultivation has been assumed on the ground of necessity (K. C. Chang 1959a); whether this era can be equated with the Shengwen horizon is a big question.

From this point on we are on surer ground (see K. C. Chang 1959a; T. K. Cheng 1959; G. D. Wu 1938; Andersson 1943; Teilhard de Chardin and Pei 1944). From a small part of north China, the part with the nuclear area as a center and including northern and western Honan, southern and central Shansi, southwestern Hopei, central Shensi, and eastern Kansu, still largely confined within the drainages of the middle Huangho, Fenho, and Wei-shui, there have been found hundreds of prehistoric sites that are grouped together by their similar stratigraphic position and by the presence of a number of common distinctive horizon markers—painted pottery, some pottery forms (pointed-bottomed jars, flat- and round-based cups and bowls, thin-necked and big-belly jars, and possibly *li*-tripods), and some characteristic stone forms (rectangular knives and round axes, mostly symmetrically edged). In terms of cultural style this was the Yang-shao horizon—which as a horizon had a solid functional basis, as will be presently seen—and in terms of ecosocial development this was the stage of the establishment of the farming villages and effective food production.

Archaeological remains of the Yang-shao horizon indicate the appearance of moderate-sized (200-300 meters to a side) nucleated villages. Approximately a dozen round or rectangular semisubterranean dwellings, or sometimes a few long, partitioned communal houses, comprised the village, which, according to the community patterning, might have sheltered one or several lineages or clans. The inhabitants engaged in farming, cultivating millet (*Setaria* and *Panicum*), and animal husbandry (dog and pig). The cultivating implements included the hoe, spade, digging-stick, and weeding knife. According to the shifting and repetitive pattern of settlement—indicated by the multiple components of the sites and the brevity of occupation of each component—it seems reasonable to assume that these early farmers engaged in slash-and-burn cultivation. Stone axes with a round or lentoid cross section and a symmetrical edge were manufactured, presumably for clearing fields in the woods. Stone implements were chipped, pecked, or ground, and pottery of a variety of paste was manufactured, by hand (often coiled) or with the aid of a mold. Most of the ceramic wares were of a domestic nature: cooking pots, water jars, storage jars, and bowls and cups; some of them (especially the cooking pots) were impressed with cord-mat-basket patterns, and others were beautifully painted in monochromic or bichromic decorations. Hunting and fishing took place, sometimes on a considerable scale, but these activities remained of a supplementary nature. The bow and arrow, harpoons, spears, and fishhooks were among the principal implements. Silkworms were raised, and hemp was possibly cultivated; the fabrics were spun (spindle-whorls), woven (loom?), and sewed (eyed needles).

Each village of Yang-shao farmers was apparently a self-contained "little community," consisting of a dwelling area, an incorporated or separate quarter with kilns, and a village cemetery. Considering that the decorative art was focused upon domestic activities, that the evidence of a religious nature points to a fecundity cult and a fertility ritual that was presumably performed on behalf of the whole community rather than for a selected portion of the inhabitants, and that the community pattern shows no symbolic orientation of outstandingly privileged personnel, one tends to conclude that the internal status-and-role differentiation of the village inhabitants was not significantly developed; presumably, such distinctions as existed were based on age, sex, and personal achievement. The tenor of life seems to have been peaceful in the main, since evidence of both defensive measures and offensive weapons is scanty.

Presumably during this stage the Yang-shao farmers were only beginning to become established, and the process of their expansion, within the limited region of the nuclear area and its peripheral surroundings, was largely confined to the gradual reclamation of immediately accessible and cultivable land by the descendant villages, which had split from their relatively overpopulated parent villages. Evidence from the Pan-shan hills in eastern Kansu and from a group of settlements in Hua Hsien in eastern Shensi shows that several neighboring villages shared a common cemetery, and this can best be interpreted in terms of the split-village situation rather than in terms of the formation of alliances of many discrete villages. The argument for this kind of expansion is also supported by the uniformity of style over the entire area of distribution of the Yang-shao horizon. Though there were minor regional variations and two possible microhorizons (Honan and Kansu), the stage shows striking stylistic uniformity over a wide area, as compared with the stage that was to follow.

Expansion of the Huangho Farming Villages and the Formation of Regional Traditions

Since the transition from food-gathering to food-producing is not documented in the archaeological record of north China, the consequences of the emergence of food production in the Huangho basin are not directly observable in the brief account we have presented so far; but from what followed, one is able to extrapolate and examine certain highly probable consequences.

The rate of growth of productivity brought about by the introduction of agriculture and animal husbandry can hardly be exaggerated. Two immediate consequences were the growth of population density and the potentiality for the elaboration of culture owing to the reserve energy released by surplus. Further consequences consisted of the fixity of settlements, the internal status-and-role specialization of communities, the frequency of warfare, the general spread of farming villages into the hitherto unexplored and underexplored areas, and the formation of a number of regional traditions that were synchronized in a widespread Lungshanoid horizon. Let us examine each of these phenomena in turn (see K. C. Chang 1959a, b; T. K. Cheng 1959; S. Y. Liang 1939; C. Li *et al.* 1934; Andersson 1943, 1947).

The Lungshanoid settlements were spread over most of China proper, but they can be grouped together on the basis of stratigraphy and a horizon style that was distinctive of this stage. These horizon-markers include the following:

(1) A great variety of pottery forms, particularly tripods (*li, ting, chia, kui*) and ring-footed vessels (*tsun, p'o,* and *tou* or fruit-stand). These forms characterize not only the Lungshanoid of north China but also areas far beyond it, and they may, together with scapulimancy, reflect the complexity of rituals in this stage.

(2) A distinctive ceramic style. One of the most striking features of the pottery of this horizon is the sharpness of the curves on every part of the body, in great contrast to the "roundness" of the pottery shapes of the Yang-shao horizon.

(3) The perforated-ring feet of fruit-stands and other forms of vessels.

(4) The decline of the art of ceramic painting, the increase of

incisions and combed marks and the appearance of checker impressions.

(5) Certain edged tools of stone, which are often square or rectangular in cross section and which have assymmetrical edges.

The ecosocial basis of these stylistic expressions is not hard to find. The Lungshanoid settlements were considerably larger than the Yang-shao ones in areal dimensions and were often of longer duration. The repetitive settlement occupation pattern had given way to settled, permanent villages, as indicated by the conditions of continuous deposition, the permanent earthen village walls, the predominance of adzes and chisels (woodworking complex) over axes (for forest-clearance primarily), and the general configuration of the settlement culture, among other things. Besides noting some basis in ecology (the wet and fertile land provided by the eastern low countries into which the farmers had expanded), we are still uncertain as to the basic factors that brought about the tendency toward permanent settlement in north China as a whole. Irrigation, the use of fertilizer, the fallowing of fields, and the improvement of cultivating implements and techniques are all possible innovations of this stage, but we have no substantial evidence of any one of them. Metals might have been used to a small extent (a few metal objects have been found from a Lung-shan-stage site in Kansu and from one in Hopei, and the sharp curves of pottery are suggestive of a metallic fashion), but it seems extremely unlikely that metal was used for making agricultural implements at this time. In fact, metal does not seem to have been widely employed for this purpose in ancient China until iron came into use in the mid-first millennium BC. From the little we do know about status-and-role differentiation and the presence of public works (the village wall), it is not altogether unreasonable to assume that the fixity of settlements during this stage resulted, to a certain extent, from a kind of organized management of manpower that could have achieved a greater efficiency than heretofore. But there is a good deal of speculation in this statement.

In the Huaiho valley, remains of rice grains were found in a Lungshanoid context, but it seems proper to assume that millet remained a leading staple in the north. Hoes, spades, digging-sticks, and sickles are the principal farming tools that are known archaeologically; and stone, clay, bone and antler, shell and presumably wood constituted the raw materials of artifact manufacture. Cattle, sheep-goats and the horse may have been added at this time. Hunting and fishing were locally important. In a word, the basic technology does not seem to have undergone any considerable improvement during this stage, and the growing productivity can be accounted for only in terms of social organization and management. The significant novelty of this stage seems to lie in its increasing population density and the growth of internal specialization and differentiation among the populace.

The internal specialization and differentiation of the villages are shown by a number of indications. In several of the Lung-shan traditions the potter's wheel was now in use. This, plus the fact that some of the black pottery was extremely finely and delicately manufactured, points to the fact that by this time pottery-making was already a full-time job. Metallurgy, as was suggested above, may have begun in this stage; what metallurgy implies in terms of craft specialization is common knowledge.

There is also some evidence of a differentiation of personnel in other terms at this stage. At the Liang-ch'eng-chen site in Jih-chao on the coastal Shantung, there was one spot where finely made jade objects were concentrated. Also at this settlement and at a site at Ta-ch'eng-shan near T'ang-shan in Hopei, the burials were both face up and prone, a suggestion of status differentiation, according to the Yin-Shang mode of interment. Furthermore, during this stage the art of scapulimancy appeared, seen all over north and central China in Hopei, Shantung, Honan, Shansi, Shensi, Kansu, Anhwei, and Kiangsu, which was presumably handled by a specialized class of shamans or priests. In this regard, the prevalence and variety of ceremonial vessels is highly suggestive. Taken together, such indications support the conclusion that in the Lungshanoid settlements there were specialized craftsmen, full-time administrators, and priest-shamans, and that there were also a theocratic art and a theocratically vested ceremonial pattern, which, no longer the common property of the entire village, was focused upon a selected portion of the villagers. From what we know of the later (Yin-Shang) practices, the basis of selection might have been founded on kinship.

Each of the Lungshanoid villages, however, seems to remain self-contained in the basic ecosocial and religious affairs, as indicated by the completeness of the functional network of the settlement culture. Relationships among settlements might have been more frequent than previously, but not infrequently the relationship was rather hostile and took the form of warfare. The earth walls of the Lungshanoid settlements at Hou-kang in northern Honan and at Ch'eng-tzu-yai in central Shantung appear too high and too thick to have served as decorations or boundary markers in time of peace. Arrowheads, daggers, spears, halberds, and clubs were among the offensive weapons. Skeletons were found at a site near Han-tan, Hopei, that show evidence of violent death, some having even been beheaded or scalped. This is hardly unexpected, for as population grew, taxing the land's capacity, people either reclaimed more land or fought for the field that was already available.

The transition from the Yang-shao stage to the Lung-shan stage seems to have started somewhere in the nuclear area (K. C. Chang 1959a). There are some two dozen sites now where the Lung-shan-over-Yang-shao-with-a-break-in-between stratigraphy has been observed, sites distributed all over the middle Huangho valley, from Kansu to northern Honan. On the other hand, in the nuclear area, in western Honan, southern Shansi, and eastern central Shensi, there are a number of sites of the transitional stage that show a mixture of the markers of both horizons, although the Yang-shao markers predominate in quantity in the lower portions of the deposit, as the Lungshanoid ones do in the upper. The famed site at Yang-shao-ts'un itself, for instance, belongs to this transitional category, though for the sake of convenience the name Yang-shao has been temporarily maintained for the horizon stage that preceded the Lung-shan. Moreover, it is in the nuclear area that an early form of the Lung-shan-stage horizon has been found (C. M. An 1959) that seems to be the prototype from which the other peripheral Lungshanoid traditions radiated.

Following the lead of the nuclear area, the Lung-shan settlers gradually developed upon the basis of the Yang-shao shifting-farmer level into the entire area on the western highlands of north China. Population pressure, among other factors, might have been responsible for causing the north China farmers to spread into the formerly unexplored or underexplored riverine, lacustrine, wooded and hilly regions in the east, north, and south. The distribution of Yang-shao sites indicates that the eastern plains, the Huaiho valley, and the Shantung uplands were not at this time significantly occupied by the farmers, if at all, possibly owing to the swampy environment. The Lung-shan settlers, however, began to penetrate into this area and build earth mounds on which village sites were located. To the north, agricultural settlements began to appear in the southern fringes of the Jehol mountains, the Liao-Sungari plains, and the southeastern Manchurian uplands. Remains of these settlements show a clear mixture of the Lungshanoid elements and the woodland and maritime Mesolithic and Subneolithic hunting-fishing inventories.

South of the Tsinling mountains and the Huaiho valley, insofar as we know at present, evidence of agriculture and animal husbandry begins with the widespread appearance of Lungshanoid horizon (K. C. Chang 1959b). Prior to this horizon, the evidence indicates that only the southwestern portion of south China was inhabited by Mesolithic food-collectors, whom some scholars have labeled the "Hoabinhian" because of the similarity of their cultural inventory to that of their Indochinese contemporaries. Subsequent to the nonceramic phase of this sheet of culture and prior to the appearance of the Lungshanoid farmers there was probably an intermediate ceramic stage, characterized by the appearance of cord-marked pottery and some polished-stone implements. These remains have been located in scatters in the southwest, on the coasts of Kwangtung, and on the island of Formosa. But evidence of both agriculture and its cultural affinities is still wanting. At any rate, the extensive exploration—at an early agricultural level—of the central and south China jungles, hills, and swampy valleys was the achievement of the Lungshanoid farmers spreading from the north. When these farmers had moved into a new ecological zone, they were forced to perform a series of important adaptive changes, which led to the predominance of rice and presumably fruit-and-root crops over millet, and the abandonment of stamped-earth structures and of lime-plastered floors. Mounds or pile-dwellings were built along the eastern coasts, and there is a generally pioneer aspect to their settlement and culture. These southern Lungshanoid farmers then began to settle down and, after receiving considerable stimulation (primarily in connection with metallurgy and decorative patterns) from the urban civilization subsequently developed in the north, a southern geometric horizon developed that was assimilated shortly before the time of Christ by the Ch'in and Han empires.

On account of the wide expanse of the area; the great environmental differences that the settlers encountered in moving into it; the hostility between settlements, with a resultant semi-isolation; and the different groups of hunter-fishers assimilated by the settlers in the new environment, the Lungshanoid horizon—although unified by its constituents' common heritage, by their similar developmental situation, and by far-reaching trade—was divided into a number of regional stylistic traditions. The most easily distinguished of these are the Honan, the Shansi-Shensi, the Kansu, the

Shantung, the southern Manchurian, the Huaiho, the Hanshui, and the southeastern coastal traditions. It was with one of these regional Lungshanoid traditions (Honan, Shensi-Shansi, or Hanshui, according to different advocates) as a base that the first Chinese civilization eventually came into being.

Emergence of Civilization in the Huangho Basin

The Lung-shan horizon of the formative stage of ancient Chinese culture in the alluvial plains of the lower and middle Huangho valley and in the Huaiho valley, in the provinces of Honan, western Shantung, southwestern Hopei, eastern Shensi, northern Anhwei, and northern Kiangsu, was followed by the first civilization in Chinese history that has been amply substantiated by archaeology, the Yin-Shang Dynasty (see C. Li 1957a; T. K. Cheng 1957). The Yin-Shang civilization has all the essential ingredients that a civilization is supposed to contain—writing, a fully developed bronze metallurgy, palaces and temples, science and the calendar, chariots and squads of warriors, a political and religious hierarchy of a royal house, class differentiation, far-reaching trade, a centralized management and redistribution of agricultural produce and other scarce goods, and a great artistic tradition. There are two settlement groups of this period that are relatively well known archaeologically, Anyang and Chengchow, both in northern Honan. Each was composed of a number of small farming and handicrafting communities, whose close ties are indicated by their clustering within eye-sight distances and their sharing of a common administrative and ceremonial center. This was Hsiao-t'un in the case of Anyang and an earth-walled town in the case of Chengchow.

The emergence of such a highly developed civilization in the Huangho basin appears to have been in itself relatively sudden and new, and most archaeologists believe that there must have been a transitional period between the Lung-shan and the Yin-Shang horizons. It must be stressed, however, that from the Neolithic Lung-shan to the bronze-age Yin-Shang there was a developmental continuation rather than a cultural break. The accompanying chart shows in a preliminary manner the Neolithic heritage of the Yin-Shang bronze-age culture and its innovations (see S. Y. Liang 1939; C. Li 1957a) (Table 2).

From the mere enumeration given in the chart it becomes apparent that in the past the "suddenness" of the emergence of the Yin-Shang civilization has been unduly exaggerated. Even the new items in the right-hand column mostly indicate a process of intensification and a change in degree. It is apparent, however, that civili-

Table 2. Neolithic-Bronze Age Continuities and Discontinuities in North China

Continuities	Discontinuities
A. Formation of village aggregates	*a*) Mature urbanism and related institutions (especially the formation of differentiated groups)
B. Raids and warfare	*b*) Class differentiation
C. Status differentiation and prone burials	*c*) New government and economic patterns (conquest, tribute, redistribution)
D. The elaborate ceremonial complex (more lineage-ancestral than community-agricultural)	*d*) Wider trade, currency
E. Cultivation of millet, rice, wheat, and hemp	*e*) New war patterns (capture of slaves and use of the chariot)
F. Use of domesticated dog, pig, cattle, sheep, horse, chicken	*f*) Chamber burials and human sacrifice
G. Stamped-earth structures	*g*) Domestication of water buffalo; possible use of wooden plow
H. Semisubterranean houses and lime-plastered floors	*h*) Highly developed bronze metallurgy
I. Industrial specialization	*i*) Writing
J. Scapulimancy	*j*) Advanced stone carvings
K. Some pottery forms (especially ritual forms with ring-feet and lids)	*k*) New pottery forms
L. The Shengwen (corded ware) tradition	
M. Some decorative motifs	
N. Some stone implements and weapons	
O. Shell and bone craft	
P. Silk	
Q. The jade complex	
R. Language (?)	

zation in China started with the Yin-Shang and not, as is sometimes asserted, with the Lung-shan stage and that these two are decisively different. First of all, the Yin-Shang witnessed the intensifications of all aspects of Chinese culture—more advanced technology, greater population density, more intensified status-and-role differentiation, greater centralization of government and economy, more frequent warfare, and more institutionalized communication in the form of writing and trade

The developmental change of society and culture during the Yin-Shang is, furthermore, most distinctively marked off by the formation of the differentiated settlement groups and the specialization of the various settlements in a settlement group in ecosocial functions. The Lung-shan communities, as previously stated, were self-contained "little communities," in spite of their sometimes large size and some degree of internal specialization and differentiation. But the Yin-Shang settlements had become specialized externally in ecosocial functions. Each community no longer worked only for its own survival and wealth, but worked for other communities and was worked for by others as well. The new horizon was marked by the appearance of centers of administration, redistribution, and ceremony, which one may call towns or cities, where officials and priests managed rather than labored. There were also farming and handicrafting hamlets, the inhabitants of which engaged in organized labor coordinated under a central control. This phenomenon, the ecosocial interdependence among specialized communities, is to this author one of the most decisive criteria of urbanization, which in turn was brought about by a change of the total social-cultural structure. Insofar as one can see from the archaeological record of this part of the world, no single factor alone makes a civilization appear.

Comment

The foregoing discussion can be summarized, in a simplified fashion (Figs. 1 and 2), in stratigraphical-typological profiles cutting through most of China longitudinally and perpendicularly, respectively.

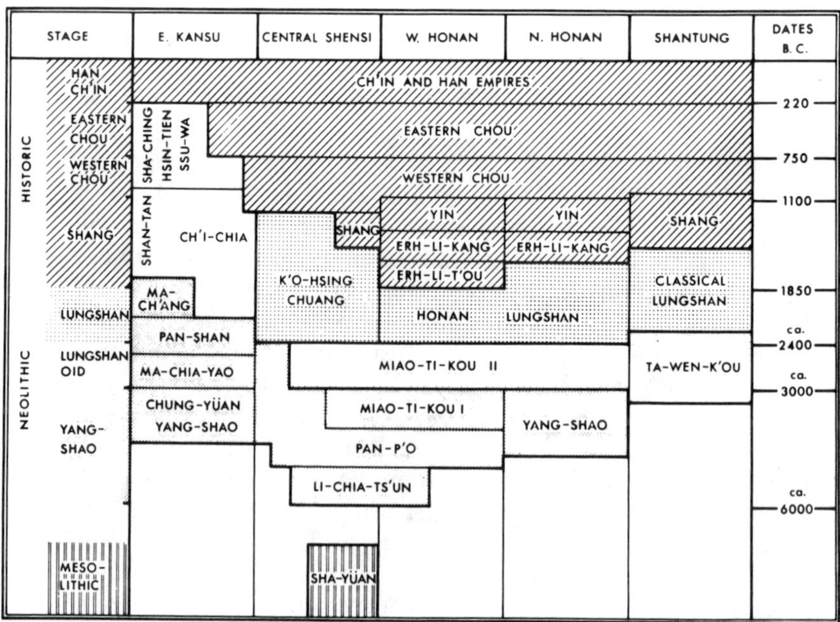

Figure 1. Ancient Culture Chronologies of North China

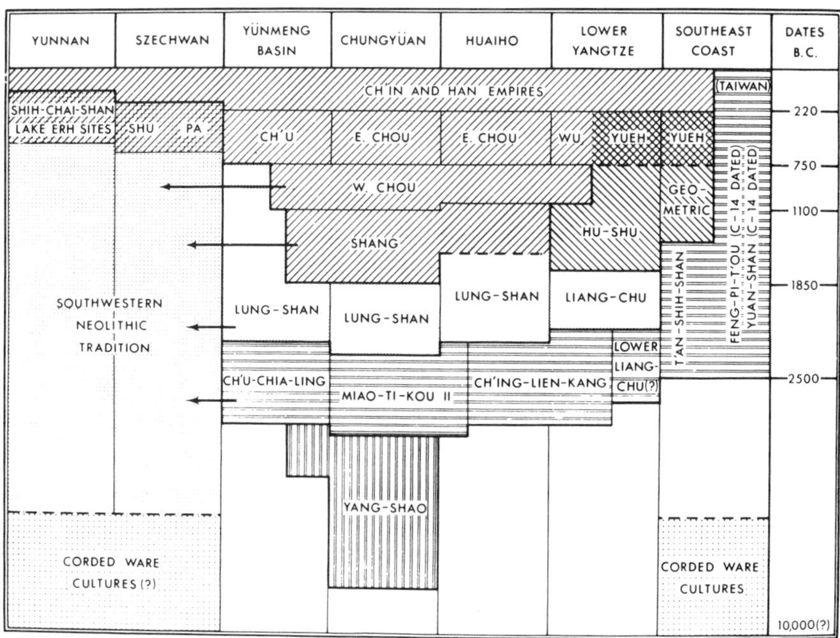

Figure 2. Ancient Culture Chronologies of South China

The tentative nature of the foregoing synthesis is most readily admitted. Indeed, it will be astonishing if, within a decade, new information that is now accumulating does not force an amplification and amendment of our scheme—perhaps even its drastic alteration. At the present time the scheme given above is the most we can do, but this is an attempt that has to be made if a world-wide consideration of cultural alternatives is to be made. Alfred Whitehead once observed that China "forms the largest volume of civilisation which the world has seen." Any consideration of the nature of civilization's growth in general cannot afford to leave China out, and China must be dealt with in the theoretical terms that anthropologists all over the globe are at home with. These theoretical terms are not those of the traditional doctrine in Chinese archaeology. It is the traditional viewpoint that in Neolithic China (and, for some obscure reason, only in a late aspect of it) there were two (or possibly three) distinctive cultural strains. The Yang-shao (or "Painted Pottery") and the Lung-shan (or "Black Pottery") are the main suggested strains, the former in the west and the latter along the eastern coast. Yin-Shang civilization was derived—the traditional viewpoint holds—from a third strain, which came to China fully developed from some source not yet fully specified. It is only now that, equipped with a good deal more data, we can begin to consider some of the major premises afresh and adopt a holistic, configurational, and functional approach that a new and probably truer picture has emerged. The prehistoric cultures in China are no longer regarded as a conglomeration of indigenous and exotic traits each of which had a separate history of development. Rather, the structural covariations and efficient causes are being stressed in terms of social mechanism and cultural pattern.

In the same manner, the problems regarding the "origins" of cultural elements in ancient China, which were the focusing point of many archaeologists and sinologues, have also received some basically fresh reappraisal. The origin and history of the development of various and sundry objects are highly interesting and instructive matters, no doubt; but it is becoming clear that the basic issues of cultural and social growth do not necessarily rely upon their solutions. It is this writer's profound conviction that ancient China owed much of her riches to loans from the outside, just as many outsiders owed their riches to loans from her. But, to the writer, the important issue lies primarily in the functional context of the development sequence itself, without an understanding of which one will never understand how and why China received outside help at a certain point of time and how and why she had such things to offer in return.

Addendum
Radiocarbon Dates from China, Some Initial Interpretations

Until recently, the technique of radiocarbon dating has been applied in Chinese archaeology only to samples from the southeastern coastal provinces of Kwangtung (Beyer 1956) and Taiwan (Stuiver 1969). Consequently, much of Chinese prehistory was dated relatively and speculatively (e.g. K. C. Chang 1966; 1968). After having attempted to put together such a speculative scheme some five years ago, I made these observations:

For all its stress on archaeology, China, whose technology is capable of producing the hydrogen bomb, has yet to establish a radiocarbon dating laboratory. It is almost certain that the chrono-

---

Note: This essay was originally published in *Current Anthropology* 14 (1973): 525-528. Reprinted with permission of *Current Anthropology*.

logical assessments made here of various archaeological cultures are due for some drastic revision when several dozen well-placed carbon-14 dates become available. (K. C. Chang 1968: 448)

Fortunately, these statements have since proved to be incorrect in every way. Not only was my prediction of "drastic revision" unwarranted, but I was wrong in my facts. A radiocarbon laboratory was established in Peking as early as 1965 within the Institute of Archaeology, in the Chinese Academy of Sciences (Chung-kuo K'o-hsüeh Yüan K'ao-ku Yen-chiu Suo). Samples from archaeological sites of known historical age were processed first, and then prehistoric materials were studied. This work was interrupted in the middle of 1966 by the Cultural Revolution, but it was resumed in late 1971. The first results, from the work done during the late 1965-early 1966 and late 1971-early 1972 periods, are reported in two articles published in the journal *K'ao-ku* (*Archaeology*), Nos. 1 and 5 Volume 1972 (Chung-kuo K'o-hsüeh Yüan K'ao-ku Yen-chiu Suo Shih-yen-shih 1972a, 1972b). These are summarized in Table 3.

For a discussion of the significance of these dates, we must take into account the Taiwan dates published earlier (Stuiver 1969; K. C. Chang et al. 1969: 265-6) and a new date from Taiwan that has just been reported by the Radiocarbon Laboratory of the Smithsonian Institution (Robert Stuckenrath, personal communications 1972). This new date (SI-1229) is that of an oyster shell Mr. Huang Shih-chiang (of National Taiwan University) and I collected in July, 1972, in the Kuei-jen district of Tainan county, in southern Taiwan, at a prehistoric site characterized by cord-marked pottery remains of a late Ta-p'en-k'eng type: 5480 ± 55 BP (5568 ± 30 half life), 5645 ± 60 BP (5730 ± 40 half life), 3695 ± 60 BC. This single date obviously requires corroboration, and the same is true of some of the Peking dates. Some important prehistoric cultures—covering vast spaces and presumably long time-spans—are still each represented by a single radiocarbon date, or at most two, and we must be very cautious in our interpretations. Some tentative interpretation is warranted, however, in view of the consistency of the dates among themselves and the fact that small clusters of such dates are available for some sites (Pan-p'o and several Taiwan sites) and some cultures (Yang-shao and the Lungshanoid cultures). The following are some first reactions (see C. M. An 1972a; 1972b).

(1) For the first time, Chinese prehistory can be placed on a rudimentary absolute-chronological basis. In this, however, there are few surprises. The only major discrepancy has to do with

Table 3. Twenty-eight Radiocarbon Dates from Ancient China

Sample	Archaeological site	Nature of sample	Associated culture	BP (b.1950)* (5568 ± 30 half life)	BP (b.1950)* (5730 ± 40 half life)	BC (5730 ± 40 half life)
ZK-38	Pan-p'o, Sian (Shensi)	charcoal	Yang-shao Culture	5890 ± 110	6065 ± 110	4115 ± 110
ZK-121	--	-	-	5730 ± 100	5905 ± 105	3955 ± 105
ZK-122	--	-	-	5670 ± 100	5840 ± 105	3890 ± 105
ZK-127	--	carbonized fruit pit	-	5420 ± 100	5585 ± 105	3635 ± 105
ZK-76	Hou-kang, An-yang (Honan)	charcoal	-	5330 ± 100	5485 ± 105	3535 ± 105
ZK-110	Miao-ti-kou, Shan Hsien (Honan)	-	-	5080 ± 100	5230 ± 100	3280 ± 100
ZK-111	--	-	Miao-ti-kou II Culture	4140 ± 90	4260 ± 95	2310 ± 95
ZK-126	Wang-wan, Lo-yang (Honan)	-	Honan Lung-shan Culture	3830 ± 90	3950 ± 95	2000 ± 95
ZK-86	Hsiao-t'un, An-yang (Honan)	-	Shang civilization	2980 ± 90	3065 ± 90	1115 ± 90
ZK-5	Wu-kuan-ts'un, An-yang (Honan)	-	-	2950 ± 100	3035 ± 100	1085 ± 100
ZK-3	Ku-wei-ts'un, Huei Hsien (Honan)	wood	Chou (Warring-States)	2170 ± 80	2240 ± 80	290 ± 80
ZK-108	Ts'ao-chia-tsui, Lan-chou (Kansu)	charcoal	Ma-chia-yao Culture	4390 ± 100	4525 ± 100	2575 ± 100
ZK-21	Ma-chia-wan, Yüng-ching (Kansu)	-	Ma-ch'ang Culture	4010 ± 100	4135 ± 100	2185 ± 100
ZK-25	Ch'ing-kang-ch'a, Lan-chou (Kansu)	burned wood	Pan-shan Culture	3900 ± 100	4015 ± 100	2065 ± 100
ZK-61	Ta-li-t'a-li-ha, No-mu-hung (Chinghai)	wood	No-mu-hung Culture	3670 ± 90	3775 ± 90	1825 ± 90
ZK-15	Ta-ho-chuang, Yung-ching (Kansu)	charcoal	Ch'i-chia Culture	3570 ± 90	3675 ± 95	1725 ± 95
ZK-23	--	-	-	3540 ± 90	3645 ± 95	1695 ± 95
ZK-17	Chao-su, Yi-li (Sinkiang)	-	ancient grave	1960 ± 90	2015 ± 90	65 ± 90
ZK-78	Shuang-t'uo-tzu, Lü-ta (Liaoning)	burned wood	Lung-shan Culture	3890 ± 90	4010 ± 95	2060 ± 95
ZK-79	--	-	-	3030 ± 90	3120 ± 90	1170 ± 90
ZK-19	Huang-shan-hsi, Tze-yang (Szechwan)	wood	"Tze-yang Man"	7270 ± 130	7485 ± 130	5535 ± 130
ZK-10	Hai-men-k'ou, Chien-ch'uan (Yunnan)	-	Hai-men-k'ou Culture	3010 ± 90	3100 ± 90	1150 ± 90

Sample	Archaeological site	Nature of sample	Associated culture	BP (b.1950)* (5568 ± 30 half life)	BP (b.1950)* (5730 ± 40 half life)	BC (5730 ± 40 half life)
ZK-55	Sung-tse, Ch'ing-p'u, Shanghai (Kiangsu)	-	Ch'ing-lien-kang Culture	5190 ± 100	5345 ± 105	3395 ± 105
ZK-49	Ch'ien-shan-yang, Wu-hsing (Chekiang)	rice husks	Liang-chu Culture	4560 ± 100	4700 ± 100	2750 ± 100
ZK-51	P'ao-ma-ling, Hsiu-shui (Kiangsi)	charcoal	new Lungshanoid culture	4160 ± 90	4285 ± 95	2335 ± 95
ZK-91	Huang-chien-shu, Hsi-ch'uan (Honan)	-	Ch'ü-chia-ling Culture	4100 ± 90	4220 ± 95	2270 ± 95
ZK-1	Ch'ang-sha (Hunan)	wood	Ch'u civilization	2330 ± 90	2395 ± 90	445 ± 90
ZK-6	--	-	Han civilization	1930 ± 80	1985 ± 80	35 ± 80

*In the original reports the C^{14} dates in both BP and BC are rendered from the 5730 ± 40 half life. For unexplained reasons, the BP dates are based on 1965 rather than 1950 as internationally agreed upon. In this chart, the BP dates have been adjusted (by deducting 15 years from the published figures), and BP dates based on the 5568 half life have been added, both to facilitate comparison with radiocarbon dates reported from other sources. The 28 dates are here first clustered by area (North China, the Northwest, the Northeast, the Southwest, and the Southeast), and within each area dates are listed from early to late.

Tze-yang Man, dated to the Upper Pleistocene on palaeontological and geological grounds but now shown to have an associated carbon-14 date of only 7500 years ago. The dating of this human fossil is far from settled, however, and since no cultural chronology is at issue here I shall leave it aside. Otherwise, the chronological judgments that have been made by Chinese archaeologists in the recent past on the basis of stratigraphy and typology have been largely borne out by the new radiocarbon dates in all three of the following respects: relative chronologies within each of the major regions of prehistoric China, the relative chronology of various prehistoric cultures across the major regions of China, and the absolute dates tentatively assigned to each of the major prehistoric cultures. This becomes immediately apparent when one plots the new radiocarbon dates onto some of the latest preradiocarbon chronological charts (e.g. K. C. Chang 1968: 443, 445, Tables 15 and 16). In one or two places, however, even though the deviation of the radiocarbon dates from the conjectured model is still within tolerable ranges, fresh thinking appears to be called for, because the new dates tend to strengthen alternative interpretations that have not been emphasized enough in the past.

Only two regions have adequate numbers of dates from prehistoric cultures to form a sequence: the Honan-Shensi area (or the north China nuclear area) and eastern Kansu. In the former, the Pan-p'o—Miao-ti-kou I—Miao-ti-kou II—Honan Lung-shan—Shang sequence, established mostly through ceramic typology, is confirmed by the new dates, although the early date of the Yang-shao Culture at Hou-kang in northern Honan (ZK-76) is not totally expected. In Kansu, the relative positions of Ma-chia-yao (earliest), Pan-shan/Ma-ch'ang, and Ch'i-chia (latest) again confirm the conclusion long since reached on relative grounds. The Ma-chia-wan date (ZK-21) of what has been identified as a Ma-ch'ang Culture site is roughly identical with (or slightly earlier than) the Ch'ing-kang-ch'a date (ZK-25) of a Pan-shan Culture site. In the past we have regarded Pan-shan as being slightly earlier than Ma-ch'ang. The two new dates point to the reverse, although additional data are needed, especially from Ma-ch'ang sites in the Huang-shui (Hsi-ning-ho) valley, before the chronological interrelationship of Pan-shan and Ma-ch'ang may be considered as certain.

For cross-regional relative chronologies, three sets of new dates are of particular significance: *First*, the Pan-p'o dates of north China (ZK-38, ZK-121, ZK-122, ZK-127) and the Tainan date of Taiwan (SI-1229) show that by at least 4000 BC two ceramic cultures existed side by side in north and southeast China. Neither can be said to represent the initial form of its ceramic tradition, and neither can at this time be seen as derivative of the other. *Second,* the Kansu Yang-shao Culture is now more than ever shown to be an extension or a late phase of the nuclear area Yang-shao Culture. *Third,* four dates from four cultures that have been referred to as Lungshanoid—Miao-ti-kou II, Liang-chu, Hsiu-shui, and Ch'ü-chia-ling—fall within the third millennium BC, to which I have also assigned the initial Lungshanoid cultures of Taiwan (K. C. Chang et al. 1969). This strongly supports the view that the Lungshanoid cultures were not only closely similar to one another in cultural makeup and in adaptive significance but also were largely contemporaneous.

However, a date from another Lungshanoid culture (ZK-55, a Ch'ing-lien-kang Culture site near Shanghai) falls within the fourth millennium BC. This, plus the fact that of all the Lungshanoid cultures Ch'ing-lien-kang and Liang-chu appear to be the earliest and all the others—Miao-ti-kou II, Ch'ü-chia-ling, and Taiwan—may be largely contemporaneous, must throw some new light on the internal chronology of the entire Lungshanoid horizon and, by necessary extension, on its origin as well. In 1968, after reviewing the common characteristics of the various Lungshanoid cultures, I speculated on their cultural relationship with Yang-shao as follows:

> As to the genetic relationship of this Lungshanoid horizon with the Yang-shao Culture, two possible interpretations present themselves. Either these cultures formed a separate cultural system (in contrast with the Chung-yüan Yang-shao Culture), and originated in southeastern China (Huaiho or Yangtze-Hanshui area), moved northwestward to establish contact with the Yang-shao Culture, and gave rise to the Lung-shan Cultures of eastern North China; or the Lungshanoid cultures were derived from the Yang-shao culture of the Nuclear Area, representing its expansion into the eastern and southeastern areas of China, and were ancestral to the various local Lung-shan cultures. Available archaeological evidence does not yet confirm either of the alternatives. We must know more about the chronology of each of the Lungshanoid cultures and their relations with each other before a final position can be taken. (K. C. Chang 1968: 146-7)

We now do "know more about the chronology of each of the Lungshanoid cultures and their relations with each other," but since only a single radiocarbon date is available for each culture (except for Taiwan) we are still far from a "final position." While in 1968 I was inclined, "insofar as the present evidence is concerned, toward the second of the above alternatives" (K. C. Chang 1968: 147), today we obviously must show renewed interest in the first. The possibility is certainly strengthened that the Lungshanoid horizon first began to form in the lower Yangtze valley and its adjacent coastal areas; in any event, the Miao-ti-kou II Culture has now further diminished in stature as *the* ancestral culture of all other Lungshanoid cultures, as I among others had at one time believed. Perhaps, indeed, the two alternatives were not mutually exclusive to begin with. As a horizon, the Lungshanoid could still have come about, on the foundation of a prior culture in the lower Yangtze valley (possibly a southern cord-marked pottery culture not dissimilar to the one represented by the Hsien-jen Cave remains in Wan-nien, Kiangsi), as the result of a strong and stimulating cultural impact from the Yang-shao Culture. The Yang-shao Culture, which contains many lithic and ceramic types (or prototypes) that are prominent in and characteristic of the Lungshanoid cultures, is shown to be some one thousand years earlier than the earliest recognizable Lungshanoid. But we should certainly reserve final judgment until many more dates are known from each of the Lungshanoid cultures.

(2) Probably by design, the samples that have been processed for radiocarbon dating included many from sites where remains of cultivated plants were found. Since most of these plants are characteristic of the area, the new chronological information should be of wide interest. This is summed up in Table 4.

Bones of dog and pig, unquestionably domesticated, were found at Pan-p'o. Cattle, sheep, and horse bones were also found there, but their numbers are small and they could belong to wild species. The best evidence of domesticated cattle and sheep came from the Ta-li-t'a-li-ha site in Chinghai, where abundant remains of wool products were uncovered (J. T. Wu 1963). The site has yielded a single radiocarbon date of 1825 BC (ZK-61). Both cattle and sheep are represented at many Lung-shan sites, none of which has yet yielded a radiocarbon date. It would be reasonable to say that both cattle and sheep were certainly raised in north China by late third millennium BC at the latest.

(3) From the point of view of the prehistory of the whole Far East, the new radiocarbon dates are of interest in several ways. The relatively early dates of the Pan-p'o sites (especially if we make adjustments for atmospheric radiocarbon variations in the past several thousand years as are thought necessary by Suess, 1970) would suggest that the initial phases of the Yang-shao Culture,

Table 4. Radiocarbon Dates of Cultivated Plants

Site (references)	Plants	Radiocarbon date (BC)
Pan-p'o, Sian (Chung-kuo K'o-hsüeh Yüan K'ao-ku Yen-chiu Suo and Hsi-an Pan-p'o Museum 1962)	millet (*Setaria italica*); leaf-mustard or Chinese cabbage (*Brassica* sp.)	4115 ± 110; 3955 ± 105; 3890 ± 105; 3635 ± 105
Sung-tse, Ch'ing-p'u, Shanghai (Huang 1962)	rice (*Oryza sativa* L. subsp. Shan)	3395 ± 105
Ch'ien-shan-yang, Wu-hsing (Chekiang Provincial Commission for the Preservation of Cultural Objects 1960)*	rice (*Oryza sativa* L. subsp. Keng); broad bean (*Vivia faba*); Chinese water-chestnut (*Trapa natans*, or *T. bispinosa*); peanut (*Arachis hypogaea*); sesame (*Sesamum indicum*, or *S. orientale*); melon (*Cocomis melo*); peach (*Prunus persica*); sour date (*Spoudias auxillaris*)	2750 ± 100
P'ao-ma-ling, Hsiu-shui (Ch'in et al 1962)	rice; peanut; peach	2335 ± 95
Ta-ho-chuang, Yüng-ching (Cheng and Hsieh 1960)	millet	1725 ± 95; 1695 ± 95

*Because it was thought that peanuts, sesames, and broad beans should not be found in China at such great antiquity, according to our present knowledge of their respective histories of cultivation, Ho (1969: 205-9) questions the stratigraphy of the remains at the Ch'ien-shan-yang site. This obviously is not a question that can be settled by reading or interpreting the original report, which gives no reasonable ground for doubt in stratigraphical issues. Note that peanuts were also found in Hsiu-shui from the same cultural level and time period.

which predate the Pan-p'o phase, may be pushed back into the fifth, if not the sixth, millennium BC. This would make the Yang-shao Culture, or a yet unknown culture in north China that is antecedent (and precedent) to Yang-shao, one of the world's first farming cultures. Since southeast Asia has a ceramic tradition of great antiquity, and it was at least in some places associated with the utilization of plants (e.g. Gorman 1972, for Spirit Cave, northern Thailand), there can be no question that there was cultural interaction between north China and southeast Asia at the time of the Pan-p'o phase, or even earlier. But, until we are shown a similar culture in southeast Asia at the same time, or earlier, that is at least as fully developed in cultural makeup and cultural style, one must regard as premature at best such attempts as Solheim's (1972: 155) to derive Yang-shao from Hoabinhian. As to further efforts to link Yang-shao directly with the Near East, the early age of Yang-shao and the relative chronology of nuclear area Yang-shao and Kansu Yang-shao should put them to rest.

The absolute dates of the Lungshanoid cultures point to the Lower Yangtze valley of east-central China as an area of innovation and intense activity in the fourth millennium BC. As research goes on, this area is likely to assume increasing importance in the study of southeast Asian and Pacific prehistories. The widespread occurrence of remains of rice in this area must mean that rice was by then an important or even leading staple. Elsewhere, there is the possibility that rice was present at Non Nok Tha in Thailand "at 3000 BC or earlier" (Bayard 1971: 32). Very likely by 3000 BC rice was cultivated throughout monsoon Asia. As of now it would appear futile as well as pointless to look further for the one region or the one spot within this vast area where rice was first grown.

The single date from Hai-men-k'ou (ZK-10) is also of considerable interest to southeast Asian chronology. At this site was found a Neolithic culture with copper axes (Yunnan Museum 1958), in many ways similar to the early copper and bronze ax strata at Non Nok Tha in Thailand. The Non Nok Tha chronology is at this time unresolved. Radiocarbon and thermoluminescence dates from the site cluster into early and late sequences. According to the early sequence, copper and bronze metallurgy began at Non Nok Tha in the early or middle third millennium BC (Bayard 1971, 1972). The Hai-men-k'ou date is, instead, in agreement with the late sequence at Non Nok Tha, which would place the beginning of metallurgy here in late second millennium BC.

3 Urbanism and the King in Ancient China

In our minds a city often stands for a fixed site, with streets, public buildings, marketplace, and temples. None of these, as monumental architecture, was of paramount importance in the earliest Chinese cities. Because of their inconspicuousness our unobstructed vision is better focused on that which really mattered, namely, people—people amassed, people organized, people with common interests and with conflicting interests, people with strong wills dominating over the land, but people who have long since been outlived by it. In this setting, standing tall and conspicuous are the essential components of the first Chinese civilization, and of civilizations elsewhere: political kingship, a religious system and hierarchy that coupled with it, segmentary lineages, economic exploitation of many by a few, technological specialization, and sophisticated achievements in art, writing, and science.

All of these we see in the earliest cities of China: Yen-shih, Cheng-chou, and An-yang (K. C. Chang 1968: 194-228). These are all names of modern cities in Honan province, and we borrow them to designate the old city ruins found in their environs left by the Shang of about 1850-1100 BC. The Shang built one of the so-called Three Dynasties, Hsia, Shang, and Chou, the earliest in Chinese history. In fact, later legends accredit Kun, father of the founder of the Hsia dynasty, as the cultural hero who first built cities. Traditionally, the Hsia dynasty is placed between 2205 and 1766 BC. I am among the many who believe in the essential validity of the historical records concerning the Hsia, although archaeologists have as yet been unable to identify any Hsia ruins despite many attempts to do so. The nature of the Hsia society as revealed by the textual records is in many, and in all essential, ways identical with that of the Shang. Yet only with the coming to power of the Shang can we describe the physical manifestations of their cities and also look with considerable confidence into the multitude of factors that may account for these manifestations. The Shang cities thus provide us with a model of the first Chinese cities, even though they themselves probably were not, literally, the first Chinese cities.

Today, none of the Shang cities leaves any significant visible trace above ground. But if we imagine the archaeologist's spade

Note: This essay was a Winslow Lecture, Hamilton College, Clinton, New York, April 7, 1973, originally published in *World Archaeology* 6:1 (1974): 1-14. Reprinted with permission of publisher.

opening up at the city sites an area of between 30 and 40 square kilometers, we would see emerging the foundation ruins of clusters of buildings of various sorts. These clusters are densest at the approximate center of the area and become sparser, with greater distances between one another, as we move away toward the peripheries. As we look more closely at the nature of the individual buildings and of the artifacts, it becomes clear that most of the clusters probably performed special functions, and that only the entire web of clusters formed a functional whole. The word web is appropriate, since the clusters of buildings form the nodules, and invisible lines of complementary relationships interconnect the nodules with one another and with the center of the web.

At An-yang, two clusters of buildings are the most noteworthy. One, Hsiao-t'un, in the southeast, has a cluster of 53 individual houses arranged in three groups, each laid out in a recognizable plan. The houses were all above-ground, wattle-and-daub, rectangular structures built on foundations of layer upon layer of compressed earth. Yet in spite of their unimpressive architecture these houses are surrounded by sacrificial burials of humans and horse chariots, by storage pits containing the turtle-shell and bone archives of the royal oracle records, and by pit-houses apparently lived in by service personnel. It does not seem at all unreasonable of the archaeologist to characterize this cluster of buildings as the palace, ancestral hall, and ceremonial area of the royal house of the Shang dynasty (Shih 1959). Just over two thousand meters to the northwest of Hsiao-t'un is the Hsi-pei-kang cemetery, where eleven large graves and more than twelve hundred small ones were excavated in the 1930s. The vast size of the large grave pits, the lavish grave furnishings, and the many human sacrificial burials that accompany them, leave little doubt that very important people were laid to rest in these chambers. Since no tombs of grander scale are to be seen anywhere else in An-yang, Hsi-pei-kang has been referred to as the royal cemetery (Kao 1959).

Outside Hsiao-t'un and Hsi-pei-kang, other clusters of buildings in An-yang include residential remains, tombs of varying degrees of elaborateness in construction and in furnishings, workshops, storage pits, and so forth. All of these, presumably remains of villages or hamlets of various sizes and sorts, were located within sight of one another; often specific kinds of artifacts are found in some of the villages but not at others. It is easy to conclude that the entire An-yang web of individual, nodular components, with Hsiao-t'un at its nerve center, was indeed a single community—an urban settlement in the sense of many people, having specialized segments, and representing the Shang capital politically relating to a number of similar urban settlements located elsewhere in north China. The Shang territory extended roughly from eastern Shensi in the west to central Shantung in the east, and from southern Hopei in the north to northern Hupei and Anhwei in the south.

In this brief picture of a Shang city, one striking feature stands out—a total absence of architectural monumentality. This is an absence that is the more conspicuous against a backdrop of written documents, sophisticated bronze metallurgy, and one of the world's greatest art styles manifested in bronze, wood, stone, bone, and a host of other materials. The Shang had stones and knew how to work them, as shown by the fine stone sculptures that have been found. Nevertheless, they built not only their houses but also their palaces and ancestral halls of nothing more durable than clay, not in the form of adobe or brick but in wattle-and-daub standing on foundations of pounded layer upon layer of pure loess. Possibly there were houses of two stories (Shih 1970b), but single story buildings seem to have been the rule, and their roofs were probably covered with nothing more elaborate than thatch. The royal tombs were formed of earthen pits and ramps, in which a wooden chamber was built to contain the coffin. Mounds are not yet known over graves, and no markers are known to have been left in place. In short, the Shang made no apparent effort to create monumental architecture to impress or to immortalize, in the way Lewis Mumford (1961: 64-70) has described for ancient Babylonia and Greece.

At Cheng-chou, where the An-yang pattern of settlement was duplicated, the palatial and ceremonial nucleus was encircled by a long clay wall of considerable dimensions. There is some question as to the dating of the remains of the wall, but even if it is indeed of Shang age it was apparently intended for purposes other than permanency, for the Cheng-chou site was short-lived as a Shang capital. According to classical texts, from T'ang, the dynasty's founder, to P'an-keng, who moved to the site at An-yang, the city that served as capital until the dynasty's fall, there were altogether seven capital cities, as follows:

Po (possibly the Yen-shih ruins)	1766-1557 BC	(209 years)
Ao (possibly the Cheng-chou ruins)	1557-1534 BC	(23 years)
Hsiang (archaeologically unknown)	1534-1525 BC	(9 years)
Keng (archaeologically unknown)	1525-1517 BC	(8 years)
Pi (archaeologically unknown)	1517-1433 BC	(74 years)
Yen (archaeologically unknown)	1433-1384 BC	(49 years)
Yin (the An-yang ruins)	1384-1122 BC	(262 years)

The precise dates given here are highly suspect, but if the durations are near the truth, then one may conclude that the capital—the topmost city in the state hierarchy of cities—was where the king was, and that the city hierarchy was determined by the political hierarchy but not the other way around.

This may be anything but unusual, but the Chinese case presents itself with a stark clarity that is rare in other areas. The location of a city may be regarded for a limited period as geomancically auspicious, and the movement from one site to another may have been dictated by divination. This we read from the following passages of *P'an-keng,* an edict issued by King P'an-keng explaining his move to Yin, as recorded in *Shu Ching* (*The Book of History*):

> P'an-keng wished to remove the capital to Yin but the people would not go to dwell there. He therefore appealed to all the discontented, and made the following protestations.
>
> "Our king Tsu Yi came and fixed on [Yen] for his capital. He did so from a deep concern for our people, because he would not have them all die where they cannot help one other to preserve their lives. I have consulted the tortoise shell and obtained the reply: 'This is no place for us.' When the former kings had any important business they gave reverent heed to the commands of Heaven. In a case like this especially they did not indulge the wish for constant repose; they did not abide ever in the same city. Up to this time the capital has been in five regions. If we do not follow the example of these old times, we shall be refusing to acknowledge that Heaven is making an end of our dynasty here. How little can it be said of us that we are following the meritorious course of the former kings! As from the stump of a felled tree there are sprouts and shoots, Heaven will perpetuate its decree in our favor in this new city. The great inheritance of the former kings will be continued and renewed. Tranquillity will be secured to the four quarters of the kingdom." (Translated, Waltham 1971: 85-86)

It was through the act of renewal that the God's favor was to be perpetuated; the locus of a city *per se* was accorded no permanent relevance as being worthy of political and ceremonial eminence. Once the capital was moved away, the old site was often transformed, in cruelly short years, into farming fields. According to *Shih Chi,* written by the great historian Ssu-ma Ch'ien around 100 BC, a few years after the fall of the Shang and the destruction of Yin, Chi Tzu, an uncle of the last Shang monarch, went by the ruins and was moved to see them covered by many acres of millet fields, with but scant trace of their former splendor. The city was the institution, not the site, and its movements from site to site was obviously at the king's option. The layout and structuring of the new capital were designed to serve him as the center of attention.

Even without additional evidence, one can see that in the Chinese case the first cities arose to serve a number of functions associated with the emergence of a ruler possessed of extraordinary political powers. To understand how cities began in China one may thus begin by describing some central features of the kingship and how they evolved.

The king presided over a hierarchy of government, economy, and religion, with himself at both top and center. If we conceive of the Shang state as a horizontal plane, the royal palace-temple complex and the royal cemetery were at the center of the urban web. Broadening our view, we see on the north China plains a large web of settlements, with the capital city at its figurative center. In the Shang conception of the world, there were five cardinal directions: north, south, east, west, and the "central Shang", the last being wherever the king and his court resided (T. Wu 1953: 26-27). This central city apparently exerted political control over the other settlements through an effective mechanism of hierarchical government. The Shang state may be referred to as the political sphere within which, or under whose umbrella, these settlements were strung together. Beyond the state lay alien and hostile powers in all four directions, with which the Shang state often engaged in varying degrees of warfare (M. C. Ch'en 1956: 269-312).

If we take a different perspective and view the state hierarchy vertically, in cross-section, we see that the king was at the apex of a markedly stratified social order. The king, his family, and his high officials enjoyed the highest quality of life at the time—aboveground houses, objects of bronze and other valuable materials, lavish feasts and banquets, and hunting as a sport. They were served by a large retinue of officials, including historian-scribes, priests, oracle-takers, and ministers of state affairs; by the armed forces, which engaged in wars outside the state and in the maintenance of law and order within; and by some of the best artists and artisans of the ancient world.

At the other end of the ladder, there were those whose whole life-needs were served by an underground pit-house a few meters in diameter, in which we will find only the remains of a few pottery cooking and serving vessels. Hundreds of these pits were found amidst and around the loci of archaeological splendor that are usually associated with the Shang civilization, but which really served only a portion of the populace. What best symbolize the relationship, or rather the social distance, between the king and the pit-house dwellers are the remains of human sacrifice associated with the construction of the royal palace-temples and the royal graves. For the burial of the master of Hsi-pei-kang tomb no. 1001, who in my opinion was none other than King P'an-keng himself, at least 164 men accompanied him to the other world (Liang and Kao 1962). For the construction of a single house in the middle segment at Hsiao-t'un, more than six hundred people were killed and buried in its southern front (Shih 1970a, 1971). There may be those who would imagine that these victims were religiously indoctrinated so that they went to their graves willingly, or even that to be sacrificed in this manner was accepted as an honor. I doubt that very much. In the year 621 BC, Duke Mu of Ch'in died. By this time human sacrifice was no longer a common practice, but in the state of Ch'in, and on this occasion, it was done. Here is a poem, presumably written at the time or shortly afterwards:

'Kio' sings the oriole
As it lights on the thorn-bush.
Who went with Duke Mu to the grave?
Yen-hsi of the clan Tsu-chü.
Now this Yen-hsi
Was the pick of all our men;
But as he drew near the tomb-hole
His limbs shook with dread.
That blue one, Heaven,
Takes all our good men.
Could we but ransom him
There are a hundred would give their lives
'Kio' sings the oriole
As it lights on the mulberry-tree.
Who went with Duke Mu to the grave?
Chung-hang of the clan Tsu-chü.
Now this Chung-hang
Was the sturdiest of all our men;
But as he drew near the tomb-hole
His limbs shook with dread.
That blue one, Heaven,
Takes all our good men.
Could we but ransom him
There are a hundred would give their lives.

'Kio' sings the oriole
As it lights on the brambles.
Who went with Duke Mu to the grave?
Ch'ien-hu of the clan Tzu-chü.
Now this Ch'ien-hu
Was the strongest of all our men.
But as he drew near the tomb-hole
His limbs shook with dread.
That blue one, Heaven,
Takes all our good men.
Could we but ransom him
There are a hundred would give their lives.
(translated, Waley 1960: 311-312)

Indeed, people were willing to die with the Duke, but for quite different reasons! This poem was composed a thousand years too late to describe a Shang burial scene, but on what basis are we to argue that the Shang sentiment was basically different?

What mechanism produced and maintained such royal powers, such stratification of society and uneven distribution of power and wealth? To answer this we may first take a brief look at the social structure of the aristocracy, at the top of which sat the king.

The king's clan was named Tzu, mythologically descending from a black divine bird. The internal structure of the Tzu clan is anything but clear, but recent studies have revealed two interesting features. The first is the possibility that at the top of the Tzu aristocracy were two lines of succession, and perhaps two discrete but related and intermarrying lineage groups, which supplied the kings to the throne in alternative generations. Thus a new king would be the old king's sister's son but in turn he would hand over the throne to his own sister's son, who was also the old king's consanguineal grandson (K. C. Chang 1963a). The second feature of the Tzu clan structure is suggested by the system of the Chou, which we know a little better. It is the rule that after a few (often five) generations some members of the lineage would move away, both from the land the lineage members tilled and from the lineage hall, in which the ancestral tablets were placed. In their new locus these splinter members would establish a new lineage, with its own land and its own ancestral hall. The same process of fission would then be repeated after a few generations, resulting in additional new lineages. This is the system that we know of as Tsung Fa from Chou texts, or as the conical clan, the ramage, or the segmentary lineage system in modern anthropological writings (K. C. Chang 1963b). A built-in feature of this lineage fission system is the dilution of political power as one moves from the senior or stem lineage outwards toward the minor and peripheral lineages. The closer one is from the stem lineage the higher one would be in ritual status and, presumably, in political power. When this is coupled with the dualistic kingship, one can easily speculate about a dualistic system of stem lineages at the heart of the aristocracy (K. C. Chang 1964).

The Tzu clan, however, could not have been the sole component of the Shang ruling aristocracy. They had to share power with at least two other groups: the clans with which the Tzu exchanged women in marriage, and the clans that were the *de facto* rulers of settlements and tribes within the state that were not under the direct rule of the Tzu princes. Thus, at least three factors were at work to distribute members of the aristocracy all over the state, but in top positions in each region: lineage fission within the clans, localization of marriageable partners, and the legitimatization of the local powers. All these localized segments of the aristocracy were obviously structured, and interacted, in a hierarchical system based for the most part upon kinship and quasi-kinship. The cities and towns were in this sense the seats of the lineages at the local level. As lineages were hierarchically organized across the state, so were the various cities, towns, and local settlements. To Fei Hsiao-t'ung (1953: 95), a walled town in recent China is "an instrument of the ruling classes in a political system where power resides in force. It is the symbol of power and also a necessary tool for the maintenance of power." These words may be used to characterize a Shang city just as well.

In Chou texts that describe town buildings, invariably the construction of the ancestral temples and the placement of lineage treasures in them were given prominent attention (e.g. poem "Sung Kao," in the *Book of Poetry*). In the city there was an eminence for the lineage temples (see *Shih Ming*). To govern the lineage was the same as to govern the town (e.g. poem "Kung Liu," in the *Book of Poetry*). Significantly, in the Shang oracle records we often see that identical names were used for a local settlement, a lineage that occupied it, and individual members of the lineage or of the settlement (P. C. Chang 1967). Thus, the immortality of the king may be said to lie in the immortality of the group, his lineage and his clan, which moved about in space, rather than the immortality of the architecture, which merely served a transient purpose.

This kinship and city hierarchy was the hierarchy of the ruling class. Beneath them, within each city and each settlement or cluster of settlements lived the people over whom they ruled. Some of the latter were skilled craftsmen, but most were farmers. Certain scholars see the possibility of some centrally planned estate farming, supervised by the aristocracy. A major piece of evidence is the discovery in a single storage pit of no fewer than 444 stone sickles, all bearing signs of use, together with valuable artifacts that rule out the pit being for rubbish (Shih 1933: 727). There were also professional soldiers, but in times of war most of the armed men were probably conscripted. The aristocracy's hold on the lower classes was obviously total, sanctioned by fiction and enforced by might. From texts we know that groups of craftsmen and probably farmers were among the spoils of war, to be possessed by one master and then by another. In archaeology, the human sacrifice is an extreme example of the master's powers.

The lineage system may explain at least in part the wide political gulf between the aristocracy and the lower classes. Under the segmentary lineage system, the members of minor and peripheral lineages could theoretically be so far removed from the stem and the center of prestige and power, that they became members of a lower class. But a major source of the members of the lower classes, especially those that had the honor of joining the king or noblemen in death—whose teeth show to the physical anthropologists (Mao and Yen 1959) signs of malnutrition—and those whose bones were found among the raw materials in a bone workshop in Cheng-chou (Chao et al. 1957: 58), must have been prisoners of war. Perhaps this was the main reason for the frequency and intensity of wars throughout the Shang period. People put to work were the major source of wealth; in that sense the bronze weapons of the Shang were a major technological breakthrough in agriculture. From the oracle records we learn of wars involving thirteen thousand troops. One of Shang's major adversaries was the Ch'iang people to the west. Oracle records frequently mention expeditions to the Ch'iang territory, and they sometimes enumerate the numbers of Ch'iang captives: three once, five another time, and as many as twenty-five at one time. Another piece of oracle record mentioned thirty thousand captured in one battle, but the name of the enemy was not preserved in the piece of bone bearing that information (S. K. Yang 1962: 20-21). Anthropometric studies of the skulls from the Hsi-pei-kang sacrificial burials have disclosed a remarkably heterogenous population (H. M. Yang 1970), giving credence to the conjecture that the Shang brought back prisoners of war from many places and many populations to fill the ranks of the lower social classes.

Such a political hierarchy must have assumed pyramidal form if it was to function effectively. The transition from the Neolithic Lung-shan Culture, which is the culture immediately antecedent in western and northern Honan, to the Shang civilization is a quantum jump of the highest order in the quality of life for the elite, yet there is no discernible corresponding change in the technology of food production. Archaeological assemblages from Shang and Lung-shan sites contain essentially the same agricultural implements of stone, antler, bone, and presumably wood, and hoes and digging-sticks were the tools of moving earth in both cultures. Persistent efforts to prove the use of cattle-pulling plows during the Shang have not yet met with any appreciable success. The sophisticated bronze metallurgy that characterize the Shang was devoted to the production of weapons and ceremonial objects; its benefits spilled over into the arena of agricultural production only occasionally, if at all, except in the labor-producing sense with weapons and war captives. The only significant difference between the Lung-shan and the Shang stone assemblages lies, in the opinion of some, in the greater abundance and variety in the Shang assemblage of harvesting knives (C. Li 1951: 533-534). Nevertheless, it seems likely that Shang farmers were able to produce, on an individual basis, more food than their Lung-shan predecessors. Perhaps the Shang used fertilizers, or made more effective or extensive use of irrigation. Certainly it must also have been the result of more effective cultivating methods; one method involved the tilling of land by team, the so-called *hsieh t'ien*, a phrase often seen in the oracle records (see Amano 1959).

I don't know how one can measure the absolute increase of food yield that resulted from such improvements. But in any event these could represent only improvements of degree, while the change in the quality of life was one of kind. Other factors being equal, the food increase that was needed to support the lavish living of the higher aristocracy, the full-time war machine, wasteful works such as the royal tombs, and the full-time craftsmen and officials, must have been enormous. Thus if changes in the technology of producing food were involved in the transition from Lung-shan to Shang, we could not possibly miss them in the archaeological record: metal farming implements, for example, or animal-pulled plows, or large-scale waterworks. A change of that magnitude could not possibly require an archaeological reading of the fine print or between the lines.

This leads to the inevitable conclusion that the Shang period witnessed the beginning in this part of the world of organized large-scale exploitation of one group of people by another within the same society, and the beginning of an oppressive governmental system to make such exploitation possible. In *Meng Tzu* ("T'eng Wen Kung II"), we read that a wise Lu state gentleman, Kung Ming Yi, had commented: "In their [the ministers'] kitchens, there is fat meat. In their stables, there are fat horses. But their people have the look of hunger, and in the wilds there are those who have died of famine. This is leading on beast to devour men" (translated, Legge 1895: 282). In modern terms such a social system in which one group of people exploits another is one in which "people eat people." This is no psychologically based metaphor (Solomon 1971: 101); it is literally true. The food-based wealth of the aristocracy could only have been accumulated at the expense of the cultivator who tilled the land, whose yields were presumably enough to feed much more than himself and his family, but who probably was not allowed to keep more than what was absolutely necessary to sustain himself and his family at or below the subsistence level. The rest of the fruits of his work, which were more abundant than in the Neolithic past, thanks mainly to the organizational improvements mentioned above, were thus the foundation of the Shang civilization, created by those whose full-time business it was to make the civilization great. In this sense, in the Chinese case the urban revolution was based not on technology or on the power of production, but on the fruit of human toil taken away from the many and given to the few. One can only conclude that the urban revolution was a revolution of the social system, and that civilization was its by-product.

The mechanisms of this exploitation cannot have been simplistic, and they must have taxed the wisdom of the kings. From the oracle records we learned that there was an enormous machinery of war, at the center of which was the horse-drawn chariot and its bronze-tipped spears, arrows, and *ko*-halberds. The purpose of this mighty force must have been for wars for spoil, as a threat and a sanction to make the tribute system work, and as garrison over the large number of farmers at the bottom of each urban pyramid. At the same time, a religious system identifying the gods with the royal ancestors contributed its share toward maintaining the social order. But the kings were no stereotypes of Oriental despots who commanded by whim and killed at will. They were more successful in leading their people, of all ranks, in wars and in other massive undertakings, when they were able to convince the masses that their interests and the king's coincided. According to *Shu Ching* (*The Book of History*), on the eve of his conquest of Hsia, T'ang made this speech.

> Come, ye multitudes of the people, listen all to my words. It is not I, the Little Child, who dare to undertake a rebellious enterprize; Heaven has given the charge to destroy the sovereign of Hsia for his many crimes.
>
> Now, ye multitudes, you are saying, "Our prince does not compassionate us but is calling us away from our husbandry to attack and punish Hsia." I have indeed heard these words of you all. But the sovereign of Hsia is guilty and, as I fear God, I dare not but punish him.
>
> Now you are saying, "What are the crimes of Hsia to us?" The king of Hsia in every way exhausts the strength of his people and exercises oppression in the cities of Hsia. His people have all become idle and will not assist him. They are saying, "When wilt thou, O sun, expire? We will all perish with thee."
>
> Such is the course of the sovereign of Hsia. And now I must go punish him.
>
> I pray you, assist me, the One Man, to carry out the punishment appointed by Heaven. I will greatly reward you. On no account disbelieve me; I will not eat my words. If you do not obey the words I have spoken to you I will put your children to death with you. You will find no forgiveness (translated, Waltham 1971: 67-68).

There are in this address persuasion and cajoling, as well as the threat of force and punishment. This is not a despot speaking, but a patriarch, who lived well and expected obedience, but knew what was good for his wards and was somehow always successful in getting them to go his way. In the Chinese dynastic cycles, such patriarchs built dynasties, but their unworthy descendants, who became despots, invariably lost them to other patriarchs who were able to swing the masses to their side. Mencius expressed it best when he said, "The people are the most important element in a nation; the spirits of the land and grain are the next; the sovereign the lightest. Therefore to gain the peasantry is the way to become a sovereign." When sovereigns' actions were undertaken against the interest of their people, they would lose their hold. "Chieh and Chou's losing the throne, arose from their losing the people, and to lose the people means to lose their hearts." Once he had lost the people's hearts, the sovereign was fated to become a "mere fellow." Mencius said that he indeed heard about the cutting off of that fellow Chou, but that he never heard of any assassination of a king (*Meng Tzu,* Chapters "Liang Huei Wang II," "Li Lou I," and "Chin Hsin II," translated, Legge 1895).

If this new social order had as its focus a characteristic form of kingship, and if urbanism was an essential facet of the new order, it becomes much easier to ask pertinent questions about the beginnings of both urbanism and kingship in China, or at least about the possible mechanisms that brought about their emergence. The advances in agricultural yields that had continued since the Neolithic periods were obviously a prerequisite, since otherwise no matter how hard farmers were squeezed they could not possibly support the vast aristocracy and its style of high and wasteful living. The development of new weaponry, particularly the horse chariot, whether a native development or an importation from the Near East, was certainly a major advance in enabling oppressive measures to be effective. Advances in industry were at least partly responsible for the highly specialized division of labor that made a hierarchical society necessary. The urban revolution in China was a qualitative leap forward as the result of accumulated changes in all of these, and perhaps many other, different aspects. One may emphasize some of these aspects as against others as the most important, and that is his privilege. But two factors must be singled out that could not possibly have played a role in this transition that was even remotely decisive; these are large-scale water-works and massive changes in the environment. One would have to be reading between the lines in the archaeological and historical record to attribute roles of any significance to them.

The Shang pattern of urbanization apparently survived the conquest by the Chou in 1122 BC. In fact, there is reason to believe that essentially the same principles governing the formation and development of the Shang cities may be applied to the Chou cities, both before and immediately after the conquest. Collective farming, large-scale and frequent warfare, and the close relationship between the kinship system and the political system were all prominently a part of the historical record of the Western or early Chou dynasty, from about 1122 to about 700 BC.

The next major change in the history of ancient Chinese cities, as in the history of ancient Chinese culture and society in general, occurred in the late Western and early Eastern Chou periods. From about 700 BC onward, not only was there a great increase in the number of cities built throughout China, but the cities themselves underwent a series of physical changes of the first magnitude. The web pattern of earlier cities changed to an aggregated mass of houses, separated by streets, served by public buildings and markets, and surrounded by an outer wall. These changes were associated with the first use of cast iron for agricultural implements, the use of cattle and plow, the archaeological and textual evidence of large-scale irrigation works, the individualization of farming, and the institution (in 594 BC) of the system of taxation of agricultural land. Space does not permit detailed discussion of this second urbanization process in ancient China, which is obviously one of great complexity and vast implications. Suffice it to say that the so-called urban revolution took two giant steps in ancient China, about a millennium and a half apart from each other. The first was a revolution of social systems, responsible for a realignment of the societal segments in their relationship to food resources and for the emergence of a great civilization. The second, perhaps made possible only by the first, was a technological revolution *par excellence,* which led to the breakdown of the parental societal system and the emergence of the Chinese empire.

4 Towns and Cities in Ancient China

In the Shang and Chou texts the local settlement was referred to as *yi*. The word—composed of two compounds, one referring to a bordered area and the other apparently a "pass" designating membership in the border area (C. T. Chin 1956: 82)—was first seen used in the oracle texts of the Shang period and continued in the same form throughout the Chou (Fig. 3). It designated settlements of various sizes and kinds. A *yi* may range from a small hamlet of some ten households[1] to large state capitals with hundreds or thousands of inhabitants. Its nature is best expressed through its taxonomic contrasts with local groups of other kinds and levels:

(1) *Yi* was contrastive with *t'ien,* farming fields. In this sense a *yi* was a group of dwellings. In a Shang oracle text, an official was quoted as reporting to the court that T'u Fang (an alien people) invaded two *yi*s in the eastern *pi* of the Shang (see below for *pi*) and Kung Fang (another alien people) invaded *t'ien* in the western *pi.* The contrast in this text between *yi* and *t'ien* is unmistakable (M. C. Ch'en 1956: 322). The same contrastive pair of words was apparently meaningful to a Chan Kuo-period commentator of *Ch'un Ch'iu* when he explained that "the word *t'ien* was used when one referred to an area with more *t'ien* than *yi,* but the word *yi* was used when the area had more *yi* than *t'ien*" (*Kung Yang Chuan,* First Year of Huan Kung). In other words, a *yi* was a nucleated settlement.

(2) Surrounded by farming fields, hunting and grazing grounds, and forests, *yi* was considered the center of things, the civilized area. The various terms designating the several land types that

---

Note: This essay was originally published in *Asia Antiqua*: *The Archaeology of East and South East Asia,* ed. Janice Stargardt (London: Duckworth, 1975). Reprinted with permission of the editor.

An earlier version of this paper was presented at the conference of "The Traditional Chinese City: Studies in Urban Social Structure," held August 31-September 7, 1968, at Wentworth-by-the-Sea, New Hampshire, under the auspices of the Social Science Research Council. Paul Wheatley's monumental book, *The Pivot of the Four Quarters* (1971), which came out after my essay was written, has rendered the essay largely obsolete in point of fact. But some of my ideas are still seemingly useful. In addition to Wheatley's volume, there are many other general and topical works on ancient Chinese towns and cities. Outstanding among them are Ōshima (1959) and Miyazaki (1957). Useful descriptions in the Western languages may be found in Granet (1930) and Trewartha (1952).

1. *Lun Yü* ("Kung-yieh Ch'ang"): "Even in a hamlet of ten households, persons of loyalty and sincerity are to be found."

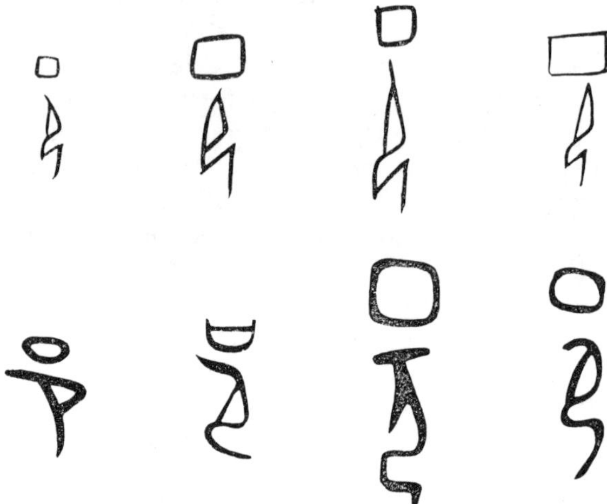

Figure 3. The character of *yi* in the oracle bone (upper row) and bronze (lower row) scripts

formed concentric circles with *yi* at the center area as follows: beyond *yi* there was *chiao,* the "suburbs"; beyond chiao was *yieh,* "wild" lands for farming, grazing, hunting, and so on; beyond *yieh, lin,* forests; and beyond *lin, chiung,* the land at the very border. This and similarly concentric schemes of terms area seen in Han texts (*Shuo Wen, Erh Ya*), but these words were comparably used in Shang and Chou literatures.

(3) Each state included in its territory a large or small number of *yi.* One of them was the main *yi,* and its name was often also the name of the state. The name of this *yi* went with its inhabitants or principal inhabitants in case of a change of locale (S. N. Fu 1930a; K. W. Wang 1956: 135). Shang and Chou, for example, were names of main cities of the states of Shang and Chou as well as the names of these states (for Shang *yi,* see *Shu Ching* and *Shih Ching;* for Ta yi Shang, see oracle texts; for Tay yi Chou, see *Shu Ching*). The main city of the Shang state changed its locale several times during the course of the dynasty, but the city was known as Shang at more than a single locality. Therefore, in this sense *yi* and the various terms meaning state, such as *kuo* and *pang,* were interchangeable synonyms (see *Shuo Wen,* under *yi, kuo,* and *pang;* see also C. T. Chin 1956: 87). This is clear in a phrase in "P'an Keng" of *Shu Ching,* in which the Shang were said to be "not permanent in their settlement of *yi,* and five *pangs* have now been built." In the sense of a state, *yi* was thus contrastive with *ssu t'u,* the Four

Earth, or *ssu fang,* the Four Sides (M. C. Ch'en 1956: 258, 319).

(4) Within the state itself there was a hierarchy of *yi* at various levels. In the oracle texts of the Shang, among the many *yi* one was a *Ta yi,* the Great *Yi.* The capital city at An-yang, Honan, for example, was referred to as *Ta yi Shang.* Before the capital was established at An-yang, the term was apparently applied to other sites where the royal house had its ancestral temples and other markers of the aristocracy (M. C. Ch'en 1956: 323). Another significant contrast in the Shang oracle texts was that between *Ta yi* and the *yi* in the *pi* areas. Ch'en Meng-chia's interpretation of *pi* as the "many small *yi* that gathered outside the *Ta-yi:* those to the east were *tung* (east) *pi* and those to the west *hsi* (west) *pi*" (M. C. Ch'en 1956: 323) is highly questionable. The text on which the interpretation is based mentions invasions by alien peoples in the eastern and western *pi,* and I cannot see that the small villages and hamlets immediately surrounding An-yang were said to be invaded. Possibly the *Tu-pi* contrast in the Chou texts was applicable to the Shang also.

In Chou (especially Eastern Chou) texts the same pairs of contrast remained meaningful. First, there was the contrast between those *yi* where there were *tsung* (lineage) temples and those where there were not. The former were called *tsung yi* (*Tso Chuan,* 14th Year of Ai Kung) or, as in the case of a state capital, *tu* (*Tsuo Chuan,* 28th Year of Chuang Kung), instead of just plain *yi.* In the more complex and highly stratified states of the Chan Kuo period, a state often had a number of *tu* presiding over their respective smaller divisions; the supreme *tu,* where the state's prince presided, was referred to as *kuo.*[2] Second, there was the contrast between *tu* and *pi.* The word *pi* probably had a number of different meanings.

2. *Tso Chuan,* First Year of Yin Kung: "Large *tu* should not exceed one third of *kuo* in size; medium *tu* should not exceed one fifth; and small *tu,* one ninth." This rule, largely fictitious as it must have been, is not totally unsupported by the archaeological remains. The following comparisons between the capital cities and provincial towns, according to data unearthed in three different states of the Eastern Chou period, are highly revealing:

	Dimensions	Area
Chin:		
Capital sites	1500-3100 m (1 side)	4,650,00 m^2
Ch'ing-yüan	980 x 980	960,400
Wei:		
An-yi	4500 x 2100	9,450,000
Yang	1300 x 580	754,000
Chao:		
Han-tan		2,940,000
Wu-chi		682,232

In this contrastive context it probably referred to areas distant from the *tu,* that is, near the border regions or in the interior of the state (see *Shih Ming*). Thus within the same state the importance of the various *yi* differed among themselves according to a scale of a maximum of four levels: ordinary *yi; tsung-yi* with temples of aristocratic lineages; *tu,* with the temples of the grand lineages; and *kuo,* with the temples of the supreme lineage of the state. In contrast to *tu* and its neighboring *yi,* the *yi* and perhaps even the *tsung yi* distant from the center of the state were grouped into four *pi:* those in the eastern, western, northern, and southern *pi* of the state.

This multifaceted taxonomy of Shang and Chou settlements suggests that ancient Chinese cities were indeed "multi-functional in character."[3] A city was a settlement that could be placed within the various taxonomic loci according to its various functions; a *tu,* for instance, was a *yi* and was identical with all *yi* in important ecological aspects. To differentiate the roles the various kinds of settlements had to play in ancient China, however, we are tempted to refer to ordinary *yi* as villages and hamlets and only to those *yi* that attained *tsung yi, tu,* and *kuo* status as towns and cities. But this would have been unduly restrictive, for in ancient literatures the attributes of a city were not enumerated and archaeological remains are mute. But I think that the city wall (*ch'eng* and *kuo*) would serve a useful purpose here. We cannot say that all wall cities—all *yi* with *ch'eng*—were *tsung yi, tu,* or *kuo,* for some, such as military fortresses, were not. But it is quite possible to say that all *tsung yi, tu,* and *kuo* were walled.

China has been called a world of walled cities (N. I. Wu 1963: 11), and the city wall is sometimes regarded as a characteristic "Chinese" feature (C. Li 1928: 57-58). Although the wall can only be as important in any study of Chinese life as what was walled within it, the city wall was an essential expression of the city itself, and a walled settlement often differed from an unwalled one in kind. It is significant to note at the outset that in ancient legends Kun, father of the founder of Hsia, the first Chinese dynasty, was credited with the first construction of walled towns and cities ("Tso P'ien," of *Shih Pen; Lü Shih Ch'un Ch'iu*). In the history of the Chou, town-building activity was said not to have begun until the

---

3. See Trewartha (1952: 73). This point may be highly relevant to the controversy between scholars who regard ancient Chinese cities as city-states in the Classic sense (Kaizuka 1956; Rubin 1965) and those who emphasize the hierarchical interrelationship of the various cities under the *feng-chien* system.

time of Ku Kung, immediate ancestor of kings Wen Wang and Wu Wang. All of these go to show that walled-town building was in the ancient Chinese conception associated with the rise of dynastic power. Moreover, these same legends ratify the truism that town walls were erected for defending the town itself.[4] The study of Shang and Chou towns and cities is, therefore, by definition an inquiry into certain physical expressions of the ancient Chinese power structure.

The material for the study of walled towns and cities in ancient China comes from historical and archaeological sources. Historic texts tell us that town building was a persistent and ever-increasing activity of major import throughout Shang and Chou life. The Hsia period before them, as just stated, witnessed the "invention" of city building. There is, however, little information about Shang cities from ancient texts or oracle bone inscriptions other than the many city names and some characters designating structures related to the city wall such as the gate-tower (H. P. Sun 1965: 244-249). Of Western Chou cities we know much, primarily from *Shi Ching* and *Yi Chou Shu,* about the construction of the royal cities at Feng, Hao, and Lo-yang. For the Eastern Chou period, data about town and city building became abundant, for not only literary sources from this period increased but also many new towns and cities were built. Ōshima Riichi, for example, has identified from *Tso Chuan* and *Kung Yang Chuan* no fewer than 78 cities that were built during the interval of the Ch'un Ch'iu period (Ōshima 1959: 53). But we know that even this is merely a fraction of the total number of cities extant then and being built, for in the state of Cheng alone 102 names of *yi* were recorded (Kimura 1965: 68), and even in such a small state as Lu of Shantung 23 cities were recorded as having been constructed during this time (W. L. Hou 1955: 205). When we come down to the Chan Kuo period, there was an even larger number of cities everywhere; for instance, 120 cities were known in the state of Ch'i alone (*Chan Kuo Ts'e*). All these are interesting and instructive data concerning the spatial expression of the various power groups of ancient China and their spatial structure of hierarchy. What these literary sources lack in details of physical layout and composition and in the overall picture of city life are to varying extents made up for by the actual ruins of towns and cities brought to light by the archaeologist's spade (Fig. 4).

4. *Lü Shih Ch'un Ch'iu* (as quoted in *T'ai P'ing Yü Lan*, vol. 193): "Kun built *ch'eng* to protect the lords and *kuo* to defend the people—such was the beginning of walled cities."

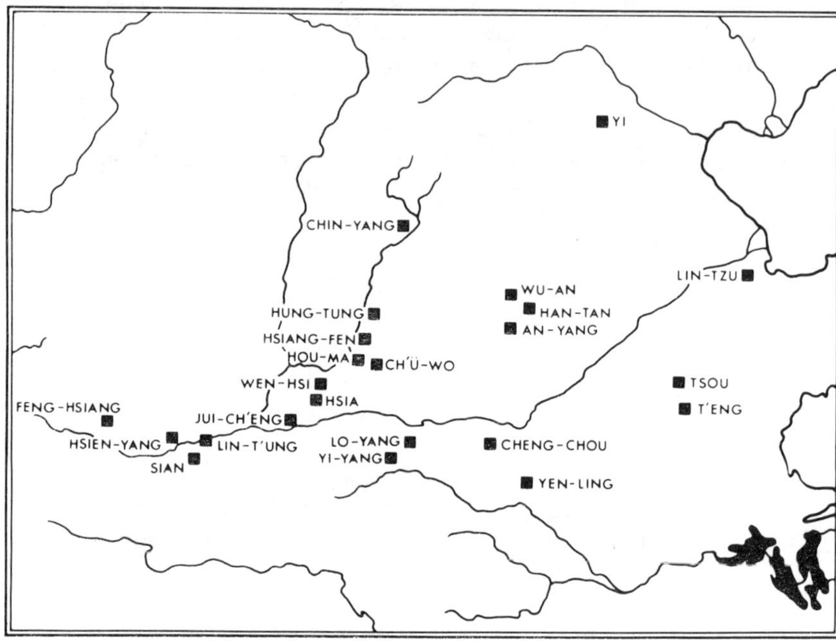

Figure 4. Locations of Shang and Chou City Ruins

The earliest walled villages of the Lung shan Neolithic cultures of north China perhaps give some substance to the legendary cities of the Hsia (C. Li et al. 1934; C. J. Shih 1945), but the ruins of the great cities Shang in Yen-shih, Cheng-chou, and An-yang (all in Honan) mark the real florescence of urbanism in ancient China (K. C. Chang 1968). Only Cheng-chou has the remains of a city wall, and even there the dating of the wall is in some dispute (C. H. An 1961: 73; C. Y. Liu 1961: 39-40; C. M. An 1961: 448-450). But the essential features of the ancient Chinese cities are present in all three, the absence of wall remains notwithstanding. Residential remains dating from Western Chou have been found widely, but towns and cities have yet to be defined by remnants of city walls. At the Eastern Chou sites walled cities are no archaeological rarity: more than a score have been found, most having been uncovered during the last fifteen years. There is no question that urban archaeology of ancient China has barely begun, but the historical and archaeological data combined are already sufficient for a preliminary characterization of the physical features and conceptual patterns of the Shang and Chou towns and cities, and, also, for a tentative formulation of the pattern of change that has taken place from the beginning of the ancient period to the end.

In physical characteristics ancient Chinese cities exhibit a number of common features. (1) The cities were in most cases located on level plains near waterways and hills.[5] (2) They tend to be walled. Throughout Shang and Chou the section of the city containing the palaces and temples was almost always walled. In Eastern Chou, an outer wall (*kuo,* as against *ch'eng,* the inner or single wall) was often erected to encompass the residences, industries, and shops. (3) The city walls were in all cases constructed of stamped earth, and the technique of *hang-t'u* or pisé construction remained identical throughout the period. The width and height of the walls vary from city to city in the archaeological remains. The base of the remaining wall of the Chou city of Lo-yang is only about 5 m wide, but the Hsia-tu (state of Yen) wall is 40 m wide. While the height of most walls can only be speculated about, because they have invariably collapsed, the wall at Han-tan (state of Chao) still stands at more than 15 m high. (4) The majority of the cities were rectangular or square in overall plan, though in rare cases the shape was irregular. Their sizes again varied: the smaller ones were about 1000 m to a side, and the largest was 8000 m east to west.[6] (5) The orientation of the city enclosure and the ceremonial and palatial structures was

5. From textual studies Kimura (1965: 74-76) concludes that most ancient settlements were built on hills or mounds, and Miyazaki (1957) believes that walled cities evolved from hill fortresses. Cities built on hills, however, are rarely found archaeologically.

6. Archaeological remains of the various state capitals of the Warring States period show that their sizes varied greatly. Han-tan of Chao measures only 2100 by 1400 m or 2,940,000m^2. Increasingly larger are Royal Chou's Lo-yang (2900 by 3000 m or 8,700,000 m^2); Wei's An-yi (4500 by 2100 m or 9,450,000 m^2): Ch'i's Lin-tzu (4000 by 4000 m or 16,000,000 m^2): and Yen's Hsia-tu (8000 by 4000 m or 32,000,000 m^2).

Ancient texts themselves give a rather confusing picture of the dimensions of the Chou cities. *Yi Chou Shu* ("Tso Lo Chieh") records that the *ch'eng* (inner enclosure) of Lo-yang was 1720 *chang* to a side and that its *kuo* (outer enclosure) was 70 *li* to a side. According to Yang K'uan (1957), one later Chou *ch'ih* equals 0.2308864 m. Thus, Lo-yang *ch'eng* was, according to *Yi Chou Shu*, 17,200 *ch'ih* or 3973 m to a side, which is not altogether off the archaeological report of the site. The outer enclosure, according to *Yi Chou Shu,* would thus be 126,000 *ch'ih* or 29,106 m to a side. At Lo-yang, no such walls have been located. No walled city of this size has been excavated anywhere in China from the ancient period.

In the Ch'un Ch'iu period city walls were apparently measured in units of *pan*, *tu*, and *chih*, which etymologically appear to have derived from words for construction technique and/or physical features of city walls. According to the lore of the lords, a hundred *chih* to a side appears to have been the maximum allowable for a city other than the capital of the state. (*Tso Chuan,* First Year of Yin Kung: "If the *tu*'s *ch'eng*

invariably guided by the four cardinal directions, with an emphasis upon the north-south axis. From the length and direction of steps and ramps it can be determined that a south orientation was important for the prominent buildings. (6) Earthen platforms or mounds served as the foundations of politically and ceremonially important and prominent structures. (7) The basic constitution of specialized quarters (palaces, temples, workshops, shops, domiciles, and farming hamlets, in various proportions and arrangements) is constant in all the cities where excavated data are sufficient for an understanding of this functional layout. A city consisted of a number of parts, no single one of which could be considered to be self-contained in economy, government, and religion—here I am speaking of the temple center, royal cemetery, workshops, and farming hamlets of the Shang cities, the twin ceremonial centers and the residential quarters of the Western Chou cities, and the palaces, the temple, the market, and the industrial and farming quarters of the Eastern Chou cities (Fig. 5).

Underlying these physical characteristics of Shang and Chou cities is the apparent fact that the core of a city was built as a unit according to a plan rather than in successive stages as the result of "natural" growth in a city's life. Speaking about the city in ancient Chinese history in general, Nelson Wu (1963: 32) observes that "it manifests an intellectual order superimposed upon a natural terrain," and Andrew Boyd (1962: 72) agrees that in ancient China "the whole city was itself a work of art."

Central to this, I think, is the fact that a city in ancient China was

---

exceeds a hundred *chih* [in length], it would become harmful to the state." *Kung Yang Chuan,* Twelfth Year of Ting Kung: "No *yi* should have a *ch'eng* a hundred *chih* in length.") There is, however, no agreement about the absolute values of these various terms. Mao's commentary of *Shih Ching* (poem "Hung Yen Chih Shih," in "Hsiao Ya") says: "One *chang* equals a *pan,* and five *pans* are one *tu*." This is not too far from Ho Hsiu's annotation of *Kung Yang Chuan,* where it is said that "eight *ch'ih* are called a *pan*; one *tu* comprises of forty *ch'ihs;* one *chih* has two hundred *ch'ih*; and a *ch'eng* is as long as twenty thousand *ch'ihs*." According to Ho, a hundred *chih* (maximum length of the city wall on one side) would thus be 4,617.728 m. But according to Tu Yü's annotation of *Tso Chuan,* there was a rather different set of equations: "Each square *ch'ang* is called a *tu*; two *tus* are called one *chih.* Each section of city wall one *chih* in length is three *chang* long and one *chang* tall." A hundred *chih,* in this calculation, would measure only 692.66 m.

In texts of Chan Kuo period, these older units of measurements for city lengths give way to *li. Meng Tzu* ("Kung Sun Ch'ou, Hsia") speaks of "*ch'engs* of three *lis* and *kuos* of seven *lis,*" and *Mo Tzu* ("Tsa Shou") also speaks of "leading ten thousand households and [making] a *ch'eng* three *lis* square." Three *lis* would be 1,247.4 m and seven *lis* would be 2,850 m., closely approximating the measurements of the city ruins of this period (see also *Chan Kuo Ts'e,* "Tung Chou Ts'e, and *Chou Li,* "K'ao Kung Chi").

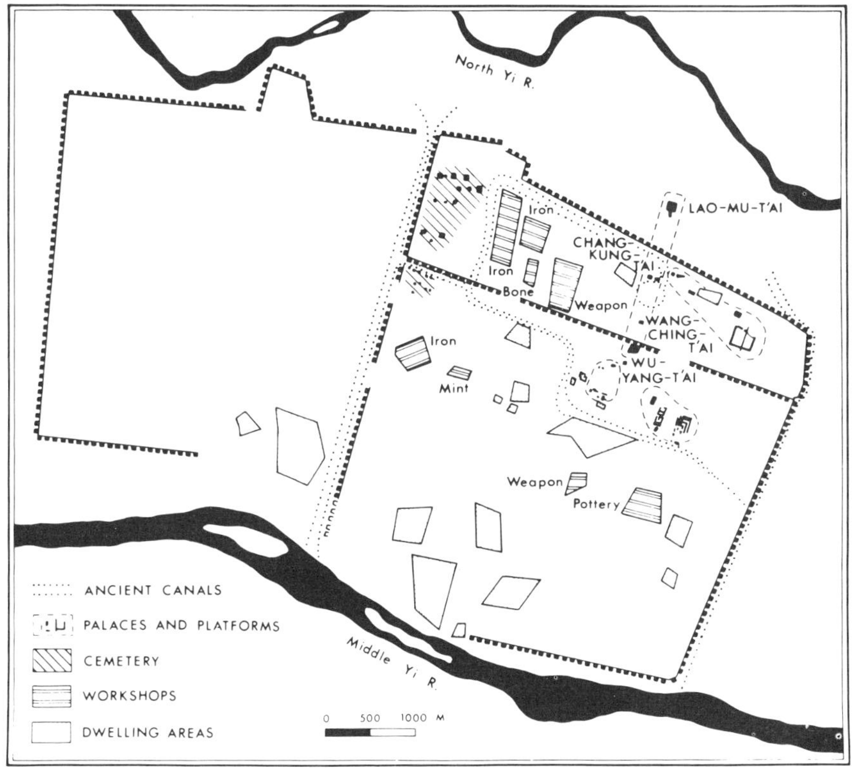

Figure 5. Ruins of the City of Hsia-tu, State of Yen. Note the layout of the various functional parts

the administrative, ceremonial, and defensive locus of the politically prominent lineages and their wealth; it was not just a settlement whose inhabitants engaged in commercial transactions and subsistence enterprises of various kinds among themselves. In *Li Chi* ("Ch'ü Li") we read, "When a superior man (high in rank) is about to engage in building, the ancestral temple should have his first attention, the stables and arsenal the next, and the residences the last. In all preparations of things by (the head) of a clan [family], the vessels of sacrifice should have the first place; the victims supplied from his revenue, the next; and the vessels for use at meals, the last" (translated, Legge 1885: 105). In ancient Chinese descriptions of town building, invariably the construction of the ancestral temples and the placement of the lineage treasures in them were given prominent attention. ("Sung Kao," in "Ta Ya," *Shih Ching*). In the city, there was an eminence for the *tsung* temples (*Shih Ming,* under "Tsung ch'iu"). To govern the *tsung* was to govern the town ("Kung Liu," in "Ta Ya," *Shih Ching*).

To explain some of the terms above: A "lineage" in one anthropological usage is

> a corporate group of unlinear kin, with a formalized system of authority; it is a single group that is assumed to be permanent, to which rights and duties may be attached as to a single unit and which may usually be represented *vis-à-vis* other groups by a single person. It is generally named and within it an accepted genealogical relationship is known between all members. It includes both living and dead. . . . A lineage may be subdivided into smaller groupings each with genealogies of shallower depth and narrower span. Each segment is then a unit in a system of segments, all being corporate groups. (Middleton and Tait 1958: 7, 34)

In the parlance of the ancient Chinese, *tsu* is comparable to a minimal segment of the lineage, and the lineage of various larger grades is referred to as *tsung.* In each *tsung,* there were several minimal segments, *tsu,* and the segments all traced their ancestry to a common lineage founder. One of these *tsu* was the stem, referred to as the *tsung,* and the others were its branches, referred to as the *tsu* in the same *tsung.* The stem *tsung* was composed of a direct line of *tsung tzu, tsung* sons, who were keepers of a *tsung shih,* the *tsung*'s ritual chamber, in which the lineage ancestor's tablets were stored. Normatively, the stem *tsung* was to be carried on by the eldest son of the primary wife. The branch *tsung* established by the younger sons and sons born to the concubines, if they were to be established, were politically and ritually subordinate to the stem *tsung;* they, in turn, however, became stem *tsung* when they themselves gave rise to branches smaller still. Thus, it is evident that the Shang and Chou lineage system had a built-in system of authority hierarchy and formal power distribution.

It is obvious that the kinship alignments provided a basically fictional order of authority but in themselves could not be sufficient for maintaining or changing the actual balance of political power. In other words, realistic political power could not be determined by kinship alone. The practical sources of power of special lineages in ancient China were both material and spiritual. The former included land tenure, effective control and protection of sizable populations, and wealth in material goods; the latter, ritual attributes associated with specific lineages by force of mythology and tradition. The town or city at which the *tsung tzu* was seated was the concrete manifestation of both material and spiritual sources of the political power at the lineage's command, but above all it provided a locus for the manipulation of the lineage wealth in the form of agricultural products, handicrafts, and, in later periods, markets. To Fei Hsiao-t'ung (1953: 95), a walled town in modern China is "an instrument of the ruling classes in a political system where power resides in force. [It] is the symbol of power and also a necessary tool for the maintenance of power." There is no reason not to use the same characterization for the Chinese cities and towns of three thousand years ago.

The identification of the ancient town both with a lineage and with its locale must explain many physical attributes of the Shang and Chou cities and towns. For instance, it explains why the ancient Chinese cities and their prominent structures were not as durably constructed as might be expected from the capability of the ancient Chinese builders and their available resources. Lineages were composed of people, whose ties with the physical loci of their ancestral temples and tablets were transitory. Lineages were constantly renewable, mobile, and ever-expanding and ramifying. The immortality of a lineage was accomplished by the perpetuation and rejuvenation of its membership rather than by the permanency of its physical shell, which could only be incidental. The concepts of longevity and posterity were expressed through the propagation of the lineage descendants, symbolized by the temples and paraphernalia of the ancestral cult, rather than through monumental architecture. The monumental symbols of immortality consisted of ritual bronzes;[7] inscriptions on many of them bore the wishful message, "Tzu tzu sun sun yüng pao yüng," or "Forever to treasure and use by you sons and grandsons." Some of the same ideological principles that Arthur F. Wright (1965: 678-679) believes are revealed by the construction of Sui and T'ang cities were already working concepts of the Shang and Chou Chinese.

7. Tu Yü's commentary to *Tso Chuan* (Fifteenth Year of Chao Kung) states that "*yi* [ritual vessels] means *ch'ang* [perpetual]."

5 The Lineage System of the Shang and Chou Chinese and Its Political Implications

The kinship and lineage systems of the ancient Chinese have been investigated by both Chinese Classicists (e.g., Wang 1956) and comparative sociologists (Granet 1939; M. J. Kuo 1930; H. P. Li 1939, 1954; Y. F. Ruey 1947, 1949, 1950a, 1950b, 1954, 1958, 1959; H. Y. Feng 1948; Ch'en and Shryock 1932). These studies have amply shown that in Shang and Chou China the kinship system and history are closely interwoven with political system and history. This paper focuses upon some of the specific features of this interweaving relationship and brings to the fore their comparative significance.

The Shang and Chou Lineage System

"(In the distinctions of the mourning) for the kindred who are the dearest, the honoured ones to whom honour is paid, the elders who are venerated for their age, and as the different tributes to males and females; there are seen the greatest manifestations of the course which is right for man" (translated, Legge 1885, Part IV:44). This piece of late-Chou early-Han text spells out with clarity and accuracy the major criteria by which a Shang or Chou Chinese distinguished different categories of his fellow men and adopted a pattern of behavior appropriate to these categories. The criteria are: sex, primacy of one of the spouses over the rest, primacy of one of the sons over the rest, and generation. Four major native categories of relatives were formulated with the application of these criteria: *tsu, tsung, hsing,* and affines.

(1) *Tsu. Pai Hu T'ung* (chapter "Tsung Tsu") defines *tsu* as "To merge and to gather together, designating those relatives who flow together and merge into a single group, including the great-great-grandfather above and the great-great-grandson below." *Erh Ya* (chapter "Shih Ch'in") states that all male cousins descending from a common great-great-grandfather are referred to as *tsu*

Note: This paper was prepared during the term of an Asian Studies grant awarded by the American Council of Learned Societies and the Social Science Research Council for 1963-64. I thank the above councils for their financial support as well as the following scholars for advice and suggestions: Floyd Lounsbury, Arthur F. Wright, Nelson I. Wu of Yale; William Davenport of the University of Pennsylvania; and Yang Lien-sheng, Max Loehr, and John C. Pelzel of Harvard.

hsiung ti, or *tsu* brothers, whereas those from a common great-great-great-grandfather are called *ch'in t'ung hsing,* or the "near relatives with the same *hsing.*" These and other pieces of evidence suggest that the Eastern Chou *tsu* was a jural community with a membership of an extended patrifamily, whose members were related by blood within five patrilineally reckoned generations descending from a particular ancestor. The statements in various chapters of *Li Chi,* that "some of the *tsung* are discontinued after five generations," that "there is no more kin at the sixth generation," and that "T'ai Kung was first buried at Ying Ch'iu [in Ch'i] but was moved back to Chou after five generations [of Ch'i dukes]," all indicate that the five descending generations assumed an important role in kinship categorization: those within it were members of the same *tsu.*

The word *tsu* appears in the oracle bone inscriptions of the Shang Dynasty, its context suggesting that the *tsu* of Shang was also an elementary unit of kin for the joint performance of many activities, particularly those in military connection (M. C. Ch'en 1956: 496-497). In *Tso Chuan,* under the Fourth Year of Ting Kung, it is stated that after the Chou conquest of Shang, six or seven *tsu* of the Shang's people were given by the king to his lord uncles as a part of their initial state establishments in eastern north China. The names of some of the Shang *tsu,* furthermore, suggest that each of them was associated with a specialized handicraft. The importance of the "fifth generation" in the Shang Dynasty is indicated by a genealogical table inscribed on a piece of bone unearthed at An-yang; this table lists names of a line of fathers and sons, but the names of a brother are given at every fifth generation from the top (M. C. Ch'en 1956: 499). The royal geneaology of the Shang, discussed in some detail below, if broken down into five-generation segments, reveals an interesting point: each segment began with a king named alternatively with the Heavenly Stem *yi* or *ting.* The significance of this will become clear in another context.

We have little data on the composition of the *tsu* during the Western Chou, the period between the Shang and the Eastern Chou. If the Eastern Chou statements about the Five Ancestral Temples system of the earlier Chou kings (see *Chou Li* and *Li Chi*) are of some validity (statements to some extent supported by Western Chou bronze texts, see T'ang 1962), then we are again faced with the mysterious number five in connection with the genealogies. It appears, in any event, to be a fair assumption that the *tsu* was a basic kinship unit throughout the Shang and Chou periods, a unit of common residence and activity and common occupation, consisting of patrilineally related members within five generations descending from a particular ancestor.

(2) *Tsung.* "A lineage," in the definition of Middleton and Tait (1958: 3-4, 7), "is a corporate group of unilinear kin, with a formalized system of authority; it is a single group that is assumed to be permanent, to which rights and duties may be attached as to a single unit and which may usually be represented *vis-à*-vis other groups by a single person. It is generally named and within it an accepted genealogical relationship is known between all members. It includes both living and dead . . . A lineage may be subdivided into smaller groupings each with genealogies of shallower depth and narrower span. Each segment is then a unit in a system of segments, all being corporate groups." The term "segmentary" is often used in reference to several types of social systems, "but the essential features are the 'nesting' attributes of segmentary series and the characteristic of being in a state of continual segmentation and complementary opposition." These and similar definitions have been made of late according to recent studies of many African and Oceanic societies, but their heuristic significance to the study of ancient Chinese lineages cannot be overstated. For *tsu,* as described above, is comparable to a minimal segment of the lineage, and the lineage of various larger grades is referred to in ancient Chinese texts as *tsung.*

Under the Third Year of Duke Chao, *Tso Chuan* quotes Shu Hsien, a noble official of the state of Chin, in commenting upon the decline of some of the Chin noble families, "My *tsung* used to have eleven *tsu,* but now only one, by the name of Sheep's Tongue, remains." *Tsu* is often mentioned in Shang and Chou texts as one of a cluster, and it appears that the *tsus* were organized into *tsung* groups. In each *tsung,* or lineage, there were several minimal segments, *tsu,* and these segments all traced their ancestry, by actual or accepted genealogies, as to a common lineage founder. One of these *tsu* was the stem, referred to as the *tsung,* and the others were its branches, referred to as the *tsu* in the same *tsung.* In time depth, the stem *tsung* was composed of a direct line of *tsung-tzu,* or *tsung* sons (whose official primary spouses were *tsung-fu,* or *tsung* daughters-in-law), who were keepers of a *tsung-shih,* or the *tsung*'s ritual chamber, in which the lineage ancestors' tablets were stored. *Pai Hu T'ung* defines *tsung* as "the respected one, having the ancestral tablets and being endowed with high rank by the *tsung* members." Eastern Chou texts indicate that the head of the *tsung* maintained considerable authority over his member *tsu:* he could execute offenders or exile members; he must be consulted by the king in any action taken against his members; and he served as leader in military campaigns (H. P. Li 1954: 195-196). In Shang oracle records, the word *tsung* takes the proto-form of *shih,* meaning the ancestral tablet. The character *tsung* in the Chou literatures consists of two radicals: the tablet below and a roof above.

(3) *Hsing.* In both Shang and Chou, members of the same *hsing* traced their descent patrilineally to a common mythological male or female ancestor and were known by a common name, *hsing,* which was derived from the mythological birth, *sheng,* the original form of the word *hsing* (H. P. Li. 1954: 7-8). The actual or accepted genealogy went beyond the level of *tsung* only to the extent that all *tsung* of the same *hsing* were branches of the stem *tsung* at some point in time, which in turn claimed actual descent from the *hsing* ancestor. The hierarchical structure of the *tsung* in one and the same *hsing* is very much like that of *tsu* in one and the same *tsung,* although there are more levels of complexity with reference to the *tsung* than to the *tsu.*

In Eastern Chou texts, frequent reference was made to an archaic society in which, within the family, "the mother was known and acknowledged, but the father was not." If this, as some scholars have asserted, indicates that there was in north China a matriarchal/matrilineal stage in the history of societal development (e.g., H. P. Li 1954: 74-77), then such a tradition must have been kept alive for at least two thousand years, which does not seem to be a fair assumption. At any rate, both the Shang and the Chou definitely fell within the patrilineal "stage," and the importance of patrilineality may go back even further. Indeed, phallic images of clay have been found from the Neolithic site at Yang-shao-ts'un (Andersson 1943: 68, 1947: 51), a site now thought to be situated chronologically between the Yang-shao and the Lung-shan Neolithic stages. And in the oracle bone inscriptions, the character for the "ancestor" (grandfather and his ancestors) unquestionably designates a phallus. This character, in fact, also resembles the shape of the ancestral tablet that is known in later texts to be located in the ancestral temples (M. J. Kuo 1952: 16-17; Ling 1959a: 1-47). To be sure, we have good reason to suspect that the worship of phalli and the cult of male ancestors may have had an early beginning in north China in the Lung-shan stage of the Neolithic at the latest (K. C. Chang 1960: 266-267).

When we come down from the Neolithic to the Shang and Chou,

we shift from inference to certainty. *Hsing, tsung,* and *tsu* were all patrilineal units, and no explicit record of any kind of unilineal kin groups other than the patrisib (*hsing*) and patrilineages is known in Shang and Chou China. The Western Chou poem of "Liao Eh" (in section "Hsiao Ya" of the *Book of Odes*) goes so far as to declare:

My father begot me,
My mother fed me,
Led me, bred me,
Brought me up, reared me,
Kept her eye on me, tended me,
At every turn aided me.
(translated, Waley 1960: 316-317)

Members of the same *hsing* descending along a large or small number of patrilines were, in the Eastern Chou period at least, normatively forbidden to intermarry, and there is evidence to show that this was strictly enforced. In both *Tso Chuan* and *Kuo Yü,* repeated references are made to the rule that having the same *hsing* taboos a union whether or not an actual relationship can be genealogically traced. *Li Chi* (section of "Ch'ü Li") dramatizes this rule by stating that in buying a concubine of unknown *hsing,* a man must divine to make sure that she does not have the same *hsing* as his own. This rule was, to be sure, occasionally broken, but those who broke it appear in history as bad moral examples. *Kuo Yü* ("Chin Yü" IV) explains why this was so:

People having different *hsing* are also different in virtue, and people of different virtues belong to different categories. Persons of opposite sexes and of different categories intermarry in order to propagate, even if they may be very close. People of the same *hsing* also have the same virtue, and people of the same virtue converge in mind, and people who converge in mind have the same goal. Persons of opposite sexes but having the same goal do not intermarry, even if they may be very distant from each other, for fear of committing incest.

The author of this passage was apparently ignorant of genetics, but some of the concepts expressed here are of significance in several ways, some of which will be commented upon below. We are not certain, however, that such marriage taboos among *hsing* members stated in Eastern Chou or later texts were applicable to early Chou or the Shang. We shall discuss this point presently.

(4) *Affines.* In Eastern Chou texts affines are referred to as "brothers" or "maternal uncles-sororal nephews." The significance of these terms and the distinctions will be discussed below.

The scheme of ramification and segmentation of the Shang and Chou patrilineal kin groups described above was highly flexible and dynamic, and the flexibility and dynamism centered around the *tsung.* Insofar as the *hsing* delineated the category of common mythological descent and the *tsu* referred to a jural community of kinsmen related patrilineally through the fifth descending generation, these two units were rather rigidly defined, at least in concept. Since the population of any *hsing* could be large or small, its generations from the mythological ancestor on down could be many or few, and the necessary number and levels of the *tsung* within it varied greatly from one to the other. The variations depended in large measure upon the actual genealogical depth to be reckoned with for the determination of the political status of the lineage in question.

Let us elaborate upon this point, since it involves the controversial interpretation of the concepts of *ta* (major) *tsung* and *hsiao* (minor) *tsung* in the Chou texts.

As long as each male member of a patrilineage had more than one son, the size of the lineage was apt to grow and lead to the fission of the lineage. Granting two sons to each nuclear family, the lineage founded by one man would inevitably grow to 31 male members after five generations, and to 256 male members at the tenth generation. Although a *tsu* of 31 males could possibly live together in a single community, a *tsu* of 256 male members in one generation would have to split up and live in separate settlements out of pure physical necessity. In addition to sheer increase in size, there were other factors at work to increase the distance between male members within the *tsu* belonging to the same generation, such as that of recognizing generation distance in regulating kinship relations: to any one of the 256 males, the other 255 men were all descendants from a common ancestor at the tenth generation ascending; half of these claimed common descent from one at the ninth generation ascending; half still were derived from one at the eighth; only three descended from the grandfather; and only one was a full brother. The distance in kinship relations as well as the distance in living space inevitably led to subdivisions within the original lineage, and to major groups and minor groups. The "major" and "minor" are, of course, relative: descendants from the ninth ascending generation formed a major group in relation to those from the eighth, but a minor one in relation to those from the tenth.

> There is a well-known order of segmentation in lineages, from maximal levels, through major and minor orders, to the minimal level, in descending scale. As a scheme of reference and a form of group organization, this order is pervasively relativistic. Thus, the minor lineage is a major segment in relation to the minimal lineage. Definition of genealogical segments therefore depends on the apical point of reference. (Smith 1956: 40)

These major and minor lineages and sub-lineages were organized under a hierarchical framework in terms of complementary opposition in political status, and the pattern of power distribution varied from society to society. In Shang and Chou China, each lineage had a "stem *tsung,*" maintaining the position of orthodoxy, and a large or small number of "branch *tsung,*" branching away both in terms of genealogical ties and political status. Normatively, the stem *tsung* was to be carried on by the eldest sons of the primary wives. And normatively, the branch *tsung* established by the younger sons and sons born to the concubines, if they were to be established, were politically and ritually subordinate to the stem *tsung;* they in turn, however, became stem *tsung* when they themselves gave rise to still smaller branches. Thus it is evident that the Shang-Chou lineage system had a built-in system of power distribution.

Under this view perhaps we can make some sense out of the controversial passages in *Li Chi* on the *tsung fa,* or the *tsung* principles. These passages contrast *ta tsung* and *hsiao tsung,* and "those *tsung* that are to be carried on forever" and "those that move away after five generations." Most of the controversies appear to stem from the erroneous identification of *ta tsung* with those carried on forever, and *hsiao tsung* with those discontinued after five generations, identifications not at all implied in the original passages. Apparently *ta tsung* and "major lineages" may be considered as interchangeable terms—and so may *hsiao tsung* and "minor lineages." Whether a *tsung,* major or minor, is to be carried on forever or discontinued after five generations is purely a political matter. Genealogical data appear to show that the *tsung* that were associated with specific land titles and political holdings (centered in the city) stood a much better chance of being carried on forever than those that were associated primarily with official titles and administrative offices.

The Identity of Alternate Generations

There is little question that there was a segmentary lineage system in Shang and Chou China and that this system was concurrent with a centralized government. But data are scarce concerning the relationship among different lineages of the same or of different sibs. We know for a fact that two points are of great relevance to this problem, even though we are not entirely sure just how. These are the identity of alternate generations and the cross-cousin marriage.

On the former, attention must be first directed to the posthumous names of the Shang kings. The royal genealogy of the Shang Dynasty is known in fragments in such pre-Ch'in texts as *Chi Nien* (*The Bamboo Annals*) and *Shih Pen,* but Ssu-ma Ch'ien's *Historical Memoirs* presents it in its entirety for the first time. It is established from these texts that the kings of the Shang Dynasty were known during life by their personal names but that after death they were given posthumous names which, except for the first segment of the royal genealogy, included one of the ten designations for the ten-day cycle of the Shang calendar. In the Shang period, as in later historical times, the day was designated by a combination of the ten Heavenly Stems and the twelve Earthly Branches, and thus there was a sixty-day cycle intermediate between the ten-day cycle (marked by the ten Heavenly Stems only) and the year, a cycle independent of, but parallel to, the lunar months. The ten Heavenly Stems are: *chia, yi, ping, ting, wu, chi, keng, hsin, jen, kuei.* The ten-day cycle, referred to as *hsün* by the Shang, was more important in ritual matters than the sixty-day cycle, and formed the basic unit for the yearly ritual calendar. The entry into a new *hsün* was considered a life crisis, and the well-being of the king during the next *hsün* was often the subject of inquiry in the oracles that were routinely taken on the last day of the *hsün* (Tung 1945).

These calendrical matters are more or less common knowledge, but the reason for making posthumous reference to the kings by the name of one of the ten-day designations is not. Chiao Chou in his *Ku Shih K'ao* says that "after death a king is referred to according to his tablet in the ancestral temple," but it is not clear why the tablet of any particular king should be referred to by one of the Heavenly Stems. After the discovery of the oracle bones in Anyang in 1899 (bones used during the Shang Dynasty for divination purposes in the royal court and sometimes inscribed with questions and, occasionally, answers), scholars have found that there is a correlation between the posthumous names of the kings and the particular day in the ten-day cycle on which rites to him were performed. In other words, rites were performed and sacrifices made to king Chia, for instance on the first day (*chia*) of the cycle, and to king Yi on the second day (*yi*), and so forth (see for instance M. C. Ch'en 1956). This explains the great ritual importance of the ten-day cycle in the Shang Dynasty, but it does not reveal why king Chia, or his tablet, was assigned to the *chia*-day of the cycle in the first place.

The earliest known explanation is found in *Pai Hu T'ung,* which says that the Shang people named a child according to the day on which he was born. This explanation has been accepted by historians of all ages, and is still the one most widely subscribed to (Ch'ü 1948). After the discovery of the oracle bone inscriptions, at least three other hypotheses have been advanced. One derives the designation from the day of death rather than birth (Tung 1951). A second theorizes that the king's posthumous name was given according to the order of his birth, ascendance to manly status, and death (M. C. Ch'en 1956). The third proposes that the designation was decided at the time of death by means of divination (H. C. Li 1957). None of these has been satisfactorily supported by available evidence, and the birth-day theory remains the best and simplest explanation.

A careful look into the genealogy of the Shang Dynasty, however, brings to light several features of these posthumous names that cannot be explained by the birth-day hypothesis. Before enumerating these features, however, the genealogy in Figure 6 must first be considered. This chart has been worked out by scholars of oracle bones on the basis of their inscriptions considered together with Ssu-ma's *Memoirs.* It includes all the Shang kings from Shang-*chia* through the last monarch before the Chou invasion (Ti-*hsin*); their more remote ancestors before Shang-*chia* are legendary and cannot be substantiated in the ritual records. The oracle records of the last two kings (Ti-*yi* and Ti-*hsin*) keep a complete calendrical schedule of the ancestral cult rites performed within a year, and the order of appearance of the kings' names on the schedule largely agrees with Ssu-ma's record, although most of the relationships between neighboring kings (father-son or brothers) must depend upon Ssu-ma's account. Neighboring kings connected by horizontal lines in the chart are fathers and sons; those connected by vertical lines are brothers. Names of spouses appear on the ritual calendar only when their sons succeeded to the throne, and they thus became, as it were, "official" spouses. This table can be regarded as only an approximation, and in a few places it still requires confirmation.

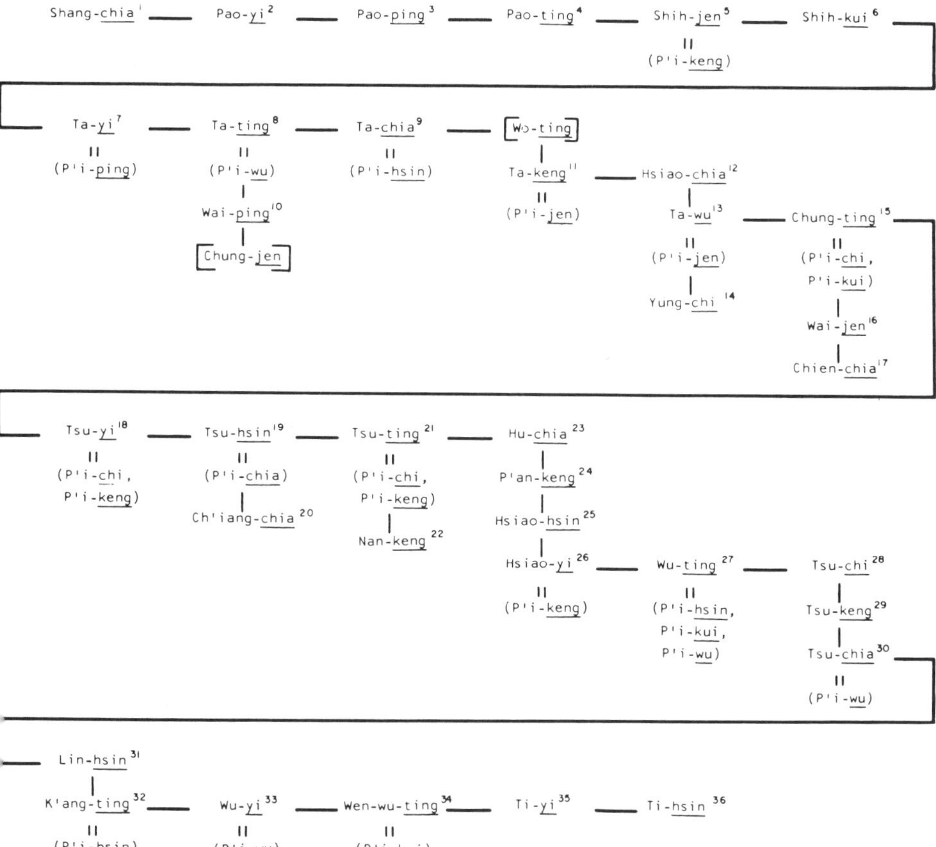

Figure 6. The Royal Genealogy of the Shang Dynasty

In the chart the parts of the names that are derived from the Ten Stems are italicized; the characters preceding them are for the most part distinguishing prefixes, and the Ten Stems are really the basic parts of the names. It is thus clear that all the Shang kings and their spouses, beginning with Shang-*chia,* have the Ten Stems as their posthumous names.

A careful examination of the chart reveals that the occurrence of particular heavenly stems in the genealogy as a whole follows strict rules and discoverable regularities.

(1) The frequency of occurrence of the stems varies greatly: There are 7 *chia,* 6 *yi,* 2 *ping,* 8 *ting,* 1 *wu,* 1 *chi,* 4 *keng,* 4 *hsin,* 3 *jen,* and 1 *kuei* among the kings, and 2 *chia,* O *yi,* 1 *ping,* O *ting,* 4

wu, 3 *chi,* 4 *keng,* 3 *hsin,* 2 *jen,* and 3 *kuei* among their official spouses. In other words, among the 37 kings with stem names, 21 used *chia, yi* and *ting,* but among all the official spouses none at all was named after *yi* and *ting.* If we adopt the birth-day hypothesis, then it appears quite legitimate to ask: How does it happen that over half of the kings were born on three days of the ten-day cycle (*chia, yi,* and *ting*), but none of their official spouses was born on two of these days and only two were born on the *chia* day?

(2) Not only do the three major stems, *chia, yi,* and *ting,* account for more than half of the kings' names, their occurrence in the genealogy is also regular insofar as the generational order is concerned. Thus, from Ta-*yi* to Tsu-*yi:*

Ta-*yi*—Ta-*ting*—Ta-*chia*—Wo-*ting*—Hsiao-*chia*—Chung-*ting*—Tsu-*yi*

The segment from Tsu-*ting* to Ti-*yi* is:

Tsu-*ting*—Hsiao-*yi*—Wu-*ting*—Tsu-*chia*—K'ang-*ting*—Wu-*yi*—T'ai-*ting*—Ti-*yi*

Thus it is seen that the stem *chia* or *yi* and *ting* occur in alternate generations. If we substitute A for *chia* and *yi,* and B for *ting:*

A - B - A - B - A - B - A - B - . . .

Three segments are not accounted for by this rule. The first is the six generations from Shang-*chia* to Shih-*kuei.* We must point out here that the actual relationships of these six kings, if they are regarded as individual personalities, are not clear. The Shang Dynasty was established by Ta-*yi,* the king following Shih-*kuei,* and it is the feeling among many scholars that the six kings preceding him in the genealogy were more in the nature of categories than actual personalities. In either case, the irregularity here is not a significant exception in this particular connection. The second segment that is seemingly exceptional to the alternate generation rule is the transition from Tsu-*yi* to Tsu-*ting.* In the chart above it has been shown that this transition is believed to be as follows:

Tsu-*yi*—Tsu-*hsin*—Tsu-*ting*
Wo-*chia*—Nan-*keng*

If so, then *yi* and *chia* appear in two successive generations before passing on to the next *ting.* But the genealogical record here is in some dispute. Evidence from the oracle bone records is conflicting, and we are not sure whether Wo-*chia* was Tsu-*hsin's* brother, as given in the chart, or his son. Wo-*chia's* spouse appears in one of the calendrical schedules worked out from the oracle records, and it is recognized as a rule that only spouses with throned sons merited this place. It is possible that the above segment of the Shang genealogy may prove to read:

Tsu-*yi* (A)—Tsu-*hsin* (B)—Wo-*chia* (A)—Tsu-*ting* (B)

If this is indeed the case, then we have a genealogical record running from Ta-*yi* through the last but one king in which *chia* or *yi* and *ting* occur in alternate generations without exception. The last king, the third segment mentioned above, is named *hsin*. This is an uncertainty but not a contradiction.

Can this remarkable rule—identity of alternate generations in posthumous designations—be accounted for by the birth-day theory? I imagine not. It is too regular to be coincident.

(3) The third regularity of the occurrence of the ten stems in the Shang genealogy is the fact that among the kings of the same generation (those who were brothers), the stems *chia* or *yi* and *ting* are mutually exclusive. There is just one apparent exception to this rule—that of Chung-*ting's* brother being Ch'ien-*chia*. But here again there is conflicting evidence from the ancient texts, and at least in one text (*Han Shu*) Ch'ien-*chia* is given as the brother of Tsu-*yi*, the following king. Chung-*ting* and Tsu-*yi* cannot be brothers, because their spouses both appear in the oracle record, and it is a rule that the spouses of only one king appear in the record in each generation. It is thus probable that Ch'ien-*chia* was Chung-*ting's* son and Tsu-*yi's* brother.

(4) The last regularity I would like to point out is that the official spouses of the kings were never designated with the same stems as those for their husbands. This has been stated before by Yang Shu-ta (1954) who speculates that perhaps in the Shang Dynasty it was the custom not to marry a woman born on the same day. This seems unlikely because in the oracle bone records we know that men did marry women with the same stem designation, but that these women were never "official" spouses.

It is obvious that the birth-day theory cannot explain the four regularities enumerated above, and it is my conviction that we can offer a more plausible explanation. We have seen that after death the kings and their official spouses (as well as other people outside this genealogical orthodoxy) were represented by tablets, and their tablets were designated with the Heavenly Stems. The designation, furthermore, follows regular patterns that remained unchanged from Ta-*yi* to Ti-*hsin*. On these regular patterns I have made the following assumptions. (1) The posthumous designation of the ancestral tablets indicates a classification of the ancestral tablets into ten categories. (2) The classification of the ancestral tablets coincides with the classification of the kings and their spouses according to their positions in the Shang lineage and kinship system. Space does not allow a detailed discussion of these assumptions, which I have given elsewhere (K. C. Chang 1963a), and only a brief summary of the general conclusions follows.

The Shang's ruling family belonged to a patrisib with the name of Tzu and with a common myth of ancestral birth. This sib was, nevertheless, basically a loose category consisting of a number of corporate lineages. Lineages differed from one another in political status, and a broad division can be made between the lineages that ruled the kingdom and those that did not, at any give time. Among the ruling lineages there appear to be two clusters that actually possessed the power to rule most of the time; these clusters are designated in the ancestral temples as *chia* and *yi* (together with their affiliated stems) and *ting* (together with its affiliated stems). When a member of the *chia-yi* lineage cluster was the king, he was probably not in the position of marrying an official spouse from the opposite cluster, *ting,* because his mother probably came from *ting,* and because any such marriage would inevitably lead to a politically embarrassing imbalance. Since the king had to marry a woman from a politically less prominent lineage, his son's political heritage was considerably diminished. But his sib brothers in the *ting* cluster had no such restrictions, and they could marry the king's sisters in the *chia-yi* cluster; hence the king's son's sib brothers, derived from two prominent clusters of lineage, had a stronger political heritage than the king's own sons. Thus when the king died, the throne was taken over, not by his own son, but by his classificatory son, who was actually his sister's son. If there was no such candidate in the opposite cluster, then the throne went to the king's sib brothers in the same lineage cluster, *chia-yi.* When the king from *ting* died, the same story was repeated, except that it was now another member of the *chia-yi* cluster who took over the throne. This member was the sister's son of the last king, but was also the grandson of the king before last. So the genealogy we see today is only half the story and the whole story can be reconstructed in Figure 7.

This reconstructed scheme of the royal succession and lineage system may appear unorthodox, but it does have ethnographic analogies and is therefore quite possible.[1] It explains satisfactorily

1. See Robert W. Williamson's (1924, vol. 1: 378-379) account of the Funafuti society of the Ellice Islands in Western Polynesia, which is quoted in Chapter 6. It not only suggests the feasibility of our reconstruction of the Shang royal lineages but also gives ground for placement of many "Old Officials" in the royal ancestral cult calendar of the Shang, as was the practice. Unfortunately, Williamson's book is not well known for reliability, and the rapid acculturation of the Ellice Islanders, particularly the Funafuti group, renders it unlikely that further evidence will come to light in this crucial respect. See Goody (1966) for similar institutions in Africa and for many interesting principles of succession that are applicable in the Shang case.

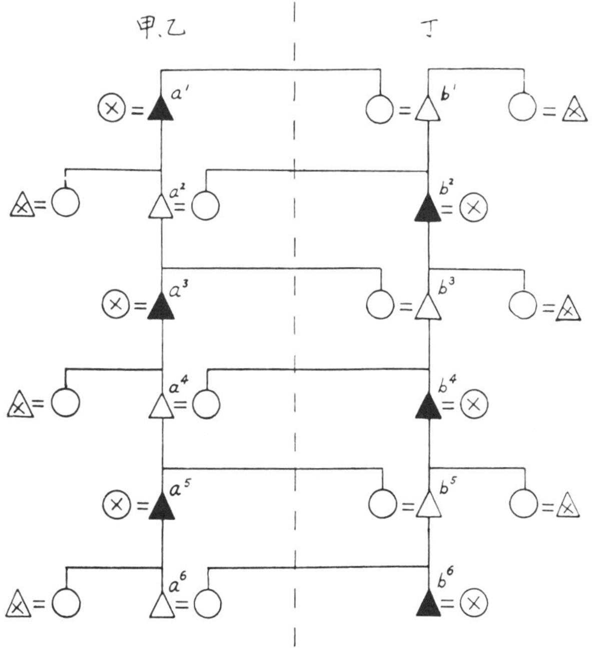

Figure 7. A Reconstruction of the Rules of Marriage and Succession of the Shang Royal Lineages

all four regularities enumerated above. In fact, I have not been able to formulate any other scheme of equally possible nature (ethnographically) that can do the same. The only modification we have to make in our data is the meaning of such kin terms as fathers, sons, and brothers; but scholars have agreed for some time that in the Shang texts the term *father* was used for all male relatives of the first ascending generation, *son* for all male relatives of the first descending generation, and *brother* for all male relatives of the same generation, and thus our modification in their meanings is not at all implausible.

The implications of this example of the study of ancient Chinese social life are clearly manifold and highly important. For one thing, it suggests a particular marriage system among members of different lineages that carries political implications. And there is evidence that such a system was not confined to the Shang alone.

The dynastic rule of China, according to the traditional history, began not with the Shang but with the Hsia. The Shang Dynasty, since the time of the discovery of the oracle bone inscriptions, has been generally accepted as a historical fact by historians, and the archaeological sites near An-yang and some other cities in northern and western Honan have been identified, by scripts and artifacts, with the historical Shang. No such substantiation avails for the Hsia, however, which remains one of the enigmae of the ancient Chinese history. This is not the place for a detailed discussion of the Hsia problem. What concerns us here is the fact that some of the legendary Hsia Dynasty kings, as recorded in *Shih Chi* and the *Bamboo Annals,* are again drawn from the Ten Heavenly stems. These names appear in *Shih Chi* in the manner shown in Figure 8. Thus, only four of the ten stems appear here: *chia, ting, keng,* and *kuei.* The three kings named *keng* are brothers, grandfathers, and grandson; the position of *ting* indicates, applying the principle of identity of alternate generations, that *ting* contrasts with *keng* and *chia* but aligns with *kuei.* There are three points of great interest: (1) *chia* and *ting* are of adjoining generations, and thus belong to separate sets, a phenomenon parallel to the Shang grouping of the ten stems; (2) *ting* and *kuei* are of the same generation class, again a parallel to the Shang system; (3) *kuei* of Hsia, a *ting* generation member, was ousted from his throne by Ta-*yi* of Shang, a *yi* generation member. If my inference that *yi* and *ting* are of parallel or

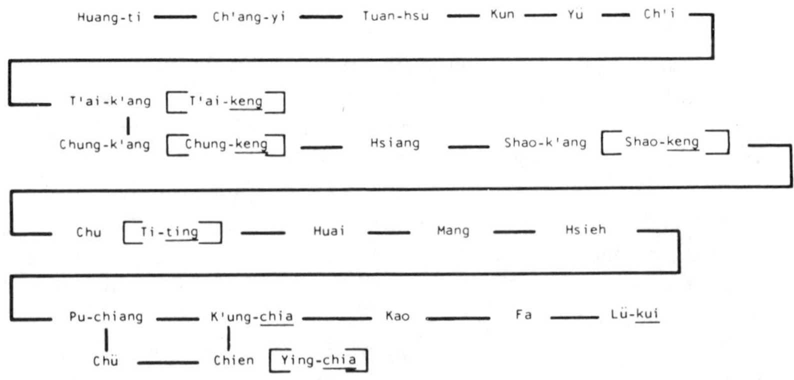

Figure 8. The Royal Genealogy of the "Hsia" Dynasty

opposite political powers is correct, then it appears that the *yi* group of Shang was responsible for the political demise of the last reigning member of the *ting* group of Hsia. Whether or not this has anything to do with the hypothesis advanced by some scholars that the Hsia Dynasty was in reality no more than an early segment of the Shang Dynasty (M. C. Ch'en 1936b), I hesitate to say. What is interestingly suggestive is that the Shang's *yi-ting* system seems to have been practiced by the Hsia, and that in both dynasties the *yi-ting* system of generation reckoning carries identical political overtones.

What appears to be an even more startling coincidence is that the Shang's *yi-ting* system shares many essential features with the so-called *chao-mu* system of the Chou Dynasty, long a much disputed system that no one after the Chou seems to know much about. This system is, like the Shang's *yi-ting,* simply an alternation of *chao* and *mu* generations as a guiding principle in the arrangement of ancestral temples of the Chou Dynasty. The words *chao* and *mu* are scattered in such Chou texts as *Shih Ching, Shu Ching,* and *Tso Chuan,* where it appears that each of the earliest Chou kings belonged to a fixed *chao-mu* designation according to the generation order he was born into, thus:

T'ai-wang (*mu*)—Wang-chi (*chao*)—Wen-wang (*mu*)—
Wu-wang (*chao*) (conqueror of Shang)—Ch'eng-wang (*mu*)—

In late Chou-Han texts such as *Li Chi* there are more elaborate explanations of the custom. The chapter "Wang Chih" in *Li Chi* says that the ancestral temples were arranged in two rows, *chao* row and *mu* row; the ancestral tablets were placed in *chao* or *mu* temples according to the generation they belonged to. Chapter "Chi T'ung" of *Li Chi* asserts that this system was for the purpose of "making explicit the generation order and kinship proximity." There are numerous speculations about the meaning of such an arrangement as well as reconstructions of the precise ways in which the system might have worked (see Ling 1959a for a latest synthesis). I would like simply to point out that in the following respects the *chao-mu* system resembles the Shang's *yi-ting:*

(1) The apparent identity of alternate generations. This is more than a matter of designations; some ritual procedures indicate the closeness of grandfathers and grandsons, and in the naming system of the Chou a new *tsung* was often given one of the personal names of the grandfather of the founder.

(2) The use of the ten Heavenly Stems for posthumous names was fairly common in the earlier part of the Chou period, as shown

by many bronze vessel inscriptions (C. C. Wu 1936). It is probable that the same principles used by the Shang in choosing names were also used by the Chou.

(3) Whenever Heavenly Stems appear in the names of Chou genealogies, their order of appearance with reference to generation relationships is identical with the Shang rules and classes. *Ting*-kung, the third duke of the State of Sung, was the great-grandson of Ti-*yi*. The founder of the State of Ch'i in Shantung was T'ai-kung; T'ai-kung's son was *Ting*-kung, whose son in turn was *Yi*-kung. The Sung dukes were direct descendants of the Shang royal family, and the resemblance of their naming system to that of the Shang is not at all strange. The dukes of Ch'i, however, belonged to the Chiang sib, having for generations had very close ties with the Chou, and the similarity of their naming system to the Shang is the more striking.

(4) The *chao-mu* system is thought to be universal in China during the Chou Dynasty, but certainly it was initiated by the royal sib, by the *hsing* of Chi. There is the likelihood that *chao* and *mu* are essentially synonyms of *ting* and *yi,* in that order. The Ch'i case is particularly instructive. The son of the founder belongs, according to the texts relating to the *chao-mu* system, to the *chao* generation, and his son to *mu*. The son of the founder of Ch'i, as mentioned above, was named *Ting*-kung, and his son, *Yi*-kung. We know that during the Shang period, rites were performed to specific ancestors on particular days of the ten-day cycle according to their names. We do not have the ritual schedules of the Chou, and the days of the ten-day cycle on which rituals were performed to particular ancestors are unknown in most cases. In a few cases, however, that are known from ancient texts and bronze inscriptions, we find that, without exception, the ancestors of the *chao* generations were sacrificed to on the *ting* day of the cycle, whereas those of the *mu* generations, on the *yi* day of the cycle. Thus it appears that, not only the *yi-ting* and the *chao-mu* systems were based on the same principles, but they may even be two names of the same thing.

In short, throughout the so-called Three Dynasties there was a persistent tendency to effect a dichotomy of the members of the same lineage according to alternate generations. All members of the alternating generations were designated with the same name and were treated alike in rituals. And at least in the case of the Shang's *yi-ting* system, it was further associated with the rules of political succession.

How is this to be explained? What kind of mechanism was behind the division of lineage members into two orders? The answer was presented in *Li Chi* itself: "The *chao-mu* system is for the purpose of distinguishing the order of father-son, far-near, elder-younger, and near-distant relationships and to avoid confusions." But this is obviously too broad to make much sense. Ancient texts can offer no more, and on this we have to enlist the assistance of social anthropology. And indeed scholars of modern comparative sociological orientation, notably Marcel Granet (1939) and Li Hsüan-po (1954), have made attempts to interprete the *chao-mu* system, and their conclusions agree in regarding this system largely as the result of marriage regulations. However there is more than one answer to the kind of marriage regulations specifically involved.

The Cross-Cousin Marriage

In ancient China bilateral cross-cousin marriage was probably practiced. The most important evidence is in kinship terminology found in Chou texts:

chiu: mother's brother; husband's father; wife's father
ku: father's sister; husband's mother
sheng; sister's son; father's sister's son; mother's brother's son; wife's brother; sister's husband; and daughter's husband

Bilateral cross-cousin marriage is a rather flexible institution, and has a wide enough range for specific adjustments under particular circumstances. The practice of this custom in ancient China has been noted as a probability by several scholars (Ruey 1947; Granet 1930: 157). What has consistently been overlooked is the fact that, within the framework of bilateral cross-cousin marriage, strong emphases were sometimes made exclusively around either the patrilateral or the matrilateral variety under certain circumstances. And the guiding principle for the shifting emphasis appears to be the political status of the intermarrying parties. To generalize: patrilateral cross-cousin marriage tended to take place among political equals, whereas matrilateral cross-cousin marriage tended to take place as a contributing factor in the delicate and dynamic equilibrium of political power between parties of unequal status. The instance of possible patrilateral cross-cousin marriage in ancient China is the Shang royal marriages between the *yi* and *ting* lineages, and there it is clearly a practice taking place between two opposite but equal parties. To what extent can we apply this finding to the rest of the ancient Chinese who practiced a *chao-mu* system is a problem of great importance but one that is not yet solved.

There are, on the other hand, several interesting facts in Eastern Chou texts that cannot be entirely accounted for in terms of bilateral or patrilateral cross-cousin marriage. These are as follows:

(1) In *Tso Chuan* intermarrying states referred to each other as "maternal uncle and sororal nephew states," and this designation is highly suggestive for the probability that the relationship between the intermarrying states was specifically constant.

(2) Such a constant relationship is referred to in *Tso Chuan* in terms that do not necessarily apply to the actual relationship between particular rulers of the two states concerned, but applies to the two states *as states,* regardless of generation. Under the Twelfth Year entry of Duke Chao, for instance, Ch'i is referred to as the "king's maternal uncle," even though there were cases where the Ch'i rulers married Chou's daughters.

(3) In the actual marriage records that I have been able to find in *Tso Chuan,* there was a distinct tendency for the marriages between different lineages of different *hsing* to be one way rather than reciprocal. Figure 9 shows some marriages between the most powerful eastern states, Lu, of Chi sib, and Ch'i, of Chiang sib. The Dukes of Lu, a brother state of Chou, married women of Ch'i lineage of the Chiang sib, among others; they rarely gave their sisters and daughters in marriage to Ch'i, but frequently married them off to other states. The Ch'i Dukes, on the other hand, married their daughters to Lu, but obtained their women mainly from other states. Even though it can be said that Ch'i (Chiang sib) married their women into the Chi sib, and also sometimes married women from the Chi sib, it is important to note that the specific lineages into which their daughters married and from which their wives came were different, even though these different lineages were all of the Chi sib. Taking the *tsung* rather than *hsing* for comparison, we see clearly that the exchange of women was much heavier one way than the other.

(4) Available records indicate that there was often a difference in political status between the maternal uncle and sororal nephew states, and that the wife receivers seem to enjoy a higher political and/or ritual status than the wife givers (see F. Hsü 1945). It is particularly illuminating to note in this connection that when a king married his daughter to one of his lords he would ask a lord from a brother state to "give the bride away," so to speak. In a commen-

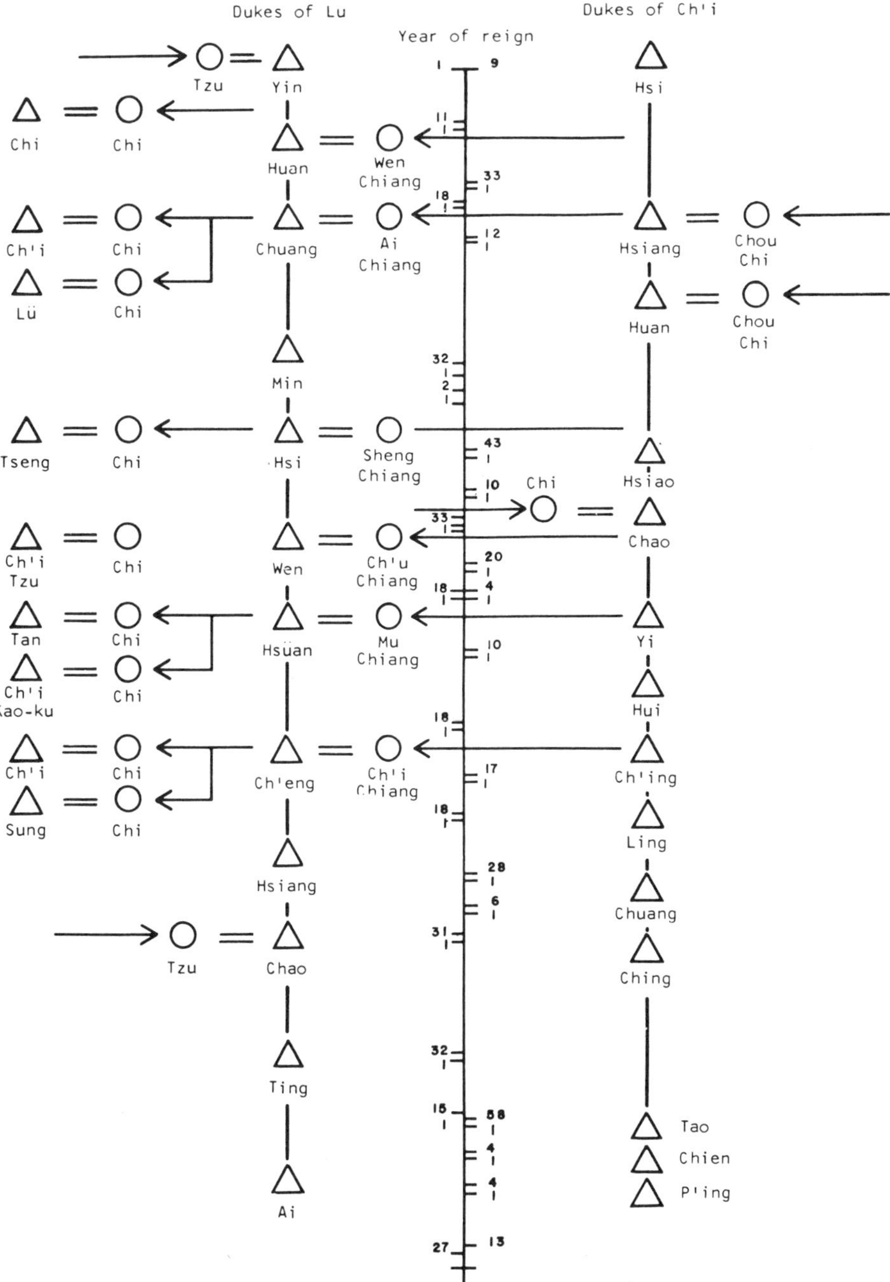

Figure 9. Marriage Relations between the Lu and Ch'i Dukes

tary to *Tso Chuan,* Tu Yü explains that this was because of the "inequity of ranks." In other words, although a king's daughter had to be married to someone whose lineage could not be politically superior to the king's, a compromise was made so that the king's lineage would not suffer a lèse majesté by an inferior alliance.

(5) Finally, the Eastern Chou nobility seems to have used an Omaha system of cousin terminology (Ruey 1958). Eyde and Postal (1961) have suggested that matrilateral cross-cousin marriage, in combination with sororate (into the same lineage), tends to produce in patrilineal societies the correct alignment of kin types for the Omaha kinship system. The presence of both Omaha terminology and sororate (H. P. Li 1944; Granet 1953) in Eastern Chou, plus the fact that in the kinship terminology the mother and the female matrilateral cross-cousin were not referred to by the same term (Ruey 1950a), thus suggests the practice of matrilateral cross-cousin marriage.

All these facts seem to suggest that in the Chou Dynasty the matrilateral cross-cousin marriage and the Omaha terminology were sometimes stressed under a general bilateral framework. If this is true, then the political implications inherent in such a system cannot be overstated.

6 Some Dualistic Phenomena in Shang Society

Isolated phenomena of a dualistic nature in various Shang institutions have long been recognized (see below), but their interrelationship and their possible relevance to a coherent dualistic system generally prevalent in Shang society cannot be clearly understood unless the various specialists on ancient China break disciplinary boundaries and collaborate with vigor and mutual understanding. This paper attempts to bring attention to some of these phenomena and to define the probable areas of research for a highly important problem in Shang studies. To begin, let us examine some interesting features at the archaeological sites of Hsiao-t'un and Hsi-pei-kang.

It is well known that the archaeological excavations at Anyang undertaken from 1928 through 1937 have brought to light a wealth of new material on the civilization of Shang China, and new chapters of Shang history have since been written according to the inscriptions on the oracle bones excavated in Anyang. Furthermore, much of the archaeological material from Anyang was made available to the average reader with the recent publication of the monographs on the structural remains at Hsiao-t'un (C. J. Shih 1959) and the royal tomb No. HPKM1001 at Hsi-pei-kang (S. Y. Liang and C. H. Kao 1962). There is now more than ever solid ground for the assertion that the archaeological sites near Anyang were the ruins of the last Shang royal capital; that Hsiao-t'un was the area of the royal palaces and temples; and that Hsi-pei-kang, less than three kilometers to the northwest of Hsiao-t'un and on the opposite bank of the Huan river, was the resting place of the deceased Shang kings.

The structural remains (mainly pounded earth floors and boulders which probably served as foundation for posts and pillars) at Hsiao-t'un were clustered into three groups, A, B, and C, arranged in a north-south axis with group A at the north end, B in the middle, and C in the southwest. The significance of this clustering, according to Professor Shih Chang-ju, is primarily chronological: Group A floors were the first to be built near Anyang, Group C floors the last. These groupings, however, also appear to be func-

---

Note: This essay was originally published in *Journal of Asian Studies,* 24 (1964) 45-61. Reprinted with permission of Association for Asian Studies, Inc. For benefits from discussions relating to the subject matter of this paper, I thank Nelson Wu, Arthur Wright, Floyd Lounsbury, Chou Fa-kao, William Davenport, Yang Lien-sheng, and Max Loehr.

tionally significant: Group A were possibly palatial foundations, Group B were sites of ancestral temples, and Group C were ritual structures. The Group B foundations were associated with a maze of human burials in the same manner in which the royal tombs at Hsi-pei-kang were associated with sacrificial human burials; this seems to give support to the hypothesis that the Group B floors were indeed sites of ancestral temples of the royal house. Twenty-one floors were excavated in Group B, but more houses had probably been constructed southeast of the excavated area in a region now submerged under the bed of the river Huan. The evidence strongly suggests that the houses in this group were arranged in two north-south rows, starting from a square earth altar at the northern end. This layout seems to resemble the arrangement of the Chou ancestral temples according to the so-called *chao-mu* system recorded in Chou and Han texts. But was the *chao-mu* system of temple arrangement already known in Shang?

We are confronted with a similar but even more perplexing problem in the arrangement of the royal tombs at Hsi-pei-kang. According to Professor Kao Ch'ü-hsün's report (Kao 1959: 1-2):

the Cemetery was divided into a Western part and an Eastern part, separated from each other by a piece of land about a hundred meters wide. Our excavations have located the western, northern, and eastern borders of the Western part of the Cemetary and, although the southern border of it has not been found, we can state with a reasonable degree of accuracy that to the south of the excavated area there are no big Royal tombs. In the Eastern part of the Cemetery about fifteen thousand square meters of field were turned over, and the northern and eastern borders of this part of the Cemetery were located. It is presumed that in the Eastern part of the Cemetery only its northwestern corner, about one fourth of the total area, has been excavated . . . In 1950, the Institute of Archaeology of the Communist Academia Sinica resumed work at Anyang and excavated one big tomb and twenty-six small graves in an area which archaeologists in the said Institute referred to as the Wu-kuan village. As a matter of fact, these tombs are within the confines of the Eastern part of the Hsi-pei-kang Cemetery, and the big tomb opened in 1950 is situated only a few meters to the south of two rows of small graves we excavated in 1935 in the northeastern corner of the Eastern part of the cemetery.

All told, 1232 tombs dating from the Shang Dynasty were excavated before World War II, and ten of these are large royal tombs, seven in the western section and three in the eastern. These big tombs are all square or rectangular, with a north-south axis. Adding to these the tomb opened in 1950, there are altogether eleven royal tombs in the Hsi-pei-kang area, seven in the west, and four in the east. This layout immediately strikes one as having some peculiar significance, and one may legitimately ask whether the north-south orientation of the royal tombs and their arrangement in an eastern cluster and a western cluster are in any way related to the arrangement of ancestral temples of the royal house in the Hsiao-t'un region. In his Hsiao-t'un report, Shih Chang-ju suggests that the construction of the royal tombs and the royal temples were related events, but he could not say how they were related. Was a temple built whenever a king was interred at Hsi-pei-kang, or was his tablet erected in an existing temple? In any event, the comparability of the Hsiao-t'un and Hsi-pei-kang layouts is striking and provocative. But why were there seven royal tombs in the western section of the Hsi-pei-kang cemetery and only four in the eastern section?

To answer such questions, we must go considerably beyond the archaeological material. I will examine some of the dualistic concepts that have been formulated according to the literary records and then come back to the Hsiao-t'un and Hsi-pei-kang ground plans to see whether some sense can be made of these phenomena.

The Chao-mu System in the Shang Royal Genealogy

The so-called *chao-mu* system is known to be a Chou institution.[1] We do not know much about it, but on the following points there is almost common agreement. (1) Authentic Chou texts indicate that this system prevailed in the early years of the Western Chou (1122-771 BC). (2) The essential form of the system is the alternate designation of *chao* and *mu* generations (one was born into either a *chao* or a *mu* generation). For instance, the conqueror of Shang, King Wu of Chou, was of the *chao* generation; his father was *mu* and his son was *mu.* (3) The *chao-mu* system was related to the descent lines of lineage segments and theoretically continued as long as the line of descent went on. When and if a segmentary lineage broke off from a parent line of descent, its founder was designated as the Ultimate Ancestor, and the Ancestor's son would initiate the *chao* generation of this new line of descent; his grandson would initiate the *mu* group. (4) Finally, the *chao-mu* system was associated with the arrangement of ancestral temples. The founder of a dynasty,

1. The names of *chao* and *mu* generations are mentioned in *Shih Ching, Shu Ching,* and *Tso Chuan,* but descriptions of the system first appear in *Li Chi.*

for instance, was worshipped in a temple at the center at the northern end of the temple compound, and his descendants' temples were arranged in two parallel rows, with the *chao* temples at the left (east) and the *mu* temples at the right (west). Not all deceased ancestors were entitled to separate temples, however. Aside from the temple of the Ultimate Ancestor, the number of temples in the two rows was fixed, and these temples were occupied by more recent ancestors. The exact number of the temples is controversial, but it is known that the king's compound included more temples than the noblemen's, and the noblemen's included more temples than the ordinary people's. The commoners probably were allowed only a single temple or merely a shrine, but the ancestral tablets were placed within it in the same two-row arrangement. Just what kind of social and ritual structure was behind the *chao-mu* system we do not know. There are some speculations that center around marriage regulations (see Granet 1939; H. P. Li 1954; Ling 1959a). We shall defer discussion of this subject for the time being.

Did the Shang Chinese have a *chao-mu* system too? Not according to the traditional history. Professor Li Tsung-t'ung has, however, pointed out long since that "the words *chao* and *mu* have thus far not been recognized in the oracle bone inscriptions [of the Shang Dynasty]. Either the Shang people were not categorized in this way at all, or they were similarly subdivided but their subdivisions were referred to by other names. Inasmuch as the subdivision is a common feature among primitive societies, the latter possibility appears to be the more likely" (H. P. Li 1954: 10). In a recent essay, "The Posthumous Names of the Shang Kings and the Royal Genealogy of the Shang Dynasty: A Sociological Analysis" (K. C. Chang 1963a), I suggest that a system closely similar to the *chao-mu* of Chou can be reconstructed for the Shang according to the distribution of the kings' names in the royal genealogy of the Shang Dynasty. Because this hypothesis is essential to the present discussion, I recapitulate the major points.

According to the oracle-bone studies and literary records, the royal genealogy of the Shang Dynasty includes the following line of kings (excluding the mythological beginnings):

Shang Chia—Pao Yi—Pao Ping—Pao Ting—Shih Jen—Shih Kuei—Ta Yi—Ta Ting, Wai Ping, and Chung Jen (successively, within a single generation)—Ta Chia—Wo Ting and Ta Keng—Hsiao Chia, Ta Wu, and Yung Chi—Chung Ting, Wai Jen, and Ch'ien Chia—Tsu Yi—Tsu Hsin and Ch'iang Chia—Tsu Ting and Nan Keng—Hu Chia, P'an Keng (first king having Anyang as capital), Hsiao Hsin and Hsiao Yi—Wu Ting—Tsu Keng and Tsu Chia—Lin Hsin and K'ang Ting—Wu Yi—Wen Wu Ting—Ti Yi—Ti Hsin.

It should be made clear at this juncture that the Shang kings were known by their personal names during their lifetimes, but that they were referred to after death by posthumous names. After death a king was known by one of the ten Heavenly Stems, the names of the days in the ten-day cycle (*Chia, Yi, Ping, Ting, Wu, Chi, Keng, Hsin, Jen, Kuei*). Rituals were performed to a specific ancestral king on the day of his name. When more than one king was known by the same day's name, distinguishing prefixes were added in later records, such as Ta, Tsu, Ti, etc. (See T. P. Tung 1951; W. L. Ch'ü 1948). Since the ten Heavenly Stems were originally derived from a system of numerals (M. J. Kuo 1952), we can conveniently substitute numerals 1 to 10 for these stems and transform the royal genealogy into the following sequence:

1—2—3—4—9—10—2—4, 3, 9—1—4, 7—1, 5, 6—4, 9, 1—2—8, 1—4, 7—1, 7, 8, 2—4—7, 1—8, 4—2—4—2—8

According to the traditional interpretation, posthumous names were conferred on specific kings according to the days (within the ten-day cycle) on which they were born. Thus, the king who was born on the second day of the cycle (*yi*) was to be known posthumously as King Yi, etc. An examination of the numeral sequence, however, makes it clear that the birth-day explanation is far from satisfactory: (a) The lopsided distribution of the ten days' names among the kings (heavy concentration in days 1, 2 and 4) is not likely the result of chance. (b) To look at this sequence through the generations, we find a tendency of alternate generations' identity; that is, the name *chia* (1) or *yi* (2) and the name *ting* (4) seem to appear in alternate generations. There are variations and exceptions to this rule, which have been discussed in detail (K. C. Chang 1963a). (c) When there was more than one king to a generation, the names *chia* or *yi* and *ting* are mutually exclusive; in other words, if there was a *chia* or *yi* king, then there was no *ting* king in the same generation, and vice versa. These regularities enable us to group the Shang kings into five classes according to their posthumous names:

(1) Chia or Yi
(2) Ting

(3) Names combined with Chia or Yi only (in the same generation or in alternate generations): Wu, Chi

(4) Names combined with Ting only: Ping, Jen, Kuei

(5) Names freely combined with either Chia or Yi or Ting: Keng, Hsin

These five classes can be further lumped into three groups, group Yi (1, 2, 5, 6), group Ting (3, 4, 9, 10), and a third or neutral group (7, 8). If we postulate that these names were not derived from birthdays but were conventional designations of the groups to which the kings belonged during life as well as after death, the analysis immediately suggests that there were two groups within the royal house of the Shang Dynasty, and that these two groups alternated in holding the power to rule. Such a system is evidently similar to the *chao-mu* system of the Chou, and I do not hesitate to equate the two.

To explain this phenomenon is an entirely different matter. The most obvious interpretation is that there was a double descent system at work here or that the kings belonged to two matrilineal groups and to a single patrilineage. In either case, this means that the kings were named posthumously according to the kinship categories of their mothers or spouses, to which they themselves also belonged by virtue of marriage ties. This is essentially in agreement with the explanation given to the *chao-mu* system by such modern scholars as Marcel Granet (1939) and Li Tsung-t'ung (1954), and it would have been satisfactory except that the posthumous names of the official spouses of the Shang kings contradict it. Many names of these spouses are known; the kings' names are seldom identical with the names of their mothers, and are never identical with the names of their official spouses. In fact, although many kings were named *yi* or *ting,* no official spouse was named either *yi* or *ting.* We are forced to conclude, therefore, that if the posthumous naming system represents a kinship network, then the network must explain the posthumous names of both the Shang kings and their wives.

My tentative hypothesis is that the royal branch of the ruling clan of the Shang, by the name of Tzu, was probably subdivided into no fewer than ten lineages. Among these ten, the *yi* and *ting* enjoyed the highest political status and held the greatest political power. Among the others, lineages *chia, wu,* and *chi* were close to *yi,* forming group Yi, and lineages *ping, jen,* and *kuei* were close to *ting,* making up the Ting group. The other lineages, *keng* and *hsin,* can perhaps be described as "neutralists." (It goes without saying that *chia, yi,* etc. were probably no more than the classifactory designations of the lineages in a ritual network, and that these lineages were presumably known by some proper names.) When a member of lineage Yi, let us say, was the king, he probably was not in a position to marry a woman from the Ting lineage for his official spouse, because of political considerations. The king's son, whose mother was a member of neither of the two politically prominent lineages, must then have inherited a political status that was relatively inferior. On the other hand, the king's clan brothers in the Ting lineage could marry women from the Yi lineage, and their sons, both of whose parents belonged to the politically eminent lineages, inherited a relatively superior political status. When the king of the Yi lineage died, the throne was therefore not inherited by his own son but by his sororial nephew in the Ting lineage into which his sisters had married. When the Ting lineage member became king, the same story was repeated, and the next king was again in the Yi lineage. The throne thus alternated between the two politically prominent lineages. Irregularities were, however, bound to occur when appropriate candidates were not available, and the throne was sometimes taken over by other lineages, in either the same or the next generation, although the group classification still regulated the candidacy. In short, from the genealogical record we can formulate: (1) the kingship alternated between two politically prominent lineages or between their respectively affiliated lineages; (2) the royal marriages were characterized by a patrisib endogamy in the manner of patrilateral cross-cousin marriage; and (3) the throne was handed down from maternal uncles to sororial nephews in two generations, or from grandfathers to grandsons in three generations. Such a rule of succession appears odd at first glance, but none of the three phenomena is unusual from an ethnographical point of view. This reconstruction explains every detail concerning the royal succession and kinship classification that one finds hitherto unexplained in the literary records. The nearest example to such a model that I have been able to find in the ethnographical literature is one from the Funafuti on the Ellice Islands in Western Polynesia (Williamson 1924, I: 378-379):

> Funafuti . . . discloses a system of alternating succession to the throne . . . According to Turner, the kingship alternated in four or five leading families, and when one king died another was chosen by the family next in turn. Hedley was told that a system had long prevailed on the island of government by a king and subordinate chief, the latter succeeding to the supreme office on the death of the

former, and being himself succeeded in the subordinate position by the later king's son. Sollas says there were two branches of the royal family, and when one king died his successor was generally chosen from the other branch . . . .

The historical evidence indicates, so far as it goes, that the curious system of double succession referred to by Hedley and suggested by Mrs. David was by no means universal, but it illustrates it to a certain extent, especially if there were only two alternating branches of the royal family. In that case we should expect that the branch which for the time being was not ruling would be of great political importance, and a member or members of that branch might well occupy the position of "subordinate king or chief." Thus it is possible that Tilotu belonged to branch A, and Paolau, who became his subordinate, was of branch B. Then on Paolau (branch B) becoming king, Tilotu's children (branch A) became his subordinates.

The occurrence of such a system in Polynesia is the more significant and interesting because the Polynesians are thought to be remotely related to the ancient inhabitants of the Chinese mainland, and other insititutions have been found that characterize both the Polynesians and the ancient Chinese.[2] Unfortunately, Williamson's book is not well known for its reliability, and the rapid acculturation of the Ellice Islanders, particularly the Funafuti group, renders it unlikely that further evidence will come to light in this crucial respect.

The passages from Williamson also remind one of the great importance attached to the many so-called "Old Officials" of the Shang Dynasty in both oracle-bone inscriptions and literary texts (M.C. Ch'en 1956). Yi Yin, for instance, is known to be an official of prime ministerial rank during Ta Yi's reign, and in the ritual cycle of the royal house he was given the same respectful treatment as the king's own ancestors. Perhaps Yi Yin was the chief of the Ting group at the time when Ta Yi of the Yi group was king. It is quite suggestive that the rites performed on his behalf were particularly abundant and elaborate during the reign of king Wu Ting, the first and the most powerful king of the Ting group during the Anyang period.

In both literary and oracle records, many other names are known

---

2. On the similarity of many Polynesian institutions to the ancient Chinese, see several recent articles by Ling Shun-sheng published in the *Bulletin of the Institute of Ethnology,* Academia Sinica, Taipei.

and are said to be those of the more remote ancestors of the Shang kings. Because these names do not include the cyclic compounds, we cannot infer whether they included ancestors of both Yi and Ting groups or ancestors of only a single group. In the legendary history of ancient China, there was a Hsia Dynasty preceding the Shang, and the historical texts record a long genealogy of the Hsia kings. Many scholars, notably Ch'en Meng-chia (1936b), have suggested that perhaps the Hsia genealogy represents no more than the legendary segment preceding the Shang genealogy, and that the Hsia and the Shang were different chronological segments of a single royal house. I think it is also just possible that the Hsia kings and the Shang kings before Shang Chia were two parallel ruling groups that were closely related. In the *Historical Memoirs* of Ssu-ma Ch'ien, the Hsia genealogy is given as follows:

Huang-ti—Ch'ang-yi—Tuan-hsü—Kun—Yü—Ch'i—T'ai-k'ang (T'ai-*keng*) and Chung-k'ang (Chung-*keng*)—Hsiang—Shao-k'ang (Shao-*keng*)—Yü (Ti-*ting*)—Huai—Mang—Yi—Ta-chiang and Chü—K'ung-*chia* and Chin (Yin-*chia*)—Kao—Fa—Lü-*kuei*

Of these kings, six were named with the cyclic Heavenly Stem compounds (including *chia, ting, keng,* and *kuei*). Applying the principle of the identity of alternate generations, we find the *chia* and *keng* belonged to the same group, and *ting* and *kuei* to another group. The contrasts between *chia* and *ting* and the affiliation of *kuei* with *ting* are both identical with the Shang rules. Another point of interest is that the founder of the Shang Dynasty (Ta Yi) took the throne from the Ting group (Lü Kuei) of the Hsia Dynasty, suggesting that the change of dynasties here involves a change of power from the Ting to the Yi. This gives ground for much speculation, but definite conclusions cannot be reached before much more material comes to light.

What is probably more important is the fact that the *yi-ting* system of the Shang and the *chao-mu* system of the Chou are similar in many ways other than the identity of alternate generations. Allow me to quote myself (1963a):

The similarities between the two systems, in addition to those described above, consist of the following:

First, it is known from bronze vessel inscriptions and other sources that the Chou continued to use the cyclic stems for posthumous names. If this usage in Shang signifies a kinship network classification, then it is highly probable that the Chou usage has a similar meaning.

Second, in some Chou genealogies, the generation order in which the cyclic names appear is identical with the Shang rule. For instance, of two *kuei* vessels dated to the reign of King Mu, one bears an inscription including the name Grandfather Hsin, and the other the name Father Yi. This order (Hsin—Yi) is identical (though in reverse) to the last two Shang kings (Yi—Hsin). The first duke of Ch'i is named T'ai Kung, whose son was Ting, Ting's son was Yi, and Yi's son was Kuei. Two points are particularly worth mentioning here. (1) The order of appearance of the three stems (Ting—Yi—Kuei, of the Ting group) is identical with both the Shang and the Hsia rules. (2) According to the *chao-mu* system, T'ai Kung was the Ultimate Ancestor of the new lineage, his son, Ting, belonged to the *chao* generation, and Ting's son, Yi, belonged to the *mu* generation. This is a first indication of a possible equation between Yi and *mu* and between Ting and *chao.* . . . The dukes of Sung are known to be the direct descendents of the Shang royal house, and one of the dukes named Ting was of the right generation in relation to the Shang kings. That the Sung institution should be identical with the Shang is not at all strange, but the identity of the Ch'i (of Chiang clan, very closely related to the royal Chou) system with the Shang customs is remarkable.

Third, what is even more striking is the fact that the royal Chou seems also to have practiced the same institution in this respect as their political opponents. We know that in the ritual cycles of the Shang the kings were worshipped in ancestral rites on the days of the ten-day cycle whose names were identical with their posthumous names. From both bronze inscriptions and literary texts, we do have some material about the days on which rites were performed to the deceased royal Chou kings and their brother dukes. In these materials we find the following coincidence: Those kings and dukes which belonged to the *chao* generation were invariably worshipped on the *ting* day, and those of the *mu* generation invariably on the *yi* day. There are some problems to be clarified before this correlation can be regarded as being conclusive, but the coincidence is rather striking.

At this point let us come back to the problem of the spatial layout of the royal tombs at Hsi-pei-kang. We have pointed out above that the four tombs for the *chao* generations were on the left (east) and the seven for the *mu* generations on the right (west). Now, Anyang is known to have been the capital of the Shang Dynasty since King P'an Keng. After P'an Keng there were eleven more kings, the last of whom, Ti Hsin, is known to have committed suicide when his capital fell to the invading Chou. The remaining eleven kings at Anyang can be grouped into two classes according to their generation order:

Ting group (*chao*): four kings (Wu Ting, Lin Hsin, K'ang Ting, Wen Wu Ting)
Yi group (*mu*): seven kings (P'an Keng, Hsiao Hsin, Hsiao Yi, Tsu Keng, Tsu Chia, Wu Yi, Ti Yi)

It is, then, quite a coincidence that there were eleven kings of Shang during the Anyang period and eleven royal tombs at Hsi-pei-kang, and furthermore, that of the eleven kings four were *chao* and seven were *mu*, and of the eleven tombs four were at the *chao* side and seven at the *mu* side. This coincidence might appear to be too good to be true, and we must bear in mind that it is by no means established without doubt that the so-called royal tombs were used for kings' burials, and that the excavations at Hsi-pei-kang are not yet completed. This is nevertheless an impressive correspondence.

If the tomb HPKM1001 described in the monographic report mentioned above is indeed the earliest tomb of the western sector at Hsi-pei-kang, according to Li Chi's stratigraphical and typological studies (C.Li 1957b, 1959), then we are tempted to suggest that this is the burial place of none other than P'an Keng himself, the founder of Anyang as the Shang capital. This identification would be a fact of great chronological and other significance. It would inevitably force a reassessment of the level of achievement of the Shang civilization at the beginning of the Anyang period, and would also lead to a reveiw of the meaning of the structural sites at Hsiao-t'un, some of which are known stratigraphically and typologically to antedate HPKM1001 at Hsi-pei-kang (C.Li 1958).

The "Conservatives" and "Progressives" in the Oracle Records

In the foregoing discussion, I have attempted to demonstrate that in the royal house of the Shang Dynasty there were probably two groups that alternated in holding the ruling power in the central kingdom. Inasmuch as the royal house was to a considerable extent the torch-bearer and molder of the civilization, the question naturally arises as to whether the Shang civilization manifested a trend toward a dualistic polarization. Inversely, any dualistic phenomena in the Shang civilization would tend to support the dualism one finds in the genealogical records. My answer to this question is that there are indeed some clues suggesting dualistic phenomena in Shang institutions. Some of these can easily be correlated with the dualistic division of the royal power group; some others cannot. Let us begin with an examination of the so-called Conservative and Progressive schools recognized in the oracle-bone inscriptions.

The late Professor Tung Tso-pin (1945, 1953) believed that "as the result of intensive chronological studies" he had

> found that during the 273 years [from the time when P'an Keng moved his capital to Anyang to the fall of Ti Hsin] the Yin institutions included an Old [or Conservative] and a New [or Progressive] school. This observation was at first based upon the difference between the two schools in the realm of the calendrical system, but later it was realized that the differences prevailed in all areas of the institution. . . . Furthermore, the Conservatives and the Progressives alternated in holding power.

The political history of the Yin period is accordingly divided into the following four stages by Tung.

Stage I: Conservative (adhering to the traditional): P'an Keng, Hsiao Hsin, Hsiao Yi, Wu Ting, and Tsu Keng
Stage II: Progressive (innovating): Tsu Chia, Lin Hsin, K'ang Ting
Stage III: Conservative (resurrection of the traditional): Wu Yi, Wen Wu Ting
Stage IV: Progressive (revival of reformation): Ti Yi, Ti Hsin

To support his hypothesis, Tung discussed in several papers the variations in the ritual cycle, calendrical system, inscription styles, and divination practices of the respective schools. The details of his evidence are too technical and minute to be described here. Suffice it to state that Tung's arguments are convincing enough insofar as the existence of two contrasting systems of institutions is concerned. The Tung hypothesis has not been accepted by Shang scholars in general, and the major point of controversy lies in the identification of the oracle texts of the reign of King Wen Wu Ting. Several scholars insist that many of the oracle texts Tung assigned to Wen Wu Ting's reign should actually be dated to King Wu Ting's reign (M. C. Ch'en 1956; Kaizuka and Ito 1953). If this view prevails, then Stage III of Tung Tso-pin would be represented by entirely inadequate data, which would render his hypothesis of cyclical rise and fall of the Conservatives and the Progressives untenable. On this highly technical point, I do not profess bias. Our immediate problem is whether the subdivision of Shang institutions, as recognized by Tung, was in some way related to the subdivision of Shang kings suggested above. In the quoted essay on the posthumous names of the Shang kings, I made the suggestion that the so-called Conservative institutions were probably the subculture of the Ting group of kings and the so-called Progressive institutions the subculture of the Yi group. I now feel that such a correlation is somewhat premature. But on the following phenomena there is probably no disagreement.

(1) The Shang institutions of the Anyang period, as seen from the oracle texts, do consist of two major variations.

(2) The oracle texts of the period of King Wu Ting, the first Ting group king of the Anyang period, are abundantly represented by remains at Anyang, and the major features of the Shang institutions during this period are well exemplified. It is clear that the transition from Wu Ting to Tsu Chia (via a vaguely understood Tsu Keng period of perhaps seven years) was marked by a sudden and drastic change of institutional characteristics. Many of the deities and ancestors Wu Ting sacrificed to were frequently neglected by Tsu Chia, and the irregular impromptu kind of ritual schedule of Wu Ting was replaced by a rigid, neat, and prearranged schedule for the rituals and sacrifices to the deceased ancestors. After a lapse following Tsu Chia, his rigid ritual schedule was revived during the reign of Ti Yi, whose institutions had many essential features in common with Tsu Chia. In other words, the variations in institutions do seem to be tied in with the subdivisions of Yi and Ting groups. The question is whether most of the oracle materials of the Yi group kings manifest the Tsu Chia and Ti Yi variety, and whether most of the oracle materials of the Ting group kings manifest the Wu Ting variety of institutions. The current knowedge of the oracle-bone specialists seems to suggest that the group-related changes of institutions are *trends* but not necessarily *requirements.* It is to be hoped that the specialists can be heard from in this respect again after they have made an intensive study with this correlation problem in mind.

(3) In addition to the points of variation detailed by Tung, other aspects of Shang institutions should also be viewed from the present perspective, so that more data concerning correlation—if any—can be brought to light. For instance, one potentially fruitful area of research is the grouping of diviners. This subject has been rather exhaustively studied by many scholars since Professor

Tung's initial discovery of the diviners' names in the oracle texts, but the purpose of the studies has been largely chronological (M. C. Ch'en 1956; T. Y. Jao 1959). The old Chinese saying has it, "yi ch'ao t'ien-tzu yi ch'ao ch'en," which can be rendered roughly as "When the Empire changed Emperors, the Court changed officials." If the Shang kings came from two contending power groups, it would be interesting to know whether the corps of diviners was overhauled with each succession involving the change of Yi and Ting groups.

Two Styles of Bronze Decorative Art

The remarkable achievement of Professor Bernhard Karlgren in the stylistic studies of Shang and Chou bronze decorative art is well known. Karlgren distinguishes three styles of this art: Archaic, Middle Chou, and Huai, of which the Archaic prevailed during the Yin and the early Western Chou (Karlgren 1936). In his "New Studies of Chinese Bronzes" published in 1937, Karlgren further subdivides the Archaic Style into three groups of decorative elements, A, B, and C. His data concern 1294 Archaic Style bronze vessels in museum and private collections throughout the world, and the distribution of the A, B, and C elements in the decor of individual bronze vessels is as follows:

> "There are . . . 517 vessels with one or several A elements (combined or not with C elements) but with no B elements; there are 549 vessels with one or several B elements (combined or not with C elements) but with no A elements. There are only 14 vessels with both A and B elements" (Karlgren 1937:72), and "the vessels that possess neither A nor B elements, but exclusively the neutral C elements . . . aggregate 214" (Karlgren 1937:75).

Karlgren therefore concludes that the Yin bronze art contains two contrasting styles, A and B, whose elements as a rule do not both appear in the decor of one vessel, but either of which could combine with a third neutral style, C. In the last decade Karlgren has studied materials brought to light after 1937, and has added some criteria of classification within his 1937 system (Karlgren 1959, 1960, 1962). His criteria are summarized below.

(1) Some common characteristics of the Archaic Style: "A store of decor elements entirely based on the animal kingdom; a stiff arrangement with confronting figures symmetrically arranged round a central figure; an invariable rule about the decorated neck

zone; and a series of 'neutral' decor features belonging to various classes of both styles (Karlgren 1962:18).

(2) A elements are: marked t'ao-t'ieh; bodied t'ao-t'ieh; bovine t'ao-t'ieh; cicada; vertical dragon; uni-decor. B elements: dissolved t'ao-t'ieh; animal triple band; de-tailed bird; eyed spiral band; eyed band with diagonals; circle band; square with crescents; compound lozenges; spikes; interlocked T's; vertical ribs. The neutral C elements are: deformed t'ao-t'ieh; dragonized t'ao-t'ieh; dragon (trunked; beaked; jawed; turning; feathered; winged; s; and deformed); bird; snake; whorl circle; blade, eyed blade; spiral band.

(3) The contrast in decorative elements between the A and B groups is related to a considerable extent to the forms and shapes of the vessels.

Karlgren's interpretation of the A-B contrast is a double-barreled one. He calls the A group of elements "primary" and the B group "secondary," believing that the latter was of later origin and derived from the former. Both groups of elements were employed during the Anyang period, Karlgren believes, but he also thinks that the A group diminished and the B group increased in importance toward the end of the period, which explains why there are very few pure A bronzes that can be accurately dated to the Chou period. On the other hand, Karlgren also suggests some sociological grounds for the origin of the B group and for the parallelism of A and B groups at Anyang.

> . . . it stands to reason that inside one such family of metal workers, in one factory handed over from father to son as a sacred legacy, the vessel types and decor types may often have been piously regarded as a sacred norm in the making of new specimens for ritual use in the ancestral temples. It may therefore have been the achievement of newly-started *rival houses* of casters to create a new style, the B style, on the basis and yet radically deviating from the earlier A style. It is quite conceivable that the head-men of the earlier house continue for generations to repeat their old decor types . . . , parallel with the activities of their more modern competitors. Conceivably the one school was in the service of one noble family, and the other in that of another noble house, a rival of the former (Karlgren 1937:91-92).

Many aspects of Karlgren's analysis are susceptible of criticism, and there has been plenty of it. On two points particularly, he is highly vulnerable. First, he has been handicapped by the nature of his data (the result of market selection, unclear provenance, and heterogeneous origins of time and place). Second, his chronological interpretation (A prior to B) is based exclusively upon the concepts of a naïve evolutionary scheme. It is not my purpose to criticize this, however. I think his A and B classification is well established by his material. His sociological interpretation of the stylistic subdivision, on the other hand, takes on new meaning under the perspective of the current undertaking. Unfortunately, his sociological inference is not at all supported by objective evidence, and this interpretation has never been seriously followed either by Karlgren himself or by his critics or adherents.

For the purpose of discerning the social significance of the stylistic dualism in the Shang bronze art, it is not enough to examine the occurrence of A and B elements in the decor of individual *vessels*; it is imperative to look for them in the decoration of vessels in the same *assemblages*. The social factors in the stylistic division must be highly complex, and the significance of stylistic distribution among different vessel assemblages is obviously manifold. Karlgren says that vessels bearing different style elements were probably cast by different families of casters. This can easily be confirmed or refuted by an examination of the clay molds found in the same factory sites, of which there are many but none which have been described in detail in publications. Furthermore, if the bronze vessels found from the same tomb all bear A or B elements, then apparently that style was favored by the man who was buried there and/or by his family. Such studies are relatively facile, but they cannot be done until more data on Shang sites are published and until we know what objects were excavated together from each house, tomb, or pit.

Now we are faced with the inevitable question of whether the dualistic division of Shang bronze art is related in some fashion to the dualistic division of Shang kings and their institutions. This is a highly complex problem because we must take into consideration not only the exact meaning of the stylistic differentiation and the changes in style during the Anyang period, but also whether similar divisions can be made in realms of art other than the decoration of bronze vessles. There is little question that the dualistic phenomena in the various realms of Shang civilization are mutually related, including those in the realm of art, because in the available data we can observe that A and B elements fail to be combined in the same vessels and that they also tend to be mutually exclusive in the decor of bronze vessels found from the same assemblages.

Of all the Shang bronze vessel assemblages that are archaeologically excavated, the most complete and detailed account available is that of the royal tomb HPKM1001 at Hsi-pei-kang. Objects of art, decorative or otherwise, are abundant in this tomb, and include stone and jade sculptures in the round, wooden beams and structures with painted and inlaid designs, engraved bone and antler pieces, white pottery, as well as bronze vessels, weapons, and horse-and-chariot fittings. An analysis of the bronze vessels according to the Karlgren classification is given below.

HPKM1133:4, Round Ting Tripod (Pl. 242:1, Pl. 245:1, in the HPKM1001 monograph quoted above): From a sacrificial human burial in the western ramp. Decor elements: C, or on the verge of becoming B.

HPKM 1133:3, Round Ting Tripod (Pl. 242:2; Pl. 245:2): Probably from a sacrificial human burial atop the wooden *k'uo* chamber. Decor elements: C, or on the verge of becoming B.

3:1622 and HPKM1133:2, Li Ting Tripod (Pl. 242:3; Pl. 245:3): Broken into many pieces, mostly recovered in the western ramp. Decor elements: C

R1068, Chüeh Tripod (Pl. 242:4; Pl. 246:2): West Ramp. B.

R11001, Chüeh Tripod (Pl. 243:1; Pl. 246:1): Probably atop the wooden *k'uo* chamber. B.

R11002, Chüeh Tripod (Pl. 243:2; Pl. 245:4): From disturbed pit. B.

R1030, Ku Vessel (Pl. 243:3; Pl. 246:3): West Ramp. B.

R11003, Ku Vessel (Pl. 243:4): Disturbed pit. C.

R11004, Ku Vessel (Pl. 244:1): Probably atop the wooden *k'uo* chamber. C.

R11021, Lei Vessel (Pl. 244:2; Pl. 246:4): Probably atop the wooden *k'uo* chamber. B.

R11028, Ting Tripod Fragment (Pl. 253:2; Pl.257:2): Disturbed pit. B.

Miscellaneous Fragments (Pl. 253-255): All from the disturbed pit. Decorative elements on them include spikes, compound lozenges, *lei-wen*ized or *yün-wen*ized t'ao-t'ieh, all elements of the B group.

All these bronze vessels were excavated from sacrificial burials in various parts of the tomb, and the decoration on all contains only B or C elements. The leading motif is a neckband of highly *lei-wen*ized t'ao-t'ieh, some of which can be called "deformed t'ao-t'ieh" and other "dissolved t'ao-t'ieh." Such characteristic B elements as circle bands, spikes, compound lozenges, and animal triple bands are found in many vessels. A elements did not occur on a single vessel.[3] On the other hand, among the other categories of objects found in this tomb, many such typical A elements as bovine t'ao-t'ieh, vertical dragon, and realistic t'ao-t'ieh are found in bone sculptures and in one type of bronze weapon. Although the significance of this discrepancy is readily evident, we are not equipped to cope with the decorative art of other artifacts than bronze vessels insofar as the Karlgren classification is concerned.

At the site of Hsiao-t'un, Li Chi (1948) reports that ten burials have yielded an aggregate of seventy-six bronze vessels. Usable data are available from six of the tombs. Their respective locations and yields are listed below:

Three Burials Near Temple Floor B7

M188: A pien (Fig. II:b, in Li Chi's report quoted above), with B elements; a p'o (Fig. 14:b), with B elements; a ting (Pl. 9:4) with B elements; and a chia (Pl. 12:2) with C elements.

M232: A ku (Pl. V:10), with B elements; a p'o (Pl. VI:1; VII:4), with B elements; another p'o (Fig. 15:b), with C or B elements; a chüeh (Pl. 16:4) and two chia (Pl. 11:2; Pl. 13:2,3), with C-like elements.

M238: A lei (Pl.L:2; Fig. 17:b) with A or C elements; a ku (Pl. 5:4) with typical B elements; two other ku (Pl. 5:11 and 12) with C elements; two square yi (Pl. 19:1, 2) with A elements; a round yu (Pl. 8:2) with A-like elements; a hu (Fig. 13:6), with A-like elements; a chüeh (Pl. 16:5) with C elements; a four-legged chia (Pl. 18:4) with C elements.

Three Burials Near House Floor C1

M331: Two tsun (Pl. 3:1,2; Pl. 7:3; Fig. 9:b), with C elements; a ku (Pl. 5:6) with B elements; another ku (Pl. 5:2) with C elements; a square yu (Pl. 8:1) with A elements; a p'o (Pl. 6:2) with C elements;

3. This tomb was heavily plundered, and most of the "spectacular" pieces have presumably found their way into various public and private museum collections. We do not know what they were, and cannot speculate about their stylistic classes. On page 3 of the HPKM1001 report, the authors state that three *ho* vessels described in Sueji Umehara (1940), plates 44-46, are known to be plundered from HPKM1001. All three of these vessels bear A-type elements, in contrast to the B-type decoration described above. Since we do not know whether these three vessels *were* indeed from HPKM1001, or which part of HPKM1001 they came from even if they were from this tomb, we can only disregard them in the present discussion.

a ting (Pl. 9:2) with C elements; two chia (Pl. 12:1; Pl. 13:5) with A elements; a hsien (Pl. 18:2) with B-like elements; a four-legged chüeh (Pl. 18:3) with A-like elements.

M333: A ku (Pl. 5:8) with C elements; a p'o (Pl. 7:2) with A-like elements; another p'o (Pl. 7:5) with C-like elements; a ting (Pl. 9:3) with B elements; a chüeh (Pl. 16:3) with B elements; a chia (Pl. 12:4) with B elements.

M388: A p'o (Pl. 3:3 Pl. 7:1) with B elements; a chüeh (Pl. 15:1) with B elements; a chia (Pl. 13:1) with B elements.

These analyses lead to the following observation. As far as the available data from the bronze vessels excavated from the Yin Dynasty tombs at Hsiao-t'un and Hsi-pei-kang are concerned, the vessels from the same tomb are decorated predominantly with either A or B elements. Accordingly, these burials can be grouped into two sets: (1) predominantly A elements: Hsiao-t'un M238 and M331; (2) predominantly B elements: HPKM1001, Hsiao-t'un M188, M232, M333, and M388. (Neutral C elements are, of course, present in both sets). The significance of this phenomenon is as yet unclear because much more material about the excavations remains to be published, but the following observations are probably warranted:

(1) Within the chronological range of the Anyang period, the relative dating of the A and B elements is inconclusively indicated by the material. But in any event Karlgren's speculation for a B-later-than-A tendency is not substantiated. On the basis of stratigraphy and bone hairpin and white pottery typologies, Li Chi (1957b-1959) believes that HPKM1001 is the earliest royal tomb in the western sector of the Hsi-pei-kang cemetery. Its bronze vessels exhibit B and C elements exclusively. The bronze-bearing burials at Hsiao-t'un, according to Li Chi's typological studies, are arranged chronologically as follows: *earliest:* M188, M232, M388; *next:* M331; *still next:* M333; *latest:* M238 (which, however, could also antedate M331 (C. Li 1948: Table 13). Of these tombs, M188, M232, and M238 are probably related to Temple Floor B7, and M331, M333, and M388 are associated with floors in Section C of the Hsiao-t'un site. Shih Chang-ju (1959) believes that Section B as a whole was earlier than Section C, and Li Chi (1958) thinks that Floor B7 at Hsiao-t'un and tomb HPKM1001 at Hsi-pei-kang are largely contemporaneous. Thus the typologically arranged chronological order of the Hsiao-t'un tombs is stratigraphically supported. Of these tombs, A elements prevailed in the later M238

and M331 burials, and B elements dominated the earlier M188, M232, and M388 burials. The one conclusion we can draw from this is that the phenomenon of vessels in one tomb having predominantly A or B elements cannot be explained purely in terms of chronological factors.

(2) The picture that has emerged so far is one that is applicable exclusively to the bronze vessels. Whether the decorative art in mediums other than bronze can be treated in the same manner and what the result may be are problems for future investigations. It is clear however that the stone, pottery, bone, and bronze artifacts in HPKM1001 were molded in different artistic styles, and that the typically A elements in the Hsiao-t'un bronzes occur more frequently in square vessels than in round vessels. It is possible that stylistic classifications overlap but do not totally coincide with industrial specializations, but this is no more than a superficial impression at this point.

(3) What is probably more important is the fact that all the excavated bronze vessels were from burials that were probably sacrificial. We have no data whatsoever on the bronze vessels within the wooden *k'uo* chambers that contained the bodies of the Shang kings themselves. Therefore, the vessel groupings indicated in the available data are not necessarily correlated with the subdivision we have made above within the royal house itself.

In addition to Anyang, Shang (or probably Shang) bronzes have been excavated from several other sites in north China and south China, but only the following sites can be analyzed from publications:

Liu-li-ko, Huei Hsien, northern Honan: Bronze chüeh, chia, and ku vessels excavated from several tombs, possibly within the same time range as the M333 at Hsiao-t'un. The decorative elements of these vessels are characterized by two leading motifs: deformed and *lei-wen*ized t'ao-t'ieh, and circle band, two characteristic B elements. Not a single instance of the A element is reported (Kuo, Hsia, 1956). *Chien-hsi, Meng Hsien, Honan:* Two bronze chüeh and one ku from a tomb, with decor again characterized by the B-category circle band and *lei-wen*ized t'ao-t'ieh (H. C. Liu 1961). *Erh-lang-p'o, Shih-lou, Shansi:* An assemblage of several vessels of unclear provenance. All illustrations that permit stylistic analysis show B elements (spikes, circle bands, and circle bands with diagonals) (Anonymous 1958). *Huang-ts'ai, Ning-hsiang, Hunan:* Several vessels of unclear provenance, all bearing typical A elements (bovine and other realistic t'ao-t'ieh) (C. H. Kao 1963). *Chu-wa-chieh, P'eng Hsien, Szechwan:* Lei and chih vessels, with realistic t'ao-t'ieh decors, typical A elements (C. Y. Wang 1961).

The homogenity of these assemblages in terms of A and B classification is remarkable, and this supports the observation made on Anyang finds that exclusively or predominantly A or B elements not only prevail in the decor of single vessels but also in the assemblages of finds. We know that the Shang royal house appointed relatives as lords of local administrative units (H. H. Hu 1944), and none of the sites listed above was a Shang capital site. Could it be that the Shang settlements in these places were ruled by lords who belonged to one of the two branches of the royal family under which the appointments of lordships were made? Did geography (south versus north China) have anything to do with the distribution of stylistic elements? These questions must remain unanswered.

Conclusions

There seems to be little doubt that dualistic phenomena existed in the Shang institutions. Furthermore, according to a sociological analysis of the royal genealogy, the dualistic phenomena in Shang institutions were probably related to the dualistic division within the ruling family. Whether the various aspects of the dualistic phenomena were all mutually related, and whether there was a single, coherent dualism that characterized Shang society, are questions worth asking. It is obvious that much in this article is speculative and that I have raised more questions than I have answered, but I am confident that studies in relevant materials, particularly the oracle-bone inscriptions, along similar lines will bear fruitful results in the future.

Dualistic phenomena are a common feature of many different societies, and many different factors are probably responsible for their existence—marriage regulations, political systems, or even geographical factors. Dualistic phenomena have been recognized in many sectors of ancient Chinese history, particularly in the early legends of the pre-Shang period. The present paper deals exclusively with Shang society, and with only some aspects of it. It cannot be stressed too strongly that I have not intended to present an overall interpretation for dualistic phenomena in different periods of ancient Chinese history, even though some of my observations may prove to be of some wider applicability.

Dualistic phenomena in Shang society are apparently related to such dualistic concepts in Shang ideology as the contrasts between *yin* and *yang* (not necessarily in such terms) and between sacred and profane. Simple equations, however, should not be made on the basis of the data presented, and the present discussion deals not with ideology but with institutions.

7 Food and Food Vessels in Ancient China

It is no accident that it is the French anthropologists (Lévi-Strauss 1965; Verdier 1969) who are working hard to make the study of the culinary art anthropologically respectable. The time has surely come for anthropological attention to be given to another noteworthy culinary art of the world, that of the Chinese (see Anderson 1970). Such attention may begin in the form of an interest in culinary history, and it is not out of mere curiosity to ask such questions as, "just when did the Chinese begin to cook and eat the way they do?"

I was more or less pushed into this study of the preparation and serving of food in ancient China. In the course of a comprehensive study of the Shang and Chou bronze vessels (see Chang 1972), I came to the conclusion that to understand these vessels we could do well first to understand the matter of eating and drinking, for which they were made. In the archaeological study of Shang and Chou China (ca. 1850-220 BC), bronze and pottery vessels provide the most abundant and essential information, but usually they are studied with reference to shape, decoration, and (if any) inscription for the elucidation of the history as well as the decorative art of the ancient Chinese, and for the chronological light they can throw on the archaeological assemblages, of which they usually form the bulk. Such studies are surely necessary and could be important. But pottery and bronze vessels were food and drink vessels more than they were archaeological instruments to probe into ancient technology and chronology. Some of them were ritual vessels, to be sure, but they served in rituals as food and drink vessels and their ritual roles were based on their food uses. In short, for the study of bronze and pottery vessels we need a study of the food habits of ancient China, and the vessels themselves provide useful data for such a study.

But there are many other data on the topic. The whole archaeological assemblages and their underground context are obviously pertinent. For example, vessels often come in sets of two, three, or more in burials as part of the furnishings, and their com-

---

Note: This essay was originally published in *Transactions of the New York Academy of Sciences* 35 (1973), 495-520. Reprinted with permission. I thank Yü Ying-shu, Hsü Cho-yun, Edward H. Schafer, and Bruce Holbrook, for their constructive criticisms of the first draft of the paper.

bination could be significant. In addition, scenes of feasts, eating, and cooking are found in the decorative designs on bronze vessels of the late Chou period, now beginning to be studied for the purpose of understanding the life of the time (Ma 1961; Hayashi 1961/62; Weber 1968).

Many more useful data are available in the written records. In the oracle bone inscriptions of the Shang period, the shapes of individual characters having to do with cooking, food, and rituals are often suggestive (Fig. 10). Similar characters are also found in bronze inscriptions of both Shang and Chou, which sometimes also describe food in ritual contexts. But the most abundant and useful information is in the historical texts dating from the two periods. One finds many vivid descriptions of feasts and food-producing activities in *Shih Ching* (*Book of Poetry*) and *Ch'u Tz'u,* and food and eating figure prominently in many profound "homilies" in *Lun Yü, Meng Tzu,* and *Mo Tzu*. But nothing compares with *Li Chi, Chou Li,* and *Yi Li,* the *Three Lis* or the *Three Books of Rites.* Hardly a page of these most solemn books goes by without some reference to the kinds and quantity of food and wine that were served during rituals.

I have not yet been able to locate a reference in ancient Chinese texts to the familiar modern form of greeting, "Have you eaten?", but perhaps in any event one cannot be far wrong to say that eating was as much a preoccupation in ancient China as it is in contemporary China. According to *Lun Yü (Confucian Analects,* Chapter "Wei Ling Kung"), when the duke Ling of Wei asked Confucius (551-479 BC) about military tactics, Confucius replied, "I have indeed heard about matters pertaining to meat stands and meat platters, but I have not learned military matters" (see translation by Legge 1893). Indeed, one of the most important qualifications of a Chinese gentleman was perhaps his knowledge and skill pertaining to food and drink. According to *Shih Chi* and *Mo Tzu,* Yi Yin, the prime minister of King T'ang of Shang, the dynasty's founder, was originally a cook. In fact, some sources say, it was Yi Yin's cooking skill that first brought him into T'ang's favor.

The importance of the kitchen in the king's palace is amply shown in the personnel roster recorded in *Chou Li.* Out of the almost four thousand persons who had the responsibility of running the king's residential quarters, 2271, or almost 60 per cent, handled food and wine. These included 162 master "dieticians" in charge of the daily menus of the king, his queen, and the crown prince; 70 meat specialists; 128 chefs for "internal" (family) consumption;

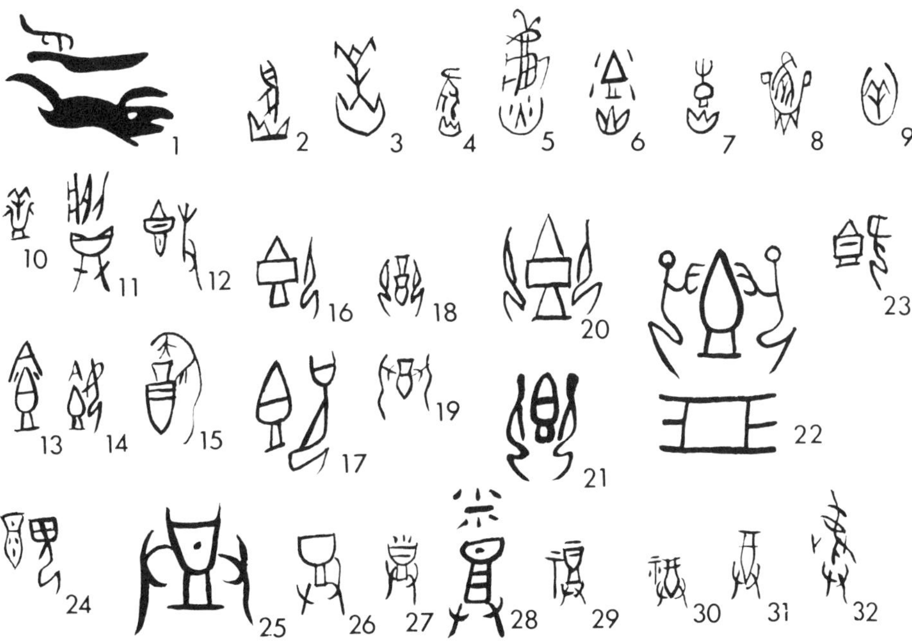

Figure 10. Characters Relating to Cooking, Eating, and Ritual Use of Food. 1: Butchering; 2-9: Cooking; 10-23: Serving in various contexts; 24-32: Ritual use

128 chefs for "external" (guests) consumption; 62 assistant chefs; 335 specialists in grains, vegetables, and fruits; 62 specialists of game; 342 fish specialists; 24 turtle and shellfish specialists; 28 meat dryers; 110 wine officers; 340 wine servers; 170 specialists in the "six drinks"; 94 ice men; 31 bamboo tray servers; 61 meat platter servers; 62 pickle and sauce specialists; and 62 salt men.

What these specialists tended to were not just the king's palate pleasures: eating was also very serious business. In *Yi Li,* the book that describes various ceremonies, food cannot be separated from ritual (see Steele 1917). *Li Chi,* which has been called "the most exact and complete monography which the Chinese nation has been able to give of itself to the rest of the human race" (Legge 1885: 12), is full of references to the right kinds of food for various occasions and the right table manners, and it contains some of the earliest recipes of Chinese dishes. It is true that the *Three Books of Rites* were probably put down during the Han period, but obviously the importance of food and eating shown in these books is as Chou as it is Han. In *Tso Chuan* and *Mo Tzu*, authentic Chou texts, references were made of the use of the *ting* cauldron, a cooking vessel, as the prime symbol of the state. I make no more confident statement than that the ancient Chinese were among the peoples of the world who have been particularly preoccupied with food and eating. Furthermore, as Jacques Gernet (1962: 135) has stated, "there is no doubt that in this sphere China has shown a greater inventiveness than any other civilization."

One may or may not like Chinese food; that is a subjective matter of habit and taste. But objective criteria may be used to measure the relative inventiveness in, and the degree of preoccupation with, food and eating among peoples of different cultures and civilizations. What peoples are more so preoccupied? Were the Chinese among them? How do we measure their degree of preoccupation as against other peoples'? Perhaps the following criteria may be used: quantitative, structural, symbolic, and psychological.

Quantitatively, the most direct measure may be taken on the food itself: how elaborately is it prepared? The absolute number of dishes that a people is capable of cooking is probably a direct indication of the elaborateness of their cuisine, but the complexity of individual dishes is certainly of significance. The more elaborately food is cooked, the more time must be consumed. A people that spends more time on cooking its food than another is probably more preoccupied with eating than the other.

The percentage of income spent on food may be used as another quantitative standard of measurement. This refers to a comparison among cultures rather than one among different families or different classes within the same culture. Between the contemporary Americans and the contemporary Chinese, for example, it is a known fact that the Chinese spend more of their income on food than the Americans, and in this sense the former is more preoccupied with eating than the latter. It is superfluous to point out here that this has a lot to do with a people's wealth. Since peoples' nutritional needs for food are probably not very different the world over, there is an absolute maximum one needs to spend on food. Poor peoples must inevitably spend, in proportion, more on food than rich peoples. But this does mean that poor peoples do require a greater percentage of their total time and energy to obtain and consume food than rich peoples, and this must make a significant difference in the relative cultural makeup of the two peoples. Furthermore, although there is an absolute maximum one *needs* to spend on food, there is no limit of how much one actually *wants* to. Two peoples may be coequals in terms of wealth, but they may differ vastly in regard to the percentage of their income devoted to actually eating.

Structurally, what different kinds of food do different cultures use on different occasions or in different social or ritual contexts? One people may use a very small number of foods and drinks for many different contexts, but another may require many. Also significant are utensils, beliefs, taboos, and etiquettes associated with various kinds of foods and drinks. All of this may be approached with a study of the terminological system of the culture's foods and their related things and behaviors. The greater number of terms that are used to designate foods and related things and behaviors, and the more hierarchical this terminological system must be arranged, the more preoccupied the people may be said to be with food.

A third set of criteria is a symbolic one. Since foods and drinks are often if not always used as media of communication, one could also attempt to ascertain among the various peoples the extent to which they are so used. Since rituals are among the most elaborate forms of symbolic behavior, the extent and the elaborateness of the use of food in rituals should give an excellent indication in this regard. The terminological system is again relevant here in accordance with Charles Frake's folk taxonomy hypothesis: "The greater the number of distinct social contexts in which information about a particular phenomenon must be communicated, the greater the number of different levels of contrast into which that phenomenon is categorized" (Frake 1961:121).

A fourth set of criteria is psychological: How much do the people think about eating in their daily life or, stated with greater seeming sophistication, how much is the anticipation of eating a factor in regulating an individual's behavior in the short run, in the same way that the anticipation of death, for example, serves as a powerful factor in regulating an individual's behavior in the long run? As Firth (1939:38) says of the Tikopia, "To get a meal is the principal work on most days, and the meal itself is not merely an interval in work but an aim in itself." Another example of psychological preoccupation may be seen in this passage of Lin Yutang (1935: 338): "No food is really enjoyed unless it is keenly anticipated, discussed, eaten and then commented upon . . . Long before we have any special food, we think about it, rotate it in our minds, anticipate it as a secret pleasure to be shared with some of our closest friends, and write notes about it in our invitation letters.'' Lin Yutang's favorite Chinese gourmet is a gentleman who lived about two hundred fifty years ago, by the name of Li Yü (or Li Li-weng). Li was fond of crabs, and he wrote in one of his literary works (Y. Li 1730, vol. 15, section ''Crabs'') that ''as far as crabs are concerned, my mind is addicted to them, my mouth enjoys the taste of them, and not a single day in my life have I ever forgotten about them.''

This brings us back to the observation that the Chinese are probably among the peoples of the world most preoccupied with eating. I have not applied all of the above criteria to measure the contemporary Chinese in this regard, although I believe that anyone who is willing to try will be amply rewarded. As to the ancient Chinese, we will come to them later. But let me first ask the inevitable question: What is so important about a people's or a culture's being more preoccupied or less preoccupied with eating? I think the answer is that this is a central focus for different cultures and peoples to be compared, and that as long as cultures and peoples are compared with one another their respective preoccupation with eating is essential to know.

But primarily these points make clear that as far as the culinary area is concerned, cultures are different and their differences go much deeper than those simply of culinary styles. In a number of recent publications, Lévi-Strauss (1964, 1965, 1966, 1968) seeks to establish some universal expressions of humanity through foods, cooking, table manners, and people's concepts about them. But food, eating, table manners, and people's concepts of them are among the sharpest symbols of their cultures, and to understand them one must first of all understand their uniqueness and the way in which they uniquely symbolize their cultures. In this sense, the Chinese preoccupation with food and eating provides its own explanation. There has been much attempt to see Chinese poverty as culinary virtue. Gernet (1962:135) explains the inventiveness of Chinese cooking in terms of ''undernourishment, drought and famines,'' which compelled the Chinese people to ''make judicious use of every possible kind of edible vegetable and insect, as well as of offal.'' This may be true, but poverty and the consequent exhaustive search for resources only provide a favorable environment for culinary inventiveness; they cannot be said to be its cause, or there would have been as many culinary giants as there are poor peoples. The Chinese have shown inventiveness in this area perhaps for the simple reason that food and eating are among things central to the Chinese way of life.

Let us go back to ancient China and examine the way in which food and food vessels uniquely express the Shang and Chou culture. The following are brief summaries of some of the available facts (see N. H. Lin 1957; Shinoda 1959).

Foodstuffs

From written documents it appears that foodstuffs are neatly categorized into cereal plants, vegetables, fruits, animals, birds, fish and shellfish, and others. Not only were words used to designate each clearly defined category, most of the words within each such category shared the same radicals or compounds: the *ho* (cereal grass) radical for cereal plants, the *ts'ao* (grass) radical for vegetables, the *mu* (tree) radical for fruits, and so on.

Of the cereal plants (see Ho 1969), the ancient Chinese had several kinds of millet *(Setaria italica, Panicum miliaceum, Panicum miliaceum glutinosa),* rice *(Oryza sativa),* and wheat. For vegetables, Li Hui-lin (1969) lists as most important the following: melon (*Cucumis melo*), bottle gourd (*Lagenaria siceraria*), taro *(Colocasia esculenta),* mallow *(Malva verticillata),* turnip *(Brassica rapa),* garlic *(Allium sativum),* Chinese shallot *(Allium bakeri),* spring onion *(Allium fistulosum),* Chinese leek *(Allium ramosum), jen (Perilla frutescens),* smartweed *(Polygonum hydropiper),* and ginger *(Zingiber officinale).* Li's listing was based mainly on an important book dating from the 5th and the early 6th century. From Chou texts, the importance of bamboo and lead-mustards is also conspicuous, and soybeans were without question an important crop. Vegetables and weeds of secondary importance are numerous. N. I. Vavilov had pointed out that "in wealth of its endemic species and in the extent of the genus and species potential of its cultivated plants, China is conspicuous among other centers of origin of plant forms. Moreover, the species are usually represented by enormous numbers of botanical varieties and hereditary forms . . . . If we take into account the enormous number of wild plants, besides the cultivated ones used for food in China, we may better understand how hundreds of millions of people managed to exist in its soil" (Vavilov 1949/50: 24).[1]

Of fruit trees, the following appear in Chou texts most often:

1. The *Book of Poetry* has this description of the collection and use of some wild

pear, haw, apricot, ballace, plum, peach, persimmon, chestnut, small chestnut, jujube date, hazel nut, ka fruit, and *Hovenia dulcis.*

The most common food animals in the Chou texts are cattle, pigs, suckling-pigs, sheep, and dogs among the domesticated, and wild boar, hare, bear, elaphure, deer, and muntjac among the wild.

Fowls and birds that were mentioned in Chou texts with frequency include chickens, pullets, geese, quails, partridges (or finches), pheasants, sparrows, and curlews. Fishes include a large number whose English equivalents are difficult to determine. Other water produces include turtles and various kinds of shellfish. Bees, cicadas, snails, moths, and frogs were among the other foodstuffs mentioned.

Condiments included various "fragrant herbs," cinnamon, and fagara.

Other materials for cooking were salt, which appears to be of a rocky variety and was often made into various shapes; lard (of "horned" and "hornless" animals); sauces; and vinegar.

Cooking Methods

One Chinese cookbook (B. Y. Chao 1972: 39) lists twenty methods of cooking: 1. boiling, 2. steaming, 3. roasting, 4. red-cooking, 5. clear-simmering, 6. pot-stewing, 7. stir-frying, 8. deep-frying, 9. shallow-frying, 10. meeting, 11. splashing, 12. plunging, 13. rinsing, 14. cold-mixing, 15. sizzling, 16. salting, 17. pickling, 18. steeping, 19. drying, 20. smoking. In Chou texts, many of these methods are encountered, although the most important appear to be boiling, steaming, roasting, simmering-stewing, pickling, and drying. A notable absence is that of stir-frying, a very important cooking method today, one that in the opinion of some tries a cook's skill more than any other.

---

plants (translated, Waley 1960: 72):

Here we are gathering duckweed
By the banks of the southern dale
Here we are gathering watergrass
In those channelled pools.
Here we are packing them
Into round basket, into square
Here we are boiling them
In kettles and pans.
Here we lay them beneath the window
Of the ancestral hall.
Who is the mistress of them?
A young girl purified.

What makes Chinese food Chinese lies, essentially, not so much in the methods of cooking as in the way in which foodstuffs are prepared before cooking, and in which they are then put together into distinctive dishes. As Lin Yutang (1935: 340) said, "the whole culinary art of China depends on the art of mixture" (see also Lin and Lin 1969: 12). Dishes are designed on the basis of combinations of flavors and ingredients. This does not mean that Chinese dishes are never made of single flavors, but from the point-of-view of the whole range of Chinese dishes, minced ingredients and mixing of flavors are characteristic. In this crucial sense, the Chou cooking is definitely "Chinese." The culinary art in Chou texts is often referred to as *ko p'eng,* namely, "to cut and cook." There were many words meaning "to cut" or "to mince," and the most common kind of dishes was *keng,* a kind of meat soup or stew, which is characteristically an art of mixing flavors.[2]

Hsiang Ju and Tsuifeng Lin (1969: 30) have suggested that "the ancient Chinese cuisine was not distinguishably 'Chinese'." This was because "there are no words for sautéing [stir-frying], for blanching [plunging and rinsing?], or any of the more refined methods of cooking," although they agreed that "the blending of

---

2. The *Keng* soup formed the basis of a metaphoric discourse by a Chou philosopher-politician, supposed to have taken place in 521 BC, as recorded in *Tso Chuan* (see translation by Legge 1872: 684): "When the marquis of Ch'i returned from his hunt, Yen Tzu was in attendance on the platform of Ch'uan, and Tzu Yu (also known as Chü) drove up to it at full speed. The marquis said, 'It is only Chü who is in harmony with me!' Yen Tzu replied, 'Chü is an assenter; how can he be considered in harmony with you? 'Are they different,' asked the marquis,—'harmony and assent?' Yen Tzu said, 'They are different. Harmony may be illustrated by soup. You have the water and fire, vinegar, pickle, salt, and plums, with which to cook fish and meat. It is made to boil by the firewood, and then the cook mixes the ingredients, harmoniously equalizing the several flavours, so as to supply whatever is deficient and carry off whatever is in excess. Then the master eats it, and his mind is made equable. So it is in the relations of ruler and minister. When there is in what the ruler approves of anything that is not proper, the minister calls attention to that impropriety, so as to make the approval entirely correct. When there is in what the ruler disapproves of anything that is proper, the minister brings forward that propriety so as to remove occasion for the disapproval. In this way the government is made equal, with no infringement of what is right, and there is no quarrelling with it in the minds of the people. Hence it is said in the ode (*Shih* IV, iii, od. II),

> There are also the well-tempered soups,
> Prepared beforehand, the ingredients rightly proportioned.
> By these offerings we invite his presence without a word;
> Nor is there now any contention in the service.

"As the ancient kings established the doctrine of the five flavours, so they made the harmony of the five notes, to make their minds equable and to perfect their government." Yen Tzu was not the only Chou philosopher who used cooking as a metaphor to convey deep thoughts. Chuang Tzu was another. He used the cutting skills of a cook to illuminate on some fine points of the Tao (Lin and Lin 1969: 23).

flavours was achieved in a remarkable way." But there are only a limited number of cooking methods, and these are current all over the world. Individual cuisine styles are distinguished, not by methods alone, but by the flavors of the products, which are achieved by the distinctive use of the ingredients.

Viands and Dishes

The results of the cooking efforts in ancient China—as in modern China— must have included hundreds or even thousands of individual food dishes that ranged from the simplest to the most complex. Because of the nature of the evidence, most of the dishes that we know something about were those used in rituals and feasts enjoyed by upper class people. Very few recipes for simple vegetable dishes, for example, are known. But whatever the complexity, many dishes were elaborately prepared, and they ranked among the best treasured enjoyments of life. Nowhere is this more vividly and convincingly illustrated than in the two poems in *Ch'u Tz'u* that "summoned the soul," asking them to return home to the good life, a life in which such good dishes satisfy the palate. In "Chao Hun" ("The Summons of the Soul"), we read (translated, Hawkes 1959: 106-7):

O soul, come back! Why should you go far away?
All your household have come to do you honour; all kinds of good food are ready:
Rice, broom-corn, early wheat, mixed all with yellow millet;
Bitter, salt, sour, hot and sweet: there are dishes of all flavours,
Ribs of the fatted ox cooked tender and succulent;
Sour and bitter blended in the soup of Wu;
Stewed turtle and roast kid, served up with yam sauce;
Geese cooked in sour sauce, casseroled duck, fried flesh of the great crane;
Braised chicken, seethed tortoise, high-seasoned, but not to spoil the taste;
Fried honey-cakes of rice flour and malt-sugar sweetmeats;
Jadelike wine, honey-flavoured, fills with winged cups;
Ice-cooled liquor, strained of impurities, clear wine, cool and refreshing;
Here are laid out the patterned ladles, and here is sparkling wine.

In the other poem, "Ta Chao" ("The Great Summons"), these were the delicious dishes, viands, and drinks that were offered as the bribes to lure back the lost soul (translated, Hawkes 1959: 110-111):

The five grains are heaped up six ells high, and corn of zizania set out;
The cauldrons seethe to their brims; their blended savours yield fragrance;
Plump orioles, pigeons, and geese, flavoured with broth of jackals meat;
O soul, come back! Indulge your appetite!
Fresh turtle, succulent chicken, dressed with a sauce of Ch'u;
Pickled pork, dog cooked in bitter herbs, and zingiber-flavoured mince,
And sour Wu salad of artemisia, not too wet or tasteless,
O soul, come back and do not be afraid!
Roast crane is served up, and steamed duck and broiled quails,
Fried bream, stewed magpies, and green goose, broiled.
O soul, come back! Choice things are spread before you.
The four kinds of wine are all matured, not rasping to the throat:
Clear, fragrant, ice-cooled liquor, not for base men to drink;
And white yeast is mixed with must of Wu to make the clear Ch'u wine.
O soul, come back and do not be afraid!

Ch'u's style of cooking was probably somewhat different from north China's, but the dishes that are described in such mouth-watering vividness in these poems are in all likelihood basically identical with those we find in the contemporary (but much more sedate) works in the north, such as *Li Chi.* Here in the north animal and fish flesh was the main ingredient of all the important dishes that were described for ritual and feast occasions. Once in a while raw meat was used, and whole animals, hair and all, might be roasted. But more often the meat was dried, cooked, or pickled. If *dried,* it was cut into squares or oblong strips, seasoned with condiments such as ginger and cinnamon, and then dried. If *cooked,* the meat was cut in one of three types: pieces and chunks with bones, slices, and minced portions. They were then boiled, stewed, steamed, or roasted. In the process, other ingredients were added. If the amount of the other ingredient was small and the purpose wholly to supplement, the result was a meaty dish. If there were important parallel ingredients to achieve "harmony" of flavors, and if the method of cooking was boiling or stewing, then there would be the meat *keng*-soup.[3]

3. Some examples of the meaty dishes are: "A suckling-pig [that] was stewed, wrapped up in sonchus leaves and stuffed with smartweed; a fowl, with the same stuffing, and along with pickle sauce; a fish, with the same stuffing and egg sauce; a tortoise, with the same stuffing and pickle sauce" ("Nei Tze," in *Li Chi*, translated,

Finally, meat was often *pickled or made into a sauce.* It appears that for this one could use both raw meat and cooked meat, but Cheng Hsüan (d. AD 200), the authoritative commentator of *Li Chi,* gave only one recipe: "To prepare *hai* (boneless meat sauce) and *ni* (meat sauce with bones), it is necessary first to dry the meat and then cut it up, blend it with moldy millet, salt, and good wine, and place it in a jar. The sauce is ready in a hundred days." This meat sauce or pickle was often used as an ingredient of a hot dish or soup. Pickling, aside from boiling and drying, also seems to be a favorite method for anthropophagy; famous historical personages that ended up in a sauce jar included the Marquis of Chiu (of Shang) and Tzu Lu (a disciple of Confucius).

The only elaborate recipes for dishes of Shang and Chou times are those of the so-called Eight Delicacies, described in *Li Chi* ("Nei Tze"), to be specifically prepared for the aged. They are the Rich Fry, the Similar Fry, the Bake, the Pounded Delicacy, the Steeped Delicacy, the Grill, the Soup Balls, and the Liver and Fat. The recipes are given at the end of the chapter.

Utensils

The archaeological classification of the Chinese bronze vessels according to their supposed uses in the food system is well known, but none of the classifications that I know of are based on an actual study of their roles in the food system of the Shang and Chou Chinese. A consideration taking into account both the past classifications of bronze vessels and the textual lexicons for food and drink utensils of all materials results in the following major categories (Fig. 11) (see Hayashi 1964):

Food Utensils

Cooking vessels: ting, li, hsien, tseng, fu, hu, and *tsao.* All of these were made of pottery and bronze, except for *tsao,* the stove, which is known only in pottery examples. *Ting, li,* and *hu* were probably for boiling and simmering-stewing; *hsien, tseng,* and *fu,* for steaming.

Preserving and storage vessels: This is a category presumed on the basis of the archaeological remains of grain-containing jars and

---

Legge 1885: 460). Examples of the meat soups are: "snail juice and a condiment of the broad-leaved water-squash were used with pheasant soup; a condiment of wheat with soups of dried slices and of fowl; broken glutinuous rice with dog soup and hare soup; the riceballs mixed with these soups had no smartweed in them" (ibid. Legge 1885: 460).

Figure 11. Major Food and Drink Vessels and Utensils of Shang and Chou. 1-4: Cooking vessels; 5: Storage jar; 6-13: Serving instruments and vessels; 14-19: Drink vessels

the record of meat and vegetable sauces and pickles. No bronze vessels are thought to have been so used, although some of the wine and water containers (see below) could certainly have been used for these purposes. But perhaps pottery jars and urns prevailed.

Serving utensils and vessels: In this category I place four principal kinds of things: chopsticks, ladles, vessels for grain food, and serving utensils for meat and vegetable dishes. Of the first two, little need be said except that they were used during the Shang and Chou periods, although hands were probably used as often as chopsticks.

Vessels for grain and vessels for dishes are complex in form and material. The former vessels, including such types as *kuei, hsü, fu,* and *tuei,* were made of bronze, pottery, and basketry; but the latter, such as *tou, pien,* and *tsu,* were mostly made of pottery, wood, and basketry. *Tou,* for example, the most important serving vessel for meat dishes, was never made of bronze during the Shang period (Shih 1969). Another way of stating this is to say that bronze serving vessels were primarily for grain food but seldom for dishes. This is an important distinction, one that we will come back to later.

Drink Vessels

Water and wine containers: bronze, pottery, wood, and so forth.

Wine drinking cups: bronze, bottle gourd, lacquered wood, pottery.

Ladles: bronze, wood, and bottle gourd.

Feasts and Meals

From the nutritional point of view, once foodstuffs are prepared into viands and dishes, they can be served with the aid of whatever utensils that exist, food enters the stomach, and there the whole affair ends. From the point of view of one whose interest lies in food as one of life's major foci, eating alone is of little consequence other than the satisfaction of hunger and anticipation, but eating together, and the pattern of behavior and the rationales behind it, is the climactical phase. Food is taken to sustain life, but food is not so much taken as given and shared. Such sentiment was expressed in this Chou poem ("Kuei Pen," section "Hsiao Ya," in the *Book of Poetry,* Waley translation):

A cap so tall,
What is it for?
Your wine is good,

Your viands, blessed.
Why give them to other men?
Let it be brothers and no one else.

And, then, in another poem, "Fa Mu" ("Hsiao Ya" section, *Book of Poetry,* Waley translation), we see feelings such as this:

They are cutting wood on the bank.
Of strained wine I have good store;
The dishes and trays are all in rows,
Elder brothers and younger brothers, do not stay afar!
If people lose the virtue that is in them,
It is a dry throat that has led them astray.

Many other poems describe the atmosphere and the provisions of feasts (Fig. 12), and from this one must agree that Creel was right in listing eating as an "enjoyment of life" in his study of ancient China (Creel 1937a: 323ff). But eating was also serious social business, governed by strict rules. As a Chou poet said of an ancestral sacrifice feast, "every custom and rite is observed, every smile, every word is in place" (poem "Ch'u Tz'u," "Hsiao Ya" section, *Book of Poetry,* Waley translation).

Let us first take a look at the physical setup of a meal. The arrangement of the table and chairs is a rather modern feature in China, not earlier than the Northern Sung period (960-1126) (Shang 1938: 119-120). In the Shang and Chou periods, the gentleman class ate individually, kneeling on individual mats; a stool was sometimes placed alongside to provide a low table or for support (Fig. 13).[4] Placed before or beside each person was a set of vessels,

4. The poem "Hsing Wei," in the *Book of Poetry* ("Ta Ya" section), describes a meal scene thus (Waley translation):

Tender to one another should brothers be,
None absenting himself, all cleaving together.
Spread out the mats for them,
Offer them stools.
Spread the mats and the over-mats,
Offer the stools with shuffling step.
Let the host present the cup, the guest return it;
Wash the beaker, set down the goblet.
Sauces and pickles
For the roast meat, for the broiled.
And blessed viands, tripe and cheek;
There is singing and beating of drums.

Again, in the poem "Kung Liu" (Waley translation):

Stalwart was Liu the Duke
In his citadel so safe.
Walking deftly and in due order
The people supplied mats, supplied stools;
He went up to the dais and leant upon a stool.

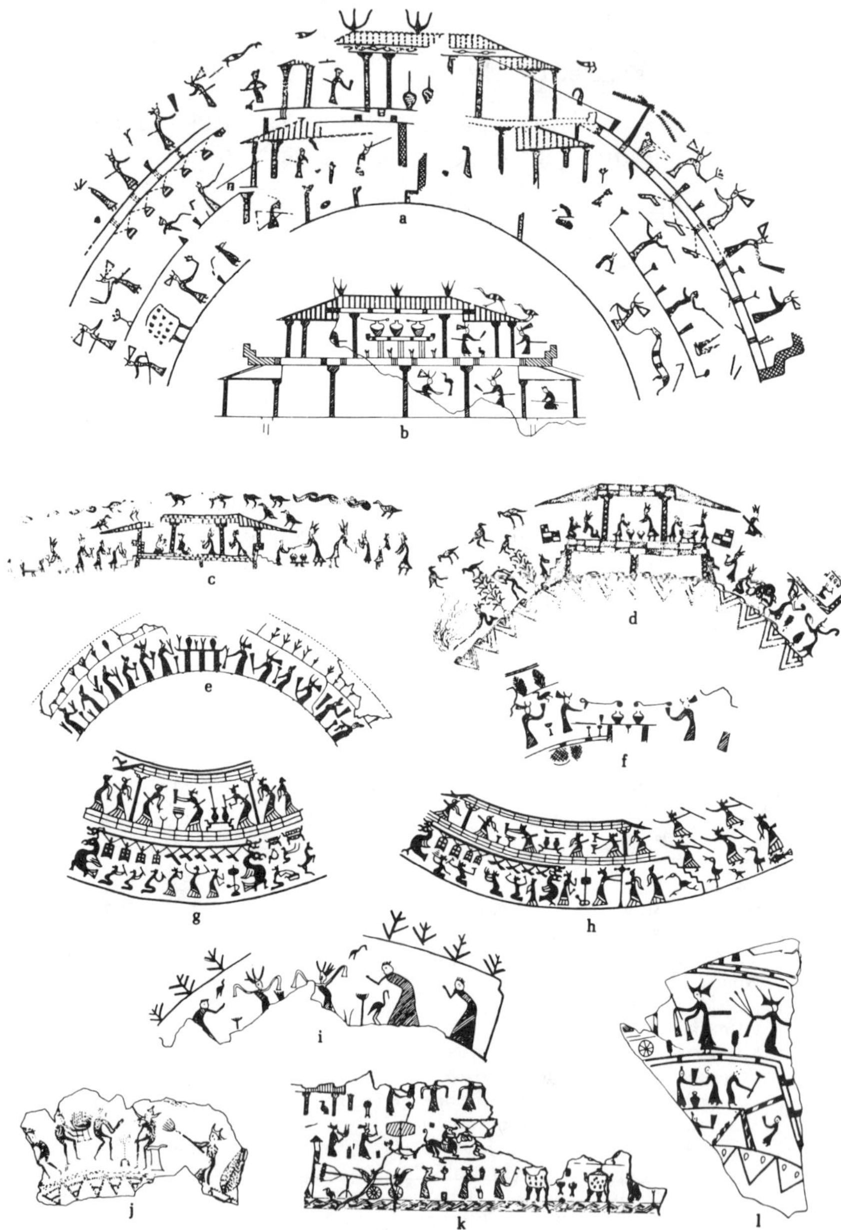

Figure 12. Scenes of Ritual Feasts from Bronze Vessel Decorations, Eastern Chou Period

Figure 13. Rubbing of a Han Tile, Offerings of Food and Drink

containing the food and drink of the meal. The definition of a meal is significant: it consists of grain food, meat and vegetable dishes, and water and/or wine. More will be said about this later. Each person was said to need four large bowls of grain to fill his stomach (poem "Ch'üan Yü", in the *Book of Poetry*), but the number of dishes varied according to an individual's rank and age. According to *Li Chi,* a minister of the upper rank was entitled to eight *tou*-dishes, and one of the lower rank, six ("Li Ch'i"). A man of sixty years may use three *tou*-dishes; of seventy, four; of eighty, five; and of ninety, six ("Hsiang Yin Chiu").

The utensils and dishes were placed in front of and beside the person in this arrangement:

> The meat cooked on the bones is set on the left, and the sliced meat on the right; the rice is placed on the left of the [person], and the soup on [his] right; the minced and roasted meat are put outside (the chops and sliced meat) and the pickles and sauces inside; the

onions and steamed onions succeed to these, and the drink and syrups are on the right. When slices of dried and spiced meat are put down, where they are folded is turned to the left, and the ends of them to the right. ("Ch'ü Li," in *Li Chi,* Legge translation, 1885: 79) The cup with which the guest was pledged was placed on the left; those which had been drunk (by the others) on the right. Those of the guest's attendant, of the host himself, and of the host's assistant;—these all were placed on the right. In putting down a boiled fish to be eaten, the tail was laid in front. In winter it was placed with the fat belly on the right; in summer with the back . . . . All condiments were taken up with the right (hand), and were therefore placed on the left . . . When the head was presented among the viands, the snout was put forward, to be used as the offering. He who sets forth the jugs considered the left of the cup-bearer to be the place for the topmost one. The jugs and jars were placed with their spouts towards the arranger. ("Shao Yi," in *Li Chi,* translation of Legge, 1885: 78-79. See also *Kuan Tzu,* "Ti Tzu Chih")

It should be mentioned in passing that children were trained at an early age to eat with their right hand ("Nei Tse," in *Li Chi*).

Finally, strict rules at the dining mat were prescribed. According to *Li Chi* ("Ch'ü Li" and "Shao Yi" sections, translations of Legge, 1885), the following rules were among the most prominent:

(a) If a guest be of lower rank (than his entertainer), he should take up the [grain], rise and decline (the honor he is receiving). The host then rises and refuses to allow the guest to retire. After this the guest will resume his seat.

(b) When the host leads on the guests to present an offering (to the father of cookery), they will begin with the dishes which were first brought in. Going on from the meat cooked on the bones they will offer of all (the other dishes).

(c) After they have eaten three times, the host will lead on the guests to take of the sliced meat, from which they will go on to all the other dishes.

(d) A guest should not rinse his mouth with spirits till the host has gone over all the dishes.

(e) When (a youth) is in attendance on an elder at a meal, if the host give anything to him with his own hand, he should bow to him and eat it. If he do not so give him anything, he should eat without bowing.

(f) When feasting with a man of superior rank and character, the guest first tasted the dishes and then stopt . . . He should take small and frequent mouthfuls. While chewing quickly, he did not make faces with his mouth.

(g) When eating with others from the same dishes, one should not try to eat (hastily) to satiety. When eating with them from the same dish of [grain], one should not have to wash his hands.

(h) Do not roll the [grain] into a ball; do not bolt down the various dishes; do not swill down (the soup).

(i) Do not make a noise in eating; do not crunch the bones with the teeth; do not put back fish you have been eating; do not throw the bones to the dogs; do not snatch (at what you want).

(j) Do not spread out the [grain] (to cool); do not use chopsticks in eating millet.

(k) Do not (try to) gulp down soup with vegetables in it, nor add condiments to it; do not keep picking the teeth, nor swill down the sauces. If a guest add condiments, the host will apologize for not having had the soup prepared better. If he swill down the sauces, the host will apologize for his poverty.

(l) Meat that is wet (and soft) may be divided with the teeth, but dried flesh cannot be so dealt with. Do not bolt roast meat in large pieces.

(m) When they have done eating, the guests will kneel in front (of the mat), and (begin to) remove the (dishes) of [grain] and sauces to give them to the attendants. The host will then rise and decline this service from the guests, who will resume their seats.

It should be remembered that the above rules of table arrangement and table manners were purported to represent the norm of late Chou upper class gentlemen. We do not know how strictly they were adhered to, whether or not they represent norms wider than north China and the upper class, or if the Chinese of the Shang and early Chou periods had identical or similar rules. From the descriptions given in many poems in the *Book of Poetry,* it appears that meals and feasts were partaken of with a lot more spirit and gusto and less formality than those recorded in *Li Chi.* When Confucius expansively proclaimed that "with coarse [grain] to eat, with water to drink, and my bended arm for a pillow;—I have still joy in the midst of these things" (*Analects,* translation of Legge 1893: 200), he was obviously thinking of a rather minimum level of a meal—without all those rules and manners—which would still, of course, constitute a meal. But was not the Master merely philosophizing? (Remember, in matters of the palate Confucius was in real life rather particular and a very difficult person to accommodate, according to another section of the *Analects*[5].) Did poor people

5. "He did not dislike to have his rice finely cleaned, nor to have his minced meat cut quite small. He did not eat rice which had been injured by heat or damp and turned sour, nor fish or flesh which was gone. He did not eat what was discoloured, or what was of a bad flavour, nor anything which was ill-cooked, or was not in

necessarily eat like a lone bum? Did they not also have their own rules in their own company? They must, but, alas, their rules are not preserved in the available records.

Is there a code in the meal system or food habits of the ancient Chinese, in the sense of the word as Mary Douglas (1971) used it in connection with meals? Was the essence of the ancient Chinese civilization codified in the rice and the dishes its people served themselves and served their guests? I would not want to call it any "code," but the following hierarchy appears to be pertinent:

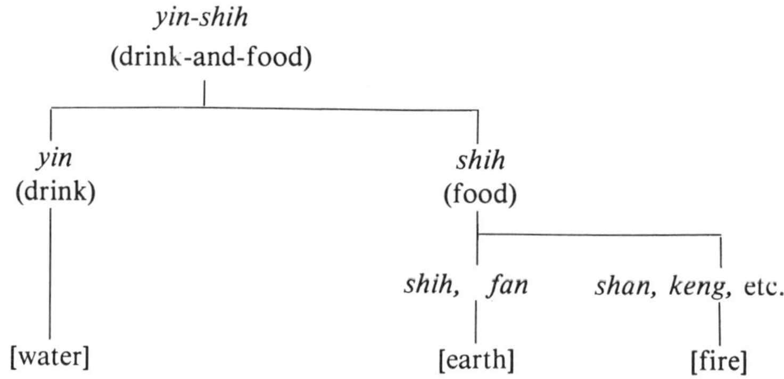

Unlike English, there is a word in Chinese (both ancient and modern) for both food and drink, that is, *yin-shih*. This, of course, is a compound word, made up of *yin* (drink) and *shih* (food). And that bifurcation is clearly shown in the texts, as we will describe later. Then within *shih* itself, there is a clear and strong dichotomy between "shih" in the narrower sense, namely, *fan* or grain food, and dishes of meat and vegetables (*"ts'ai"* in modern parlance). This regime of word classes and their associated beliefs and rules is in my opinion the structural essence of the Chinese way of eating, and it has not changed from at least the Chou period to this day.

In ancient texts, wherever enumeration of things to eat and drink appears, the same hierarchy of food (grain vs. meat and vegetable dishes)-drink contrasts is shown. The following are some outstanding examples (italics added):

Admirable indeed was the virtue of Huei: *With a single bamboo*

season. He did not eat meat which was not cut properly, nor what was served without its proper sauce. . . . He did not partake of wine and dried meat bought in the market. He was never without ginger when he ate. He did not each much" (Chapter "Hsiang Tang," translation Legge 1893: 232-233).

dish of shih (*grains*), *a single gourd dish of yin* (*drink*), and living in his mean narrow lane, . . . he did not allow his joy to be affected by it. (*Analects,* Chapter "Yung Yeh", see Legge 1893: 188)

"[Ch'ien Ao], *carrying with his left hand some shih* (*grain*), *and holding some yin* (*drink*) *with the other,* said to him, 'Poor man! Come and eat' (*Li Chi,* Chapter "T'an Kung," Legge, 1885: 195).

With coarse shih (*grain*) *to eat, with shui* (*water*) *to drink,* and my bended arm for a pillow:—I have still joy in the midst of these things. (*Analects,* Chapter "Shu Erh," see Legge 1893: 200)

The people brought baskets of shih (*grain*) *and jars of chiang* (*water*), to meet your Majesty's host. (*Meng Tzu,* Chapter "Liang Huei Wang," see Legge 1895: 170)

These passages make it clear that a minimum meal consisted of some grain (millet mostly) and some water. But when we proceed up the scale of elaborateness of meals, dealing with the meals of the ministers and the kings, we find that a third item is added, namely, the "dishes." In *Li Chi,* Chapter "Nei Tze" ("Internal [Family] Regulations"), the category of *shan* is added between *fan* (= *shih*) and *yin*. Under it are listed twenty *tou*-dishes, containing various preparations of meat. In *Chou Li,* the officer Shan Fu is stated to be in charge of the king's *shih, yin,* and *shan-hsiu.* The last refers to various kinds of dishes. Thus, within the category *shih* (= food, meal), there is an important contrast between *shih,* in the narrower sense (= grain food), and foods other than grains, namely dishes. Since the dishes often contained meat, the contrast was often made between *shih* (grain) and *keng* (meat soup): "[*Keng*] soup and *shih* boiled grain were used by all, from the princes down to the common people, without distinction of degree" (*Li Chi,* Chapter "Nei Tze", Legge 1885: 464). "A small basket of *shih* (grain) and a platter of *keng* (soup)" (*Meng Tzu,* Chapters "Kao Tzu" and "Chin Hsin"). "*Fan* (grain food) of beans and *keng* (meat soup) of weeds" (*Chan Kuo Ts'e*).

The contrast between grain and "dishes" within a Chinese meal is a living institution of major importance. As Mrs. Chao pointed out in her cookbook (1972: 3):

A very important idea everywhere is the contrast between *fan* (in a narrow sense), "rice", and *ts'ai,* "dishes." Most people who are poor eat much rice (if that) or other grain food as the main food and only a little *ts'ai* or dishes. The dishes only accompany the rice . . . Whenever they can, Chinese children like to eat little rice and much of the dishes, . . . but even children in well-to-do families are called good when they are willing to eat much rice. All this to make clear the opposition between rice and dishes in a Chinese meal. If there are noodles or steamed bread, they are considered "rice," that is, grain food.

Compare this with the following statement about Confucius more than two thousand years ago: "Though there might be a large quantity of meat, he would not allow what he took to exceed the due proportion for the *shih* (grain)" (*Analects,* section "Hsiang Tang"). One must assume that there is some very strong reason for both Confucius and Mrs. Chao's Chinese children (or their parents) to make a clear distinction between the grain food (which is the starch staple and the minimum, basic, absolutely important food) and the dishes (which is used to *p'ei* or "supplement" or "complement" the grain, to make it easier and more enjoyable to eat), and to refrain from overindulgence in the dishes.

It may be important that the contrast between grain and dishes may be seen as a significant difference between food that is of grain, and food (primarily meat) that is cooked with fire. In *Li Chi,* Chapter "Wang Chih", we find the following classification of "barbarian" peoples on the four sides of the Chinese people:

> The people of those five regions—the Middle states, and the Jung, Yi (and other wild tribes round them)—had all their several natures, which they could not be made to alter. The tribes on the east were called Yi. They had their hair unbound, and tattooed their bodies. *Some of them ate their food without its being cooked with fire.* Those on the south were called Man. They tattooed their foreheads, and had their feet turned in toward each other. *Some of them ate their food without its being cooked with fire.* Those on the west were called Jung. They had their hair unbound, and wore skins. *Some of them did not eat grain-food.* Those on the north were called Ti. They wore skins of animals and birds, and dwelt in caves. *Some of them did not eat grain-food.* (see Legge 1885: 229)

Clearly both eating food (meat) without its being cooked with fire and not eating grain food were regarded as being non-Chinese, but these two things are not equated. One could eat grain but also eat raw meat or one could eat his meat cooked but eat no grain. Neither was fully Chinese. A Chinese by definition ate grain and cooked his meat. Clearly grain and cooked meat (main ingredient of dishes) were contrastive items in the Chinese regime of eating.

But apparently meat is something that is, in the whole scheme of things, regarded as of secondary importance, a luxury that a minimum subsistence would not require. The secondary nature of dishes relative to grain food is shown not only in the use of the same word, *shih,* for food or meal in general and for grain food in particular; it is also shown in the mortuary taboo recorded for the Chou Chinese: "After the burial," according to *Li Chi* ("Sang Ta Chi"), "the presiding mourner had only coarse grain and water to drink—he did not eat vegetables or fruits . . . After the change of mourning, towards the end of the year, they ate vegetables and fruit; and after the subsequent sacrifices they ate flesh" (Legge 1885: 183-184). It means that grain and water were the basics, and when one went beyond the basics vegetables and fruits would come before meat. When one resumed eating meat, he would first eat dried meat and then fresh meat (*Li Chi,* "Sang Ta Chi" and "Hsien Chuan").

These two points may be said to be quite firmly established: that within the food category there was a "grain"–"dishes" contrast, and that of the two grain was superior to or more basic than the dishes. In the Chou texts we find two separate accounts for the origins of rituals, one revolving around grain, and the other around the use of fire for the cooking of meat. First, the grain and ritual theme appears in the origin legend of the Chou people as related in the poem "Sheng Min" ("Ta Ya" section, *Book of Poetry,* translated, Waley 1960: 241-243):

She who in the beginning gave birth to the people,
This was Chiang Yüan.
How did she give birth to the people?
Well she sacrificed and prayed
That she might no longer be childless.
She trod on the big toe of God's footprint,
Was accepted and got what she desired.
Then in reverence, then in awe
She gave birth, she nurtured;
And this was Hou Chi ["Lord Millet"]
Indeed, she had fulfilled her months,
And her first-born came like a lamb
With no bursting or rending,
With no hurt or harm.
To make manifest His magic power
God on high gave her ease.
So blessed were her sacrifice and prayer
That easily she bore her child.

Indeed, they put it in a narrow lane;
But oxen and sheep tenderly cherished it.
Indeed, they put it in a far-off wood;
But it chanced that woodcutters came to this wood.
Indeed, they put it on the cold ice;
But the birds covered it with their wings.
The birds at last went away,
And Hou Chi began to wail.
Truly far and wide
His voice was very loud.
Then sure enough he began to crawl;
Well he straddled, well he reared,
To reach food for his mouth.
He planted large beans;
His beans grew fat and tall.
His paddy-lines were close set,
His hemp and wheat grew thick,
His young gourds teemed.
Truly Hou Chi's husbandry
Followed the way that had been shown.
He cleared away the thick grass,
He planted the yellow crop.
It failed nowhere, it grew thick,
It was heavy, it was tall,
It sprouted, it eared,
It was firm and good,
It nodded, it hung—
He made house and home in T'ai.
Indeed, the lucky grains were sent down to us,
The black millet, the double-kernelled,
Millet pink-sprouted and white.
Far and wide the black and the double-kernelled
He reaped and acred;
Far and wide the millet pink and white
He carried in his arms, he bore on his back,
Brought them home, and created the sacrifice.
Indeed, what are they, our sacrifices?
We pound the grain, we bale it out,
We sift, we tread,
We wash it—soak, soak;
We boil it all steamy.
Then with due care, due thought
We gather southernwood, make offering of fat,
Take lambs for the rite of expiation,
We roast, we broil,
To give a start to the coming year

High we load the stand,
The stands of wood and of earthenware.
As soon as the smell rises
God on high is very pleased:
"What smell is this, so strong and good?"
Hou Chi founded the sacrifices,
And without blemish or flaw
They have gone on till now.

Here meat is mentioned, but Hou Chi was above all the "Lord Millet", and the ritual one in which grains played central roles. The other story is about the relation of rituals and cooked meat, and is related in the "Li Yün" section of *Li Chi.* This section contains many ideas and concepts that scholars have long suspected of being Taoist (M. Kao 1963: 38-41), and perhaps the following account (see translations of Legge 1885: 368-372) was closer to the folk-peasant tradition than the previous poem, which was in the tradition of the Chou rulers:

At the first use of ceremonies, they began with [food] and drink. They roasted millet and pieces of pork; they excavated the ground in the form of a jar, and scooped the water from it with their two hands; they fashioned a handle of clay, and struck with it an earthen drum. (Simple as these arrangements were), they yet seemed to be able to express by them their reverence for [ghosts and gods].

(By and by), when one died, they went upon the housetop, and called out his name in a prolonged note, saying, "Come back, So and So." After this they filled the mouth (of the dead) with uncooked grain, and (set forth as offerings to him) packets of [cooked] flesh. Thus they looked up to heaven (whither the spirit was gone), and buried (the body) in the earth. The body and the animal soul go downwards; and the intelligent spirit is on high. Thus (also) the dead are placed with their heads to the north, while the living look toward the south. In all these matters the earliest practice is followed.

Formerly the ancient kings had no houses. In winter they lived in caves which they had excavated, and in summer in nests which they had framed. They knew not yet the transforming power of fire, but ate the fruits of plants and trees, and the flesh of birds and beasts, drinking their blood, and swallowing (also) the hair and feathers. They knew not yet the use of flax and silk, but clothed themselves with feathers and skins.

The later sages then arose, and men (learned) to take advantage of the benefits of fire. They moulded the metals and fashioned clay, so as to rear towers with structures on them, and houses with windows and doors. They toasted, grilled, boiled, and roasted. They produced must and sauces. They dealt with the flax and silk so as to form linen and silken fabrics. They were thus able to nourish the living, and to make offerings to the dead; to serve the spirits of the departed and God. In all these things we follow the example of that early time.

Thus it is that the dark-coloured liquor is in the apartment (where the representative of the dead is entertained); that the vessel of must is near its (entrance) door; that the reddish liquor is in the hall; and the clear, in the (court) below. The victims (also) are displayed, and the tripods and stands are prepared. The lutes and citheras are put in their places, with the flutes, sonorous stones, bells, and drums. The prayers (of the principal in the sacrifice to the spirits) and the benedictions (of the representatives of the departed) are carefully framed. The object of all the ceremonies is to bring down the spirits from above, even their ancestors; serving (also) to rectify the relations between father and son, and the harmony between elder and younger brother; to adjust the relations between high and low; and to give their proper places to husband and wife. The whole may be said to secure the blessing of Heaven.

They proceed to their invocations, using in each the appropriate terms. The dark-coloured liquor is employed in (every) sacrifice. The blood with the hair and feathers (of the victim) is presented. The flesh, uncooked, is set forth on the stands. The bones with the flesh on them are sodden; and rush mats and coarse cloth are placed underneath and over the vases and cups. The robes of dyed silk are put on. The must and clarified liquor are presented. The flesh, roasted and grilled, is brought forward. The ruler and his wife take alternate parts in presenting these offerings, all being done to please the souls of the departed, and constituting a union (of the living) with the disembodied and unseen.

These services having been completed, they retire, and cook again all that was insufficiently done. The dogs, pigs, bullocks, and sheep are dismembered. The shorter dishes (round and square), the taller ones of bamboo and wood, and the soup vessels are all filled. There are the prayers which express the filial piety (of the worshipper), and the benediction announcing the favour (of his ancestors). This may be called the greatest omen of prosperity; and in this the ceremony obtains its grand completion.

Each of these two accounts, *Sheng Min* and *Li Yün,* relates mainly to one side of the grain–dishes contrast. Why this contrast? Why are they differentially emphasized in separate accounts? One may be tempted to explain this basic contrast within the Chinese meal system in terms of a mixture of two (class or ethnic) traditions. It is also interesting to note that the food that is considered the major partner of the pair is the much more recent invention, and it is also the invention that is identified with the Chinese as opposed to the barbarian. But all this, plus a detailed analysis of the two accounts of ritual origins, must be the object of further studies. In the present connection, I rather think that the dichotomy in meals is a part of the dualism that permeated throughout the whole Chinese civilization, and that the *yin* and the *yang* concepts are playing a role here also. Complete or even satisfactory demonstration of all these is not in sight, but I would like for now to return to food vessels and to archaeology, for it is in these areas that I see a flicker of light.

I had maintained earlier that Shang and Chou bronze and pottery vessels may be studied in the context of the Chinese food habits of the period. Now that we have provided a beginning of such a context, what, if any, new insight have we gained insofar as the archaeology of food vessels is concerned?

The most important for me is the realization that the study of vessels as food vessels must not be confined to those of a single material. In archaeology we are used to studying bronzes, pottery, lacquer ware, and so forth, as separate categories. In actual use of the vessels for meals and for rituals, there is usually a mixture of them made of different materials: bronze, pottery, bottle-gourd, wood, lacquer ware, ivory, bone, and so forth. An intriguing question is, in addition to the presumable—though not always apparent or provable—correlation of use and material on account of the physical properties of the various materials, were there rules that governed the mixture of vessels of different materials?

One evident rule, which has not been hitherto obvious, is that, insofar as serving vessels are concerned, bronze was for the most part the material confined to those for grain food and for drinks made from grain. *Pien* and *tou,* the two most important vessels for meat dishes, were made of wood, basketry, and pottery. They are not known to have been made of bronze during the Shang and early Chou periods. *Tou* appeared in the latter half of Chou in bronzes, but presumably there were many more pottery and wooden *tou* than bronze ones even during this brief interval, and from the beginning of Han onwards *tou* was again an almost exclusively wooden utensil (Shih 1950: 10). Shih Chang-ju tried to explain the failure of the Shang to make bronze *tou* by appealing to the physical properties of the bronze:

Most bronze vessels of the Yin period were objects that were suitable for liquids but unsuitable for solids. *Tou* appears to be a utensil for solid objects. Wooden *tou* vessels, when engraved and painted in red, were the most glamorous-looking. The reason that the Yin period lacked bronze *tou* was possibly because the bronze was not suitable for casting *tou,* or because bronze *tou* could not achieve the desired appearance due to the low level of metallurgical skills. (Shih 1969: 79)

An alternative interpretation is that the Shang grouped the food and drink serving vessels into those whose contents were made of or from grain (cooked grain or fermented grain or wine) and those whose contents included meat. Clay, wood, and basketry could be used to make vessels of both kinds, but bronze could be cast for vessels of the grain kind only, not the meat kind. That is, bronzes were not for serving dishes.

We can only speculate as to why this was so. Perhaps food and drinks were classified by the Shang and Chou into different categories, and in a ritual context different vessel materials could come into contact only with certain kinds of food and drinks, according to specific rules. We don't know how far back we can trace the idea of the "five elements"—metal, wood, water, fire, earth. According to Liu Pin-hsiung (1965: 108), not only did the Five Elements exist in the Shang period as a pervasive, basic cosmological conceptual system; they were even related to the social divisions of the royal house. But, according to others (e.g. H. S. Li 1967: 47), both the Yin-Yang theory and the Five Elements theory had a much later origin. In any event, in Warring States (*Mo Tzu*) and early Han (*Huai Nan Tzu* and *Shih Chi*) texts, the element fire and the element metal were regarded as conflicting and antagonistic elements, and when they did come into contact fire usually prevailed over metal. Earlier we have shown that grain food was in the Chou conception associated with earth, and that "dishes," in which cooked meat was a major ingredient, were associated with fire. Earth and metal were harmonious elements, whereas fire and metal were disharmonious. If this idea has an earlier origin, perhaps it would help explain why "dishes" should not be served in bronze containers. To be sure, meat was not a necessary element of every dish, and some dishes could be of vegetables only. But meat was invariably a part of ritual dishes cooked for and by the rich, and bronze vessels were used for and by the rich also. When the ritualists avoided using bronze for certain categories of vessels, there must have been some reason. In *Li Chi* (chapter "Chiao T'o

Sheng''), we find various references to the nature of food and the appropriate vessels:

> In feasting and at the vernal sacrifice in the ancestral temple they had music; but in feeding (the aged) and at the autumnal sacrifice they had no music: these were based in the *yin* and *yang*. All drinking serves to nourish the *yang;* all eating to nourish the *yin*. . . . The number of *ting* and *tsu* was odd [yang], and that of *pien* and *tou* was even [yin]; this also was based in the numbers belonging to the *yin* and *yang*. The *pien* and *tou* were filled with the products of water and the land. (see Legge 1885: 418-419)
>
> At the (Great) border sacrifice, . . . The vessels used were of earthenware and of gourds; they emblem the natural (productive power of) heaven and earth. (Legge 1885: 427-428)
>
> The pickled contents of the ordinary *tou* were water-plants produced by the harmonious powers (of nature); the sauce used with them was from productions of the land. The additional *tou* contained productions of the land with the sauce from productions of the water. The things in the *pien* and *tou* were from both the water and the land. (see Legge 1885: 434)

Thus, drinking is *yang*, and eating is *yin*. But within eating itself, some food was *yang* and some *yin*. Meat dishes cooked by fire were probably *yang*, and food and drink from grain (from the earth) were probably *yin*. Metal was probably *yang*, but pottery and gourd were probably more *yin* than *yang*. There may be rules of what food may be served by vessels of what materials, and the overall rule may be that *yang* combine with *yin* and vice versa. We do not know any of the rules, but here in food and food vessels we probably encounter once again the dualistic principles that we had encountered in the area of social organization (Chang 1964). And just how this *yin-yang* dualism worked together with the Five Elements is a most intriguing question.

Some related questions involve the possible correlation between the decoration of the vessels and their roles in the food system of the Shang and Chou Chinese. Was there any attempt to decorate the vessels with the images of some of the animals whose meat was to fill them? On the surface the answer may be an easy no, for mythological animals are obviously not foodstuffs, and the animals that decorate the Shang and Chou bronzes were certainly mythological. But mythological animals were almost always based on actual animals, the most commonly represented being cattle, sheep, and tigers. They were probably all food—and ritual—animals, and so were probably the other less-frequently represented animals such as deer, elephant, rhinoceros, and goat. Birds were among the prominent decorative motifs. Although their species are difficult to determine, there is no question that birds of many kinds were a major food item. And so was fish (Fig. 14). The question is, thus, not one easy to dispose of without much additional research.

It is also interesting to note that many of the mythological animals have been referred to, since the Sung scholars, as "t'ao-t'ieh." We do not know whether or not *t'ao-t'ieh* is an appropriate name for all split animal images, but at least *t'ao-t'ieh* is certainly among the bronze decorative motifs of Chou (*Lü-Shih Ch'un-Ch'iu*: "Chou *ting* are decorated with *t'ao-t'ieh*"). *T'ao-t'ieh*, according to *Tso Chuan* (18th Year of Wen Kung), is the name of an ancient villain known for his gluttonous greed, one who ate and indulged too much for his own good. In *Mo Tzu* (chapter "Chieh Yüng", or "Moderation of Expenditures", part 2), we find that the ancient sage-kings are said to have authorized the code of laws regarding food and drink, saying:

> Stop when hunger is satiated, breathing becomes strong, limbs are strengthened and ears and eyes become sharp. There is no need of combining the five tastes extremely well or harmonizing the different sweet odours. And efforts should not be made to procure rare delicacies from far countries.
>
> How do we know such were the laws?
>
> In ancient times, when Yao was governing the empire he consolidated Chiao Tse on the south, reached Yu Tu on the north, expanded from where the sun rises to where the sun sets on the east and west, and none was unsubmissive or disrespectful. Yet, even when he was served with what he much liked, he did not take a double cereal or both soup and meat. He ate out of an earthen liu and drank out of an earthen hsing, and took wine out of a spoon. With the ceremonies of bowing and stretching and courtesies and decorum the sage-king had nothing to do." (Mei 1929: 120-121)

This is, of course, Mo Tzu's own philosophy, but overindulgence in food and drink was probably cautioned against in ancient times as well as today. Confucius, we recall, "did not eat much." It is possible that *t'ao-t'ieh* was used on food vessels as a reminder for restraint and frugality, and if what is recorded about the eating and drinking of the Shang is true, such reminders obviously went unheeded.

But overindulgence was something only the upper class—the

Figure 14. Food and Water Bowls Decorated with Fish Designs. Did they serve fish in them, or was fish a symbol of, say, fertility? (*Lower,* Yang-shao Culture at Pan-p'o, Sian, *ca.* 4000 BC; *Middle,* a bronze *p'an* of Shang or early Western Chou; *Upper,* a Ch'u pottery *tou* from Ch'ang-sha, Hunan.)

users of bronzes—could afford. For the most people, pottery was probably the most basic material for vessels (Fig. 15). And of all materials, at least those that are durable and archaeologically important, pottery seems to be acceptable for all essential uses: cooking, preserving, storing, drinking, serving both grain and dishes. Archaeological remains do indicate that in pottery vessels one finds the whole range of food needs served. In the two groups of archaeological burials of the Chou period, from the beginning to the end, one near Sian (Chung Kuo K'o Hsüeh Yüan K'ao Ku Yen Chiu Suo 1962) and the other near Loyang (Chung Kuo K'o Hsüeh Yüan K'ao Ku Yen Chiu Suo 1959), a large number of graves contained pottery vessels. In the overwhelming majority of graves, vessels that served the whole range of food uses were found in sets in individual burials, including vessels for cooking and serving grain (*li* and *kuei*), vessels for serving meat dishes (*tou*), and vessels for drinking (*hu* and *kuan*). This serves to show that the hierarchical taxonomy that we have worked out of the Chou texts is archaeologically significant. It also goes to show that in the archaeological study of ancient China, including the study of bronze and pottery vessels, the textual materials, and the kind of information only textual materials provide, are indispensable.

The Eight Delicacies

For the Rich Fry, they put the pickled meat fried over rice that had been grown on a dry soil, and then enriched it with melted fat. This was called the Rich Fry.

For the Similar Fry, they put the pickled meat fried over the millet grains, and enriched it with melted fat. This was called the Similar Fry.

For the Bake, they took a suckling-pig or a (young) ram, and having cut it open and removed the entrails, filled the belly with dates. They then wrapped it round with straw and reeds, which they plastered with clay, and baked it. When the clay was all dry, they broke it off. Having washed their hands for the manipulation, they removed the crackling and macerated it along with rice-flour, so as to form a kind of gruel which they added to the pig. They then fried the whole in such a quantity of melted fat as to cover it. Having prepared a large pan of hot water, they placed in it a small tripod, which was filled with fragrant herbs, and the slices of the creature which was being prepared. They took care that the hot water did not cover this tripod, but kept up the fire without intermission for

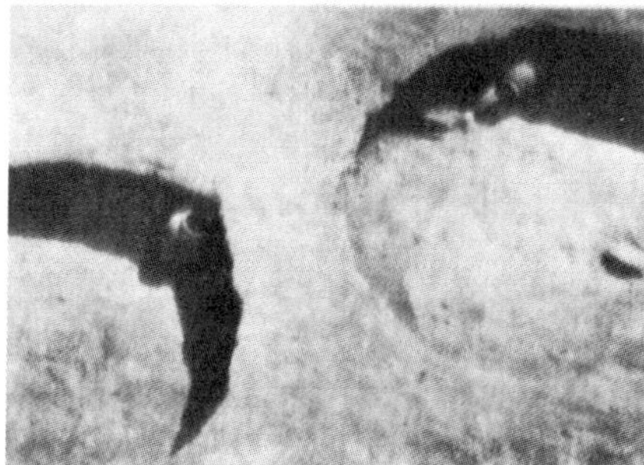

Figure 15. Different Social Classes Had Different Foods and Food Vessels (*Upper,* reconstruction of a Shang feast; *Lower,* two pit-house floors with remains of food vessels, Shang period, at An-yang, Honan.) The contrast between the two ways of life is obvious.

three days and nights. After this, the whole was served up with the addition of pickled meat and vinegar.

For the Pounded Delicacy, they took the flesh of ox, sheep, elk, deer and muntjac, a part of that which lay along the spine, the same in quantity of each, and beat it now as it lay flat, and then turning it on its side; after that they extracted all the nerves. (Next), when it was sufficiently cooked, they brought it (from the pan), took away the outside crust, and softened the meat (by the addition of pickle and vinegar).

For the Steeped Delicacy, they took the beef, which was required to be that of a newly killed animal, and cut it into small pieces, taking care to obliterate all the lines in it. It was then steeped from one morning to the next in good wine, when it was eaten with pickle, vinegar, or the juice of prunes.

To make the Grill, they beat the beef and removed the skinny parts. They then laid it on a frame of reeds, sprinkled on it pieces of cinnamon and ginger, and added salt. It could be eaten thus when dried. Mutton was treated in the same way as beef, and also the flesh of elk, deer, and muntjac. If they wished it dry, they ate it as eaten (at first).

For the (Soup) Balls, they took equal quantities of beef, mutton and pork, and cut them small. Then they took grains of rice, which they mixed with the finely cut meat, two parts of rice to one of meat, and formed cakes or balls, which they fried.

For the Liver and Fat, they took a dog's liver, and wrapped it round with its own fat. They then wet it and roasted it, and took it in this condition and scorched it. No smartweed was mixed with the fat. (translated, Legge 1885: 468-470)

8 A Classification of Shang and Chou Myths

This article presents a classification of myths of the Shang and Chou Dynasties in ancient China for the purpose of historic interpretation. Before presenting the classification, it appears advisable to make clear at the beginning the nature of the materials under discussion.

Even though there is little common agreement among students of myths as to what constitutes a myth, a detailed discussion of this problem would be out of place here. I will only say that the data that meet all the following three criteria will be dealt with here as myths: (1) Our materials are *stories* (Lévi-Strauss 1958: 228-235). (2) The story must involve something "out of the ordinary"—supernatural, sacred, mystical, etc. Either the actor or the action, or both, are unrealistic according to our knowledge. (3) But everything is real to the storyteller. The story is not merely believed in with firmness and stubborn conviction, if at times no more than explicitly, but serves as the basis upon which the storyteller's or his fellow-citizen's actions and behaviors are based and directed (Bidney 1953: 294, 297; Bain 1947: 61). In ancient Chinese texts, all stories that meet these conditions are considered as *myths*, and will be included under the present classification.

The period in ancient Chinese history that is our immediate concern consists of two dynasties, Shang and Chou. The traditional chronology places these dynasties at 1766-1122 BC and 1122-221 BC respectively. The Chou Dynasty is subdivided into two segments, Western Chou and Eastern Chou, being marked by a change in the royal capital from near Sian in the west to near Loyang in the east, an event that took place in 771 BC. Both Shang and Chou were literate civilizations, and largely speaking were within the Bronze Age, although iron implements began to appear extensively in the archaeological sites after the middle of the Eastern Chou.

Throughout Shang and Chou the principal form of documents presumably consisted of wooden and bamboo tablets inscribed with brush-written characters (Tsien 1962; P. Ch'en 1953a, 1953b;

Note: This essay was originally published in *Bulletin of the Institute of Ethnology,* Academia Sinica, 14 (Autumn 1962): 47-94.

K. Jung 1941; S. H. Li 1954; H. P. Sun 1934; H. H. Chin 1959). Most of these bamboo and wooden books, unfortunately, have perished; a few are preserved intact in tombs at a few Ch'u sites in Central China, but the texts written on them afford little historic information. During the Shang Dynasty, inscriptions were incised onto oracle bones; these pertained to the questions asked and, sometimes, to the answers obtained during the process of divination. Significant information on the Shang culture, particularly its religious aspects, can be found on these. Throughout the entire period, short or long texts were also cast or incised on ceremonial bronze vessels of the royal and princely courts, in most cases memorials of royal gifts; these also contain a significant amount of historic data. Fragmentary characters and texts have occasionally been found on some other artifacts of pottery and in one case a long document written on a piece of silk was excavated in a site at Ch'ang-sha. Aside from writings, archaeology can provide such supporting evidence in connection with our study as decorative motifs of bronzes and pottery which may be religiously or otherwise symbolic or representational.

But the overwhelming majority of Shang and Chou mythological data are contained in the traditional historic texts. These, in cases where a pre-Ch'in Dynasty (or pre-221 BC) date is reasonably certain, were presumably also written originally on bamboo and wooden tablets but were later transcribed onto paper and into later styles of characters. These documents pose for us, in many cases, serious or even insurmountable problems of chronology and authenticity. These problems can be summarized into something like the following: Our aim is to study myths of the Shang and Chou Dynasties, but (a) are the historic texts which are traditionally alleged to be of Shang and Chou dates genuinely Shang and Chou literature? and (b) could post-Chou historic documents also contain Shang and Chou myths that were not recorded until a later period? These questions may look simple enough, but any sinologist knows just how much controversy they involve. Not to burden the readers with technical minutae, I must nevertheless clarify these points as briefly as accuracy permits.[1]

1. According to Ku Chieh-kang (1935), skepticism in the legendary accounts of the ancient heroes and sages began as early as in the Eastern Chou period when much of these data were put down on paper. But, obviously, it was not until the 20th century for the historians to critically analyze these legends and myths for the purpose of historical study of the Shang and Chou periods. The earliest such studies were Ku Chieh-kang (1923), and Maspéro (1924). Soon afterwards, a number of mon-

In the first place, most scholars believe that genuine Shang Dynasty texts preserved intact probably do not exist. In *Shu Ching,* there are a few chapters, such as "T'ang Shih", "P'an Keng", and "Kao Tsung Jung Jih", that are traditionally attributed to the Shang Dynasty, but they are highly suspect to say the least. Some passages and even some of the general concepts underlying these chapters may represent a Shang ideology, but there is little question that their composition in the present form was a Chou Dynasty undertaking. The chapter of "Shang Sung" in *Shih Ching* was probably composed during the Eastern Chou Dynasty by the elite of the Sung State, which is known to have been founded by the descendants of the Shang royalty. The data contained therein may thus be utilized for the study of the Shang culture, but only to a limited extent and only as supporting evidence. For the mythology of the Shang Dynasty, therefore, we necessarily rely heavily upon the oracle bone and bronze inscriptions that are found archaeologically.

For the Western Chou period, the situation hardly improves. A few chapters in *Shu Ching* and a few poems in *Shih Ching* (particularly in the "Ya" section) very possibly date from this period, but otherwise the data are scanty and suspect. The practice of inscribing oracle bones became a lost art, thus leaving the bronze vessel inscriptions, of which there fortunately are plenty, as the sole major supplementary source of mythological data. In short, if we collect data on the mythology of Shang and Western Chou Dynasties recorded *during* these periods, we have at our disposal primarily these sources, and little else.

In the Eastern Chou period, particularly the second, Warring States, half (ca. 450-221 BC), authentic historic literatures drastically increased in number relative to former periods, and from the records of philosophers (Confucius, Lao Tzu, Chuang Tzu, and Mencius), *Shu Ching, Shih Ching, Ch'un Ch'iu* and its three *Chuan, Kuo Yü,* and *Ch'u Tz'u,* we find a considerable amount of data that are of relevance to our subject matter. *Shan Hai Ching* in part was definitely composed during the Eastern Chou period, and in *San Li* (*Li Chi, Chou Li,* and *Yi Li*) and *Yi,* there are unquestionable Eastern Chou elements, although it is at times quite difficult to separate them out. *Shih Pen,* a very important reference

---

ographic studies appeared in press (Y. P. Shen 1925; Granet 1926; C. K. Ku, ed., 1926; Erkes 1926; Ferguson 1928; C. Hsüan 1928, and C. C. Feng 1929). Topical studies in depth by mythologists began to proliferate after about 1931, but the critical foundation of the study of Chinese mythology may be said to have been laid down during the period 1923-29.

consulted by Ssu-ma Ch'ien when the latter author compiled his *Shih Chi* in the beginning of the first century BC, has since unfortunately been lost, and the fragmentary passages quoted by various historic writers during subsequent dynasties as being from *Shih Pen* may or may not represent the original version. In 281 AD (according to one version of the story), a Warring States period tomb was alleged to have been uncovered in Chi Hsien, Honan, in which a number of bamboo books was said to have been found, including *Chou Shu, Chi Nien, Suo Yü,* and *Mu T'ien Tzu Chuan*, among others. Except for *Mu T'ien Tzu Chuan,* none of these is preserved for us in a reasonably complete form, although passages of *Chi Nien, Suo Yü,* and *Chou Shu* were quoted and thus preserved in books of subsequent historic periods when the then scholars were still fortunate enough to have made use of them.

The abundance of mythological and historic data in the Eastern Chou literatures poses a serious problem for us, a problem which is again brought to the fore when the Han Dynasty texts are taken into consideration, in which even more mythological data can be found in such volumes as Ssu-ma Ch'ien's *Shih Chi* and *Huai Nan Tzu,* that related mythological and historic events not heretofore seen in the existing literature. The problem, which I have already mentioned above, is this: Could it be that some Shang and Western Chou myths were not *recorded* until the Eastern Chou Dynasty, and could it be that some Shang, Western Chou, and Eastern Chou myths were not *recorded* until the Han Dynasty? To put it differently, can we use Eastern Chou literatures for the purpose of studying Shang and Western Chou mythology, and can we use Han texts for the purpose of studying Shang, Western Chou and Eastern Chou mythology (see Y. P. Shen 1925:22; Karlgren 1946, Eberhard 1946)? In order to answer this question, one surely must take each particular work of literature for discussion and examination, but to stay at a general level one of three broad answers is possible.

a) The Eastern Chou versions of the pre-Shang, Shang, and Western Chou events that did not appear in the existing Shang and Western Chou literatures (archaeological and historical) and the Han versions of the pre-Shang, Shang, and Chou events that did not exist in the existing Shang and Chou literatures (archaeological and historical) were essentially fabricated by Eastern Chou and Han politicians and philosophers for a variety of purposes, and thus can be dismissed *a priori* from the mythological data that we can use.

b) On account of the facts that literacy and knowledge began to descend to the lower classes during the Eastern Chou and that Chinese civilization significantly expanded once during the Eastern Chou and again during the Han and thus absorbed into it many alien local cultures that were previously peripheral to or distant from the nuclear Shang and Western Chou civilizations, many oral traditions of the common folk and of the non-Shang and non-Western Chou cultures that were not previously recorded now found their way into the historical texts and can thus be utilized for the purpose of studying the mythology of an earlier period.

c) No matter whether these later versions of earlier periods were fabrications or were truthful but belated records, the fact that these were recorded during the Eastern Chou or the Han Dynasty makes it unequivocal that these data are the mythological data of the Eastern Chou and Han Dynasties themselves, and must first of all be studied as such, whereas the question whether some of these versions might also have had a previous unrecorded history is of secondary importance to the contemporary mythology and of doubtful value as pre-contemporary data, although in specific cases some of these data can be used as supporting evidence for an earlier period.

It should be clear, from the way these three choices are stated, that my preference is for c), which I do not deny is a bias, but for which explanations can be given.

The fact that a myth appeared in the historic records in a particular period but not in another period may be entirely accidental, or there may be a reason for it. In China of the Bronze Age, when the use of writing was not widespread, and when there was no printing and thus documents were scarce, historical accident must be taken into consideration when one maintains that a certain historical event did *not* take place or that a certain mythological story did *not* exist simply because we have no evidence for it. Over such accidents we have no control, but I do not believe we have to wait for the day when we are sure that we have had enough data to make our interpretations. And I have a number of reasons for my belief.

In the first place, I share the belief of most students of mythology that myths belong to, express, and are articulated with, primarily and essentially, the culture and society of which they are a part. Myths of the Eastern Chou, for instance, were alive, being told, and being recorded during the Eastern Chou period, and can and should be studied, first and foremost, as the myths of the culture of the Eastern Chou China. For the myths of the Shang, Western Chou, and Han Dynasties, we do likewise. Thus, on the positive side, we have the mythologies of the Shang, Western Chou, and Eastern Chou. None of these probably can ever be complete, and whenever new data appear for any one of these periods we make additions. When additions become significant qualitatively, we make revisions of our working hypotheses for the interpretation of the history of mythologies of these periods. We certainly do not wait for completeness for any one of these periods before we make our interpretation, nor can we pull some data from a later period to push into an earlier period other than to supplement or support the mythology of that earlier period of which we already know.

In the second place, from history and archaeology alike, we have had a fairly good picture of cultural development of ancient China from Shang through Han. When we study the mythologies of these periods we are not studying them in isolation, but have a highly reliable series of cultural contexts in which myths existed. If the absence of a certain mythological motif is compatible with a certain cultural and social context, but its presence is compatible with another context, then the absence may not be accidental. In other words, when we make a judgment on the history of myths, we have good and reliable contextual checks, and are not playing games or guessing.

Last but not least, a literate documentation of the entire period of our concern does exist, although it is not complete and never will be. From the Shang Dynasty on, there is an unbroken chain of written documents relating to a variety of events and phases of life. There is certainly an imbalance of the kinds of literatures that are preserved intact, but as far as their contents are concerned there is no valid reason to maintain that the existence and non-existence of specific mythical stories are entirely due to a skewed probability of preservation. Moreover, myth occupied a frontal and vital position in ancient Chinese ideology, a fact that is amply indicated by the wide occurrence of mythological elements in almost every Eastern Chou text. Therefore, the existence and non-existence of specific mythological motifs in the existing documents of different periods are significant *in themselves.*

I would be the last to say that the historical data for making a thorough and complete interpretation of ancient Chinese mythology exist. But I foresee no immediate possibility of discovering more written documents of Shang and Chou periods that will qualitatively increase our present knowledge, and I believe that with whatever data we already have a working hypothesis for the interpretation of ancient Chinese myths is not only necessary but also possible.

This paper initiates such studies with a classification of the principal types of ancient Chinese myths. I propose to group the Shang and Chou myths into four categories: nature myths; myths of the world of gods and its separation from the world of man; myths of the natural calamities and human saviors; and myths of ancestral heroes. (For other classificatory schemes, see Y. P. Shen 1925; C. Hsüan 1928; T. K. Cheng 1932; Izushi 1943; Mori 1944; Yüan 1960; Bodde 1961.) Needless to say, the boundaries of these categories are diffuse, and overlapping between types is a rule rather than an exception.

Nature Myths

A natural order confronted any early civilization in any part of the world, and it remained for the people to characterize and deify the landscape, in which they lived and on which they made a living, in a distinctive manner that distinguishes the early religion of one people from that of another. From the oracle bone inscriptions and from such Chou texts as *Chou Li,* one gains an insight into the conception of the natural order of the Chinese people during the Shang and Chou periods as well as the religious beliefs and rituals of its concern. Moreover, the conception and religious beliefs and rituals changed during the time span of these two ancient Dynasties.

In the oracle bone inscriptions, there are records of rituals and sacrifices made to the various deities of nature, and indications that the various natural phenomena were regarded as possessing spirit and influence. There was a Supreme Being, the *Ti* or *Shang Ti;* there were spirits of the sun, the moon, clouds, wind, rain, snow, earth, the four directions, mountains, and rivers (M. C. Ch'en 1956: 561ff; M. C. Chen 1936a; 1936b). There were possibly stories relating to each of these natural spirits in the Shang oral tradition, but the information of such stories, if they indeed existed, is largely lost. Such a natural order and the world of natural gods continued into the Chou ideology, as attested by many literary references to the various natural spirits recorded in *Shih Ching* and in a number of Eastern Chou and later documents, such as *Li Chi*. Stars also figured in the Chou conception of nature,[2] but its absence in the Shang records may just be an accident.

Mythological data concerning the natural order during both the Shang and the Chou Dynasties are singularly rare. We can describe, in this connection, no more than some brief references to the Supreme Being, Shang Ti, his court, the concept of Heaven, and the deities of the sun and moon.

The oracle bone inscriptions made frequent references to Ti or Shang Ti (M. C. Ch'en 1936a; 1936 b; 1956); the latter term shows that Ti is located somewhat "above" (*shang*), although there is definitely no evidence that it was identified with the sky or with an abstract concept of Heaven. Shang Ti was, in Shang's view, the Supreme Being, having the ultimate authority over the human world—its harvest, outcome of warfare, building of a city, and the welfare of the profane king. It was also the ultimate cause for starvation, flood, sickness, and other misfortunes. It had a court, consisting of several natural spirits, such as the sun, the moon, the wind, and the rain; when the court was referred to as a group, it was characterized as a court of five officers. These officers carried out errands for Shang Ti, and executed its wishes. The kings of the Shang, however, did not appeal directly to Shang Ti for requests, and there is no record in the oracle bone inscriptions that sacrifices were made to it or given in its name. Shang Ti was accessible to the ancestors of the kings, and whenever the king made a request for harvest or for good weather, he made it directly to the spirits of the ancestors, who in turn made it known to the Supreme Being. In fact, there are a number of indications that the separation of the Supreme Being from the ancestors was not at all a clear-cut one,

2. Poem "Ta Tung," in "Hsiao Ya" of *Shih Ching:*
In Heaven there is a River Hal
Looking down upon us so bright.
By it sits the Weaving Lady astride her stool
Seven times a day she rolls up her sleeves.
But though seven times she rolls her sleeves
She never makes wrap or skirt.
Bright shines that Draught Ox,
But can't be used for yoking to a cart.
In the east is the Opener of Brightness,
In the west, the Long Path.
All-curving are the Nets of Heaven,
Spread there in a row.
In the south there is a Winnowing Fan;
But it cannot sift, or raise the chaff.
In the north there is a Ladle,
But it cannot scoop wine or sauce. (translated, Waley 1960)

and that the Supreme Being can probably be regarded as either a sum total or an abstraction of the remote ancestors of the kings. In this connection it is interesting to note that this Shang conception of Shang Ti was not carried over by the Chou rulers. In the Chou world view, there was also a Shang Ti, similarly playing the role of a Supreme Being, but Shang Ti of Western Chou became identified with Heaven and separated from the world of ancestors.

Both the name of sun and of moon appeared in oracle bone inscriptions in ritual connections, but there are also references to a *tung mu* (Eastern Mother) and a *hsi mu* (Western Mother) (M. C. Ch'en 1936a:22, 131-132). In *Shan Hai Ching,* the Supreme Being is referred to as *Ti Chün,*[3] and among Ti Chün's wives and consorts there is a *Hsi Ho,* who gave birth to ten suns, and a *Ch'ang Hsi,* who gave birth to twelve moons. In *Li Sao* of *Ch'u Tz'u* reference is also made to Hsi Ho as the goddess of the sun, but in *Chiu Ko* (also of *Ch'u Tz'u*) the sun is referred to as Tung Chün (The Eastern Lord). The Western Mother, the moon goddess, becomes personified in the Eastern Chou texts as a powerful deity dwelling in K'un-lun Mountain in the west. *Shan Hai Ching* pictures the Hsi Wang Mu (Western Queen Mother) as a queer-looking creature, with a tail like a leopard and teeth like tiger, but in *Mu T'ien Tzu Chuan* she becomes a highly sophisticated monarch ruling a paradise and capable of composing poems.

Differing from the above picture of natural spirits, which in the main seems to have been carried into the Shang and Chou civilizational periods from an animistic basis, a system of cosmogonic formations and constructions did not appear in the ancient Chinese literature until the Eastern Chou period. There is only negative evidence for the apparently extreme view that the Shang and Western Chou Chinese did not consider the questions of the origin of the natural order worth asking, but there is positive indication that such interest was not widely documented until the Eastern Chou period.

In the Eastern Chou Chinese conception, the cosmos was in the beginning a chaos, which was dark and without bounds and structure. The natural order as it existed in the contemporary period came into being subsequently in two separate ways. We may call one of these the Separation Thesis and the other the Trans-

3. Hsüan Chu (1928, vol. 2, p. 86) was perhaps the first to state that "The supreme god in Chinese mythology may be the so-called Ti Chün." See also T. K. Cheng (1932: 146); M. J. Kuo (1945: 8-9); and P. C. Hsü (1946).

formation Thesis. These two conceptions apparently prevailed during the Eastern Chou period, independent of each other.

The Separation Thesis applies the principle of multiplication: The Chaos was One, which was divided into two elements (which in some texts were referred as the *yang,* or masculine, and *yin,* or feminine); the Animate and Inanimate Nature was formed from the original Two Elements. Similar in principle to the widespread World Parent myths, this Separation Thesis of cosmological formation is not fully represented by the existent pre-Ch'in literature as myths, although it was widely subscribed to by philosophers of the Eastern Chou. But its existence is unquestionably implied in *Chuang Tzu* and *T'ien Wen* of *Ch'u Tz'u*. *T'ien Wen* also refers to the eight pillars on earth that supported Heaven ("How are the Ladle's Handle and the Cord tied together? How was Heaven's Pole raised? How do the Eight Pillars of Heaven keep it up? Why is there a gap in the south-east?" translated Hawkes 1959: 47), and to a giant turtle on the back of which the Heaven is sometimes said to have been supported "When the Great Turtle walks along with an island on his back, how does he keep it steady?" (Hawkes 1959: 51). In Han documents fuller forms of the World Parent myths are seen to have developed and diversified, bringing about such different cosmogonic myths as the Fu Hsi and Nü Wa tale (Y. T. Wen 1956) and one version of the Pan Ku story.[4] For the Shang and Western Chou periods, the only suggestion of a World Parent myth is seen in a Shang Dynasty wood carving (C. Li 1957a: 26) which depicted what may possibly be seen as the prototype of the coiled pair of snakes which in Eastern Chou and Han definitely symbolized Fu Hsi and Nü Wa. The wide distribution of the World Parent myth in the Pacific regions (Rooth 1957: 501) is also indicative of its great antiquity.

The Transformation Thesis, better documented by Eastern Chou texts, is less ambitious. It simply states that certain natural elements were transformed out of the bodily parts of mythical creatures, but makes no explicit claim that this was the cosmological origin. In *Shan Hai Ching,* no less than three creatures performed such deeds:

4. *San Wu Li Chi,* by Hsü Cheng, as quoted in *T'ai P'ing Yü Lan,* vol. 2: "The universe was opaque like egg. P'an Ku grew within. After eighteen thousand years, the heaven and the earth became separated; the *yang* and the clear became heaven, and the *yin* and the unclear became earth. In between, P'an Ku underwent nine transformations each day, and was god to Heaven and sage to Earth. Heaven rose one *chang* each day, and Earth thickened by one *chang* each day, and P'an Ku grew by one *chang* each day. This happened for eighteen thousand years. Heaven was extremely high, and Earth was extremely deep, and P'an Ku was extremely tall. Consequently, Heaven is separated by Earth by ninety thousand *lis.*"

Chu Yin: The deity of Chung Mountain is called Chu Yin. Day arrives when he opens his eyes, and night falls when he closes them; his heavy breaths make winter, and his light breaths make summer; he does not drink, eat, or breathe; when he breathes he brings about the wind; his length is a thousand *li*, and he lies to the east of Wu Ch'i; his appearance: a human face, a snake body, and of red color; he lives under Chung Mountain (*Hai Wai Pei Ching,* paraphrased).

Chu Lung: At Mountain Chang Wei is a deity with a human face, snake body, and red color . . . . When he closes his eyes comes darkness and when he opens them comes the light . . . . (*Ta Huang Pei Ching,* paraphrased).

Nü Wa: There is a country called Shu T'u, occupied by the descendants of Tuan Hsü. There are ten deities, called the intestines (or the abdomen) of Nü Wa, out of which they were transformed . . . . (*Ta Huang Hsi Ching,* paraphrased).

Although Nü Wa did not, in the record of *Shan Hai Ching,* give rise to natural beings, he (or she) must have played a part in the formation of the world, as testified to by the questions asked in *T'ien Wen,* "How was Nü Wa fashioned?" In Ying Shao's *Feng Su T'ung,* compiled in the Eastern Han Dynasty, Nü Wa is said to have made human beings out of the clay. Whether the question in *T'ien Wen* made reference to Nü Wa as a human creator or to Nü Wa as a transforming mythic creature during the Eastern Chou period, there is no evidence to indicate. Hsü Shen, in *Shuo Wen,* also an Eastern Han text, says that "Wa was a divine woman in ancient times, known to have been transformed into the natural entities," seeming to suggest the latter possibility. Another version of Pan Ku's creation of the world, in which he was transformed into the natural entities rather than instrumental in the separation of Heaven and Earth[5], can be viewed as a final complete version of the Eastern Chou Thesis of Transformation.

The World of Gods and Its Separation from the World of Men

Throughout the Shang and Chou periods, there was a persistent conviction that the world of gods was accessible to the world of

5. *Wu Yün Chi Nien Chi,* by Hsü Cheng, as quoted in *Yi Shih,* vol. 1: "In the beginning P'an Ku was born. As he died he was transformed: breath became wind and clouds, voice became thunder, left eye became sun, right eye became moon, four limbs and five bodies became four poles and five mountains, blood became

men but, whereas in earlier periods such accessibility was taken for granted, in later periods the communication between the two worlds in some traditional versions became difficult and in others was completely severed.

In the oracle bone inscriptions of the Shang Dynasty, the act of the ancestors in meeting the gods was referred to as *pin*. Dead ancestors were often seen, in the records of the kings, to *pin* Shang Ti, in the course of which the kings' requests from the profane world were turned over to the Supreme Being (M. C. Ch'en 1936a: 122; 1956:573; H. H. Hu 1959). Records of ancestors' meetings with the sun god are also preserved. In Eastern Chou literatures, traditions of such nature have yet to appear. In *Yao Tien* (of *Shu Ching*), the Emperor Yao was said to *pin* the deities of the Four Doors, asking advice about the virtue of his possible heir, Shun; in *Meng Tzu* (chapter of Wan Chang), the ancient Emperor Yü is said to have visited Ti frequently; in *Mu T'ien Tzu Chuan*, King Mu of Chou was said to *pin* the Western Queen Mother, possibly a sophisticated version of the earlier Moon Goddess. Of particular significance is the record of the visit to Heaven by Ch'i, allegedly the founding ancestor of the Hsia Dynasty. In *Shan Hai Ching*, we find the following myth:

> Beyond the Southwestern Sea, south of the Ch'ih-shui River, and west of the Floating Sands, a man wears two black snakes in his ears and rides on two dragons. He is the Lord K'ai [or Ch'i in other texts, both meaning "to open"] of the Hsia. K'ai visited Heaven three times, and brought down to Earth the *chiu pien* and the *chiu ko* (*Ta Huang Hsi Ching*, paraphrased).

Chiu pien and *chiu ko* are interpreted as the prayers, dances, and songs used on ritual occasions, and this myth is in ancient China a rare "charter" for the rituals in the Malinowskian sense. In *T'ien Wen* of *Ch'u Tz'u*, practically the same story is repeated, but K'ai (referred to as Ch'i in this context) is here said to have visited the Supreme Being himself. Kuo P'u's annotation to *Shan Hai Ching* says that the same story is also recorded in the *Bamboo Annals.*

---

rivers, veins became landforms, muscles became soil, hairs of the head and beards became stars, skins and skin-hairs became grasses and trees, teeth and bones became metals and jades, marrows became precious stones, sweat became rains and lakes, and bodily worms and fleas became the common people." *Wu Yün Li Nien Chi,* as quoted in *Kuang Po Wu Chi,* vol. 9: "Lord P'an Ku had dragon bones and a snake body. His breath turned into winds and rains, his blow became thunders and lightnings; daylight came when he opened his eyes, and night came when he closed them."

In the Eastern Chou period, in addition to such mythological tales about the intercommunication of the world of gods with the world of ancestors, there appeared in the literature additional records concerning a world different and separate from our own, which was beautified, idealized, occupied by gods and men of a totally different age, but still sometimes accessible by human efforts. There are three kinds of such world.

The first is the world of gods, such as the K'un-lun and Hsüan-p'u described in *T'ien Wen, Mu T'ien Tzu Chuan, Chiu Chang,* and in such Han and later texts as *Huai Nan Tzu. Mu T'ien Tzu Chuan* says that in the Hsüan-p'u, "there are creeks and fountains, the climate is mild and windless, and birds and animals live an easy life." Such a gods' world was accessible in some cases through a tree trunk, and *Chiu Chang* says that when people go to the K'un-lun they "live as the heaven and the earth and illuminate as brightly as the sun and the moon." *Huai Nan Tzu* divides the K'un-lun and Hsüan-p'u world into three levels: going into the first level makes a man immortal, going into the second level makes him capable of making the wind and the rain, and going into the top level makes him a deity.

The second is the world of foreign lands, such as the country of Chih Min, the country of Wo, and the country of Tu-kuang in *Shan Hai Ching,* and the country of Chung-pei and the country of Hua-hsü in *Lieh Tzu,* where people live a paradisial life, do not die, and enjoy nature and its animals (C. Hsüan 1928, vol. 1: 99-105).

The third is the world of remote antiquity, separated from the contemporary age by a fathomless depth of time, as is the above world separated by a fathomless distance of space. The most famous worlds of this kind are those mentioned in *Chuang Tzu* when the world was ruled by such ancient sages as "Jung-ch'eng Shih, Ta-t'ing Shih, Po-huang Shih, Chung-yang Shih, Li-lu Shih, Li-hsü Shih, Hsüan-yüan Shih, Ho-hsü Shih, Tsun-lu Shih, Chu-jung Shih, Fu-hsi Shih, and Shen-nung Shih, when people made cords and used them, enjoyed their food and clothes, content in their customs and habitation. Neighboring countries were within sight and each heard the sounds of chickens and dogs made in the other countries, but their inhabitants did not intercommunicate throughout their lives." It is possible that in formulating this world of the ancient sages the Eastern Chou Chinese utilized oral traditions of their pre-civilizational stage of culture or of their Neolithic neighbors. But in the present connection these concepts are significant for picturing a paradisial world different from that of the Eastern Chou Chinese.

The significance of the Eastern Chou elaboration and diversification of the world of gods is made clear and instructive by another group of Eastern Chou myths in which, however, the central theme is the separation of the world of gods from the world of ancestors by a pair of gods, Ch'ung and Li. *Shan Hai Ching* and *Shu Ching* both have brief references to Ch'ung and Li and their roles, but the most complete story is preserved in *Kuo Yü* (*Ch'u Yü* chapter):

King Chao of Ch'u (515-489), puzzled by the *Shu Ching's* statement about the separating of Heaven from Earth, asks his minister: "If it had not been thus, would the people have been able to ascend to Heaven?" To which the minister, after making denial, supplies his own metaphorical explanation: Anciently, men and spirits did not intermingle. At that time there were certain persons who were so perspicacious, single-minded, and reverential that their understanding enabled them to make meaningful collation of what lies above and below, and their insight to illumine what is distant and profound. Therefore the spirits would descend into them. The possessors of such powers were, if men, called *hsi* (shamans), and, if women, *wu* (shamannesses). It is they who supervised the positions of the spirits at the ceremonies, sacrificed to them, and otherwise handled religious matters. As a consequence, the sphere of the divine and the profane were kept distinct. The spirits sent down blessings on the people, and accepted from them their offerings. There were no natural calamities.

In the degenerate time of Shao-hao. . . . , however, the Nine Li (a troublesome tribe. . . .) threw virtue into disorder. Men and spirits became intermingled, with each household indiscriminately performing for itself the religious observances which had hitherto been conducted by the shamans. As a consequence, men lost their reverence for the spirits, the spirits violated the rules of men, and natural calamities arose. Hence the successor of Shao-hao, Chuan-hsü, charged Ch'ung, Governor of the South, to handle the affairs of Heaven in order to determine the proper places of the spirits, and Li, Governor of Fire, to handle the affairs of Earth in order to determine the proper places of men. And such is what is meant by 'cutting the communication between Heaven and Earth' (paraphrases by Derk Bodde).

The significance of this tale in the Eastern Chou context will be further discussed in another article, but in the present connection it helps to clarify certain points concerning the myths mentioned so far under the present heading. It suggests, first of all, that the communication between the world of gods and the world of men was carried out, in practice if not in conception, by priests, shamans, and/or magicians. But this does not apply to the Shang conception, where the deceased ancestors visited the Shang Ti in person. The Shang kings, when alive, had to communicate with the Shang Ti through deceased ancestors by the medium of rituals, and in this sense the world of gods and the world of ancestors were in direct communication, but access to the world of gods *and* ancestors must be through the world of men by means of rituals and priests. The Ch'ung Li story, therefore, suggests that the "medium" interpretation for the communication between the worlds of gods and ancestors *and* the world of men indicates a separation of the world of ancestors from the world of gods. It further suggests that "cutting the communication between Heaven and Earth" may mark a contemporary effort to set the world of gods apart from the world of ancestors *and* men, which helped to make the world beyond the contemporary society become a paradise for idealization and anxiety.

Natural Calamities and Human Saviors

As mentioned above, in the Shang cosmology the world of nature and the world of men were essentially in harmony but basically distinguishable. Ancestors and gods were sometimes interchangeable, and their worlds overlapped even if they did not totally coincide. This attitude seems to prevail in the Western Chou period, according to the small number of literary data at our disposal, but starting in the Eastern Chou period the two worlds became significantly separated. There is, moreover, additional information from the Eastern Chou period to suggest that these two worlds not only underwent separation but also became dichotomized. The world of gods, by virtue of the presence of the Supreme Being and of the natural powers upon which men depended for living, constantly presided over the world of ancestors and men, but its authority was being questioned or even challenged in the Eastern Chou myths. In the contest of men against gods, men were often the losers, but occasionally the roles were reversed. Whatever the outcome, the mere fact that men challenged the authority of the world of gods, for which they often showed contempt instead of reverence, is a highly significant fact.

There is, for instance, the story of K'ua-fu, who, as told in *Shan Hai Ching,* tried to race with the moving sun, but ended up dying of thirst. There is, again in *Shan Hai Ching,* the story of Hsing

T'ien, who struggled against the Supreme Ti for authority and was decapitated by Shang Ti, but who stayed unconquered in spirit, using nipples for eyes and navel for mouth and playing with a spear and a shield.

Then there is the story recorded in Ssu-ma Ch'ien's *Shih Chi* about the insult King Wu-yi gave to Heaven by playing with a wooden figure that was given the name of God of Heaven, and by shooting a leather sac filled with blood and calling this act "the shooting of Heaven." The same thing is said to have been done by Duke Yen of Sung, a descendant of Shang, but both he and King Wu-yi of Shang are said to have died a violent death.

Finally, there is the well-known story about Kung-kung's struggle for power against the Shang Ti, his failure, and his knocking himself, in remorse or in anger, against Mountain Pu-chou, felling a pillar supporting Heaven on the earth, and causing the southeastern corner of Heaven to fall down. Kung-kung's story is recorded in *Huai Nan Tzu* in the Han literature, but fragmentary references have been made to the same story in such an Eastern Chou text as *T'ien Wen*.

The Eastern Chou texts are also flooded with stories about natural calamities and human saviors, seeming to imply that the world of gods, besides being remote and inaccessible, was not to be relied upon and was often responsible for human suffering, and that it was the deeds of ancestral saviors who rescued men from calamity. Occasionally the calamity was brought about as a punishment from the gods for human evil, but more often it just came for no reason at all. The natural calamities took a variety of forms, such as a rain of blood, the descent of ice during summertime, the reverse of day and night, and the widespread appearance of queer and powerful animals and birds who were maneaters; but the most important and severest calamities were two: drought and flood.

Drought and flood are known to have been the two natural enemies of China as well as mankind in general since the beginning of historic record, and the mythical treatment of these calamities is essentially a reflection of historic phenomena. The oracle bone inscriptions of the Shang Dynasty made references to both catastrophes, and such references can be found throughout the Chou literature. It is significant to point out, however, that myths concerning drought and flood did not begin to appear in the literature until the Eastern Chou period, and there they appeared in symbolic juxtaposition with contemporary cultural and mythological contexts.

The drought myth took the form of making ten suns in the sky, causing tremendous heat and famine. In Eastern Chou literatures, there is no complete record of a whole myth of the ten suns, but according to fragmentary references in *Chuang Tzu, T'ien Wen, Chi Nien,* and *Shan Hai Ching,* one can patch together an Eastern Chou version of the complete myth that appears in the Han text of *Huai Nan Tzu:*

> Ten suns appeared in the sky, burning the grains and killing the plants. The people became starved . . . . Yi [the Archer] undertook to shoot the ten suns.

The story of the ten suns and that about Yi the Archer seem to have had separate origins, and it has been frequently suggested that this myth represents the survival version of an ancient story associated with sun worship and the saving of the sun from eclipse (Kaizuka 1947: 4; Sugimoto and Mitarai 1950). No matter what the origins of the constituent themes of this myth are, in this myth the ten suns appeared as a natural calamity and Yi appeared as a human savior, and it is in this perspective that it must be considered as a story having a structural meaning.

The flood, in Eastern Chou myths, came as the result of several different phenomena. In *Meng Tzu,* a flooded China is described as the primeval condition of the land, and in many other contexts flood came on account of Kung-kung, either because he knocked down a part of heaven and made the flood pour in, or because of his evil doings the Ti flooded China to punish man. The human saviors, in this case, are Kun and Yü (C. K. Ku 1930; T. H. Chao 1954). It is often said that Kun tried to build dikes and dams to stop the deluge from spreading, but failed. Kun was killed by the Emperor as a result, according to some versions. Yü, described by some texts as Kun's son, succeeded to Kun's assignment and accomplished his task by changing to the ditch method. Again, the gods' evil efforts against man in the form of flood were in vain, thanks to ancestral saviors. In the course of Kun's efforts to save the world from deluge, *Shan Hai Ching* records, he was desperate enough to have tried to steal some magic earth from the God in order to fill the water. His theft was discovered, and Shang Ti executed him, not considering that the theft was undertaken for human welfare.

Heroes and Their Descents

The three types of myths described above are all cosmogonic in nature; in them are found the origin and, to a lesser extent, the structure of the natural order and the human world in the context of nature. The number and contents of these myths will probably strike any one who is familiar with the mythology of many other lands as being characteristically impoverished (C. Hsüan 1928, vol. 1: 7-8). In fact, references made in Shang and Chou myths exclusively about nature and its various spirits are few, and are more often than not made only in connection with the relation of the world of nature with the world of man.

Hero stories constitute another major category of ancient Chinese myths, and in these we can make no complaint about the paucity of data. In fact, scholars are heard to complain that in ancient China there were too many mythical heroes and not enough stories. It is plain that many of the Chou heroes were euhemerized gods and spirits of nature and the animal kingdom, and this overabundance of heroes of a historic nature can account, at least in a large part, for the rarity of nature myths.

We can describe and discuss the Shang and Chou hero myths under two subcategories: those concerning the birth of founding ancestors of kin groups, and those about the genealogical relationships among the various ancestral heroes and their activities.

Ting Shan (1956: 32) claims that he is able to distinguish, from the oracle bone inscriptions, no less than two hundred names of "totemic clans" during the Shang Dynasty. We may question his specific identifications, but have hardly any reason to doubt that ancient China was occupied, from a kinship point of view, by a large number of different kin groups that warrant the use of the term "clan" or "sib." It is as reasonable to assume that each of these clans had its own myths concerning its original founding. In Western Chou, there were presumably as many clans with their respective origin myths. In fact, we have good reason to assume that the earlier segments of Chinese mythological history were characterized primarily by a panorama of the origin stories of ancestors, as observed by Ku Chieh-kang (1926: 61):

> It is my opinion that during the time period from the Western Chou [and Shang, we might add] through the beginning of the Spring-Autumn period, the people did not trace their origins into remote antiquity. . . . They regarded only the founders of their own groups as the ancestors, and lacked any conceptualization concerning more remote forebears. They recognized that each group had its own ancestors, but did not think there were ancestors shared by many groups in common.

Among these "many" myths of clan ancestors, however, there is a record during the Shang and the Western Chou of the origin myths of only two of these groups, the Tzu clan and the Chi clan. Obviously this is because the Tzu clan happened to be the ruling clan of China during the Shang Dynasty, and the Chi clan the ruling clan during the Chou.

The Tzu clan's origin myth is preserved in such Eastern Chou texts as *Shih Ching* and *Ch'u Tz'u* (*T'ien Wen* and *Li Sao*). In these it is said that Chien Ti, a girl of the Yu-jung "tribe," conceived as a result of contact with a bird. The conception was achieved in several ways according to different versions of the myth: in some versions it was simply stated that the bird caused Chien Ti to be pregnant, and in others Chien Ti conceived by swallowing the egg of a bird. The bird is given in all texts as *hsüan niao,* which is traditionally interpreted as a black (*hsüan*) bird (*niao*), or swallow, but Kuo Mo-jo and others think the term designates a mystic or divine (*hsüan*) bird, meaning, specifically, phoenix. M. J. Kuo (1945: 11) further maintains that, whether swallow or phoenix, the bird is a symbolic expression of the male sexual organ. Furthermore, in these myths Chien Ti is said to have had certain relations with Shang Ti. The poem *Ch'ang Fa* (in *Shang Sung,* in the *Shih Ching*) simply says that "Ti gave birth to Shang," whereas "Hsüan Niao" (in *Shang Sung*) states that the *hsüan niao* was sent by Heaven (Heaven and Ti became identified in the Chou period, it has been noted). *Ch'u Tz'u,* on the other hand, implies that K'u or Kao-hsin, euhemerized versions of the Supreme Being in the Eastern Chou period as well as the Ti-ancestor of the Shang, had something to do with Chien-ti's conception. All of these versions combine to present an origin myth of the Tzu clan, the ruling clan of the Shang Dynasty, in which Chien Ti gave birth to the founding ancestor as a result of contact with a bird, and the birth was further identified with the Shang Ti. It is significant to note that *Shang Sung* is generally considered as being composed by the people of Sung, historically known as the descendants of the Shang Dynasty (K. W. Wang 1956), and that Ch'u, where *Ch'u Tz'u* was composed, inherited a considerable amount of the Shang culture (K. Yang 1941: 151-153). It follows, therefore, that the myths of Shang origins, as recorded in *Shang Sung* and *Ch'u Tz'u,* both of the Eastern Chou period, probably represent an original Shang Dynasty version. Furthermore, the names of K'u, the Supreme Being identified with the ultimate ancestor of the Shang Dynasty's ruling clan, and Chien-ti are held to be found in oracle bone inscriptions as objects of ritual sacrifices. Besides, Fu Ssu-nien (1935) has shown convincingly that the myths of the origin of clansmen from birds or bird eggs were characteristic of the Eastern Yi groups in ancient China, to which the Yin people were closely related in culture (See also Mishina 1948). There is therefore little question that the bird-birth or birth-egg-birth myth of the Shang ruling clan, Tzu, is an authentic piece of the Shang lore (S. T. Yang 1954: 32-33, 40-41; H. W. Yü 1959: 60-69).

The origin myth of the birth of Hou-chi, the founding ancestor of the Chou's Chi clan, by Chiang-yüan, is recorded in *Sheng Min* and *Pi Kung,* in the *Ta Ya* section of *Shih Ching,* generally conceded to be genuinely Western Chou literature, and there is no problem concerning its authenticity and antiquity (C. K. Ku 1926: 61; Y. T. Wen 1956: 73-80). In *Sheng Min,* Chiang Yüan is said to have "trod on God's footprint in the acres (fields)" and became pregnant as a result. After birth, Hou-chi was abandoned in an alley, in a forest, and again on ice, but he survived and grew up under the protection of cattle, sheep, and birds to become the founding father of the Chi clan.

The origin myths of the Shang and Chou ruling clans are the only two such tales that were recorded during the Shang and Western Chou times as far as is known. In the Eastern Chou literature, however, one finds a sudden proliferation of myths on the birth of heroes, who are often referred to as ancestors, and also those on their activities and mutual relations. In the succeeding essay I will attempt to explain why this was so. I shall first suggest here that these new myths may have had the following sources.

The first are the origin myths of old and traditional clans which had not been recorded during the Shang and Western Chou, as far as the literary evidence goes, but were written during the Eastern Chou period. There may be manifold reasons for their appearance at this later time, but I think the following two are the most relevent: that the use of writing was no longer limited to the ruling family and documentation became widespread; and that the ruling Chi clan of Chou began, in Eastern Chou, to lose their dominance and iron grip over the lesser clans, which increased in power, claimed ancient origins, and demanded literary documentation of their forebears. Eastern Chou myths of this source can be exemplified by those of Shao-hao and the so-called Chu-jung Pa Hsing (the Eight Clans of Chu-jung) (H. P. Li 1954: 10-13; Y. T. Wen 1956: 81-116).

A second source of the new Eastern Chou origin myths may lie in the peripheral cultures with which the expanding Eastern Chou Chinese gradually came into contact. It has been pointed out that the Eastern Chou period was one of explosive civilizational expansion, which resulted, among other things, in increasingly frequent contacts with peripheral alien cultures and in the absorption of these cultures into the greater Chinese civilization. It is highly probable that because of this the origin myths of alien clans now found their way into the Eastern Chou literatures. Possible examples of this sort are the stories of Yü, which Ku Chieh-kang considers as having a southern origin, and of Fu-hsi, the "First Ancestor" of the modern Miao people in southwestern China (Ruey 1938).

A third and final source, which is also probably the most important, is the euhemerization of ancient as well as contemporary gods, deities, and mythical animals in Chinese traditions into legendary heroes (C. K. Ku 1926; Maspéro 1924; 1950). One example is the famed Huang-ti, or Yellow Emperor, which is regarded by many scholars as the euhemerized version of the Supreme Being, Shang Ti. Yang Kuan (1941) has devoted a huge volume, *Chung-kuo Shang-ku-shih Tao-lun* (*An Introduction to the Ancient History of China*), and Sun Tso-yun (1941; 1943; 1944a; 1944b; 1945; 1946; 1947) worked out a long series of articles, on the thesis that many of the Eastern Chou and (later) heroes and legendary ancestors were euhemerized versions of mythical beings. Yang Kuan concludes (1941: Preface):

> The sage sovereigns and emperors in the ancient historic legends, after final analysis, have turned out to be nothing but the deities of heaven and earth. The original forms of these [ancient heroes] are as follows.
>
> a) Supreme Being, or Shang Ti: Chün, Ti K'u, Ti Shun, T'ai Hao, Tuan Hsu, Ti Yao, Huang Ti, T'ai Huang
> b) Earth God: Kou Lung, Ch'i, Shao Hao, Hou Yi
> c) Agricultural deity: Hou Chi
> d) Sun and fire gods: Yen Ti, Chu Ming, Chao Ming, Chu Jung, Tan Chu, Huan Tou, Yen Po
> e) River and water deities: Hsüan Min, Feng Yi, Kun, Kung Kung, Shih Ch'en, T'ai Yi
> f) Moutain god: Ssu Yü, Po Yi, Hsü Yu, Kao T'ao
> g) Deities of metal, law or animal husbandry: Wang Hai, Ju Shou, Ch'i, T'ai K'ang
> h) Deities of birds, animals, plants, and trees: Kou Mang, Yi, Hsiang, K'ui, Lung, Chu, Hu, Hsiung, P'i

Some of these identifications are possibly doubtful, but Yang's conclusions in general are valid for demonstrating in many cases the history of change from mythical creatures to ancestral heroes. A possible interpretation for such changes will be presented in the following essay, and elsewhere the nature of some of the mythical animals will be examined more closely.

From these three sources and possibly others, the Eastern Chou origin myths of ancestral heroes multiplied. These heroes, furthermore, were often genealogically related. The genealogical tables worked out according to *Kuo Yü, Shih Pen,* and *Ta Tai Li* are presented in the Chinese text of this paper, published in the *Bulletin of the Institute of Ethnology,* 14. There one finds that practically all ancestral heroes recorded during this period are recorded as descendants of Huang Ti; others that do not belong to this huge genealogical tree of descent likewise cluster around a small number of central figures. Ch'i, the founding ancestor of the Tzu clan, now becomes a descendant of Huang-Ti and a half-brother of Hou-chi, son of Chiang-yüan, the founding mother of the Chi clan of Chou. Even the Chu-jung group is tied into the same system. Many scholars have taken great pains to identify these clusters of genealogical relationships and have advanced the hypothesis that they represent the ethnic classification of ancient China before the Shang Dynasty (P. C. Hsü 1946; W. T. Meng 1933; T. Y. Sun 1941, 1943, 1944a, 1944b, 1945, 1946, 1947; Eberhard 1942). Duly respectful of and sympathetic with such efforts, I must still say that such undertakings cannot be very fruitful. To explain why this is so, we must understand the reasons behind the euhemerization and hierarchal relationships of these ancient heroes, a subject to be discussed in the following essay.

Remarks

On the basis of the evidence presented above, one can divide the Shang and Chou periods in ancient Chinese history, in the context of which the myths presented above made their appearance, into three major stages: Shang, Western Chou, and Eastern Chou. In the Shang Dynasty, the myths consisted of the origin myths of ancestral heroes and the organization of the natural deities. Ancestors and deities were diffuse and their respective worlds overlapped. The Supreme Being was conceptually identified with the ancestors in abstraction or with one certain legendary ancestor. As far as the literary evidence goes, the myths on the origin of the cosmic order, on the separation of the ancestral and the gods' worlds, and on the natural calamities and human saviors did not appear or, if they did, they were not socially and religiously important enough to appear in the extensive literatures left from that dynastic period.

The same can be said for the Western Chou. Again as far as the literary evidence is concerned, there were myths of ancestral heroes as well as myths of gods and deities belonging to the natural order. There is no existing evidence of the other types of myths. There is, however, one decisive difference between the Shang and the Western Chou mythology: whereas the Shang world view did not clearly distinguish the worlds of ancestors and of gods, the Western Chou Chinese advanced a major step in this direction by placing the Supreme Being in Heaven and by giving the king the status of "Son of Heaven" instead of identifying his ancestors with the gods and the Shang Ti.

A number of new characteristics and profound changes in the realm of mythology came with the Eastern Chou period. (1) The number of ancestral heroes multiplied in the literature. (2) Many of the gods and deities of a supernatural world became euhemerized into legendary heroes. (3) These ancestral heroes became blood relatives clustering around a small number of genealogical trees. (4) The world of ancestors and that of the gods became separated, each developing and being elaborated distinctively. (5) These two worlds became further dichotomized into more inimical than close and friendly relationships. (6) The human world was persecuted by the gods, but was saved by ancestral heroes. (7) The origin and formation of the natural world, becoming a separate entity from men and ancestors, was explained in a number of rudimentary myths of genesis.

I am by no means the first to point out such changes, nor the first one to try to explain them. Many scholars are of the opinion that such characterizing terms as "rarity," "less developed than other civilizations," and "abundance" primarily reflect the negative nature of the evidence and the hopeless situation in regard to Chinese texts, few of which are preserved and those by accident. In other words, what we know about ancient Chinese mythology is only a fraction of what actually existed. It follows, according to such reasoning, that the existing evidence provides insufficient data for any ambitious attempt to interpret it and the latter is bound to fail. Other scholars have tried to fill the gaps by a so-called "ethnological" method, whereby a complete mythology of each period in ancient China is said to have been worked out by utilizing materials which had existed earlier and had survived into the periods in which they were recorded.

Other scholars accept what there is as reliable and representative data and have attempted to interpret the mythological history of ancient China as it is known. It has been suggested, for instance, that the rarity of nature myths results from the interest of the ancient as well as the modern Chinese in the realm of the human world and in practical politics and social relations, and thus from a corresponding indifference or lack of interest in natural science or fiction (Bodde 1942; 1961: 405). Some scholars of note have even advanced such explanations as that the Chinese, living in a difficult environment not richly endowed in natural resources, had to work hard and thus had no time to indulge in dreams (as quoted in C. Hsüan 1928, vol. 1: 8-10).

But most scholars agree to a very powerful and reasonable interpretation: the euhemerization of mythical figures, which was the ultimate explanation for the lack of myths and the plentitude of legendary history in ancient China, is viewed both as a conscious effort on the part of Eastern Chou and Han scholars of the Confucian school to rationalize their mythological legacy from their less knowledgeable and more superstitious ancestors, and as a result of a humanistic and renaissance movement (K. Yang 1941: 125-126; P. C. Hsü 1946; C. C. Feng 1929; K. Yüan 1960: 17). In reviewing the growth of culture history in general in the Huangho Valley, one readily recognizes that the Eastern Chou period was one of revolutionary changes in ancient Chinese society in the realms of economy, political institutions, technology, and art style. It marks a period of intensification and expansion of the Chinese civilization both in depth and in dimension. Technology and knowledge became widespread and even commercialized, and in such an atmosphere a humanistic and renaissance movement must account for the awakening of a large part of the Chinese gentry and peasants alike to a knowledge of the world and thus for a correspondingly diminishing power of the myths to exercise sanctions on the social and political order. There is no question in my mind that this is the answer, held by historic scholars for many centuries, for a general interpretation of the mythological history of ancient China.

I am not, however, completely satisfied. I am not dissatisfied with the answer as such, but rather that it does not go deep enough to explain the specific mechanisms and bring them into focus. In the following essay and elsewhere, I shall present a hypothesis of ancient Chinese mythological changes, which parallels the rationalization theory but further specifies the details of change and links the change in mythology concretely with the change in other realms of culture. Briefly, I wish to advance the hypothesis that myths in ancient China were primarily oriented around kin groups, that kin groups determined not only members of kinship but also relative status of political authority and prestige, that the political system in ancient China in its connections with kinship changed from the Shang to the Eastern Chou, and that myths changed in spirit and in composition concurrent, concomitant, and compatible with such changes in the realm of kinship and kingship.

9 Changing Relationships of Man and Animal in Shang and Chou Myths and Art

Introduction

This essay concerns a small point, but I wish also to make a point which is less small. My specific subject has to do with some aspects of the meaning and function of animals in the mythology and art of the Shang and Chou Dynasties in ancient China, but the larger point I wish to make, which is actually evident, is that it is not enough to consider the animal in mythology and art in isolation in order to understand their meaning and function; it is necessary to consider them also in their mutual relationships and in respect to other aspects of the Shang and Chou civilizations. Also, these relationships can best be recognized and specified, not only in a static situation, but more particularly in a context of change.

Animals figured importantly in the mythology and the art of the Shang and Chou Dynasties. I hardly need to elaborate upon this statement. In myths, the roles played by animals range from progenitors of whole groups of people to agents of gods; from companions of ancestors and heroes to devilish monsters against which heroes fought legendary battles. Furthermore, it is the belief of some historians, such as Yang K'uan (1941: 2-13), that nine out of ten among the ancient sages in Chinese legends were euhemerized versions of animal deities. Others, such as Sun Tso-yün (1941, 1943, 1944a, 1944b, 1945, 1946, 1947), think that many mythological and legendary heroes were in reality chiefs of ethnic and social groups having animals for totemic ancestors. Whether or not this is true, I think it is not an overstatement to say that in the Shang and Chou myths animals were among the most important categories of actors. Throughout the art of the Shang and Chou Dynasties animals of one kind or another, or bodily parts of animals, constituted the majority of decorative elements on such objects as bronze vessels (K. Jung 1941), weapons, utensils, and horse-and-chariot fittings; on several varieties of pottery; on sculptures and inlays of wood, bone, and jade; on lacquer ware; and on personal ornaments of bronze and bone. In addition, they were the leading motifs for

---

Note: Based on a public lecture delivered on December 6, 1962, at Princeton University, Princeton, New Jersey. This essay was originally published in the *Bulletin of the Institute of Ethnology,* Academia Sinica, 16 (Autumn 1963): 115-146.

wood carvings and stone sculptures in the round (Sirén 1929; Bachhofer 1946). Most of these animals are recognizable and identifiable: water buffaloes, deer, rhinoceri, tigers, elephants, sheep, oxen, and other mammals; snakes and other reptiles; silkworms and cicadas; and a variety of birds and fish (C. Li 1957c). Others are animals more mythological than realistic, such as the *t'ao-t'ieh,* the dragon, and the phoenix. It is probably not an overstatement to say that the Shang and Chou art was, on the whole, an animal style of art.

Scholars of ancient China have devoted scores of volumes of work and many lifetimes to both the Shang-Chou myths and the Shang-Chou art. To be sure, controversial issues still abound. But no one can say that this is an unexplored, virgin field of research. In order not to duplicate efforts unnecessarily, I aim to make just a small contribution to the study of these problems, which will concern some aspects of the meaning of animals. It is largely agreed that both mythological and artistic animals assumed some kind of religious and ritualistic significance in the Shang and Chou Dynasties (Waterbury 1942; van Heusden 1952; Ackerman 1945; T. Y. Sun 1944b; Creel 1937b), and I should like to clarify some of the meanings of these animals by demonstrating the functional place they occupied in the Shang-Chou religious and ritualistic life in particular and in their cultural and social life in general.

For without an understanding of the function of these animals in myths and in art, one can hardly appreciate their meaning. The term "animal style of art" or "animal style of mythology" is a category almost as broad as "agriculture" or "pottery," and, thus, it assumes no meaning in the Chinese context unless and until its place in this context is made clear. In commenting upon the works of art in ancient Egypt and Mesopotamia, the late Henri Frankfort ventured to say that one recognizes in these works of art the "outcome not of intellectual calculations but of artistic inspiration." "There was not," he says, "in the mind of the ancient artist, the question, 'How can I render the King as god or as hero?' In his mind was merely, 'Now I must picture His Majesty,' and according to his being an Egyptian or an Assyrian the result was as we have seen" (Frankfort 1948: 11). "Meaning," as a well-defined and abstract concept imposed by us upon the ancient work of art or religion, can serve as a basis for neither structural research nor historic comparison. I therefore wish to concentrate upon the problem of how we recognize and identify subjective perspectives on the part of the authors of myth or art by examining their attitudes toward mythological animals as revealed in their eventual product.

Changing Attitudes of Man toward the Animal

I will proceed with the argument by examining relationships in a context of change. Let us now begin to examine the changing attitudes of man toward the mythological animals as revealed in a changing art, in changing myths, and in other provinces of a changing civilization.

Very broadly, three different and successive styles of bronze art of the Shang-Chou period are distinguishable; they are called Archaic, Middle Chou, and Huai by Bernhard Karlgren (1936, 1937), and Classic, Decadent, and Renaissance by Kuo Mo-jo (1945). The criteria for making such distinctions include inscriptions, the form of the vessels, and the decorative patterns, but we are concerned only with the animals in the decorative art. In the Archaic style, the decorative animals are many and various, forcefully rendered, and emotionally vigorous. The leading single motif is the *t'ao-t'ieh* mask, which often constitutes the central theme of a whole vessel's decoration and around which minor decorative elements center (Fig. 16). "Mysterious," "mythical," vigorous," "potent," and "fantastic" are some of the words that have been used to characterize these animals of the Archaic style, which are indeed awe inspiring, apparently charged with power derived from mythological sanction. Human figures seldom appear; when they do, they usually play a subordinate and submissive role in relation to the decorative animals (Figs. 17, 18).

The Archaic style prevailed during the latter part of the Shang Dynasty and the first years of the Western Chou. Beginning around 950 BC, according to Karlgren, the decorative art was suddenly dominated by the Middle Chou style, which is characterized by the conventionalization of many of the animal figures, the diminishing influence of their mythological and vigorous potency, and the near disappearance of the *t'ao-t'ieh* mask. Animals still dominated the decorative constitutions of many vessels, but their mythological character and vigor were much less apparent. The same trends of development were further intensified after about 650 BC, in the middle of the Spring-and-Autumn period of the first half of the Eastern Chou, when the Huai style came into being. Many of the Archaic style forms and the *t'ao-t'ieh* motif were revived, but they became even more conventionalized and appeared to possess none of the mythical and vigorous power that was inherent in their Archaic style antecedents. For one thing, these conventionalized animals often were small constituent elements, and seldom, if at all, filled any appreciable part of the vessel surface. On the other hand,

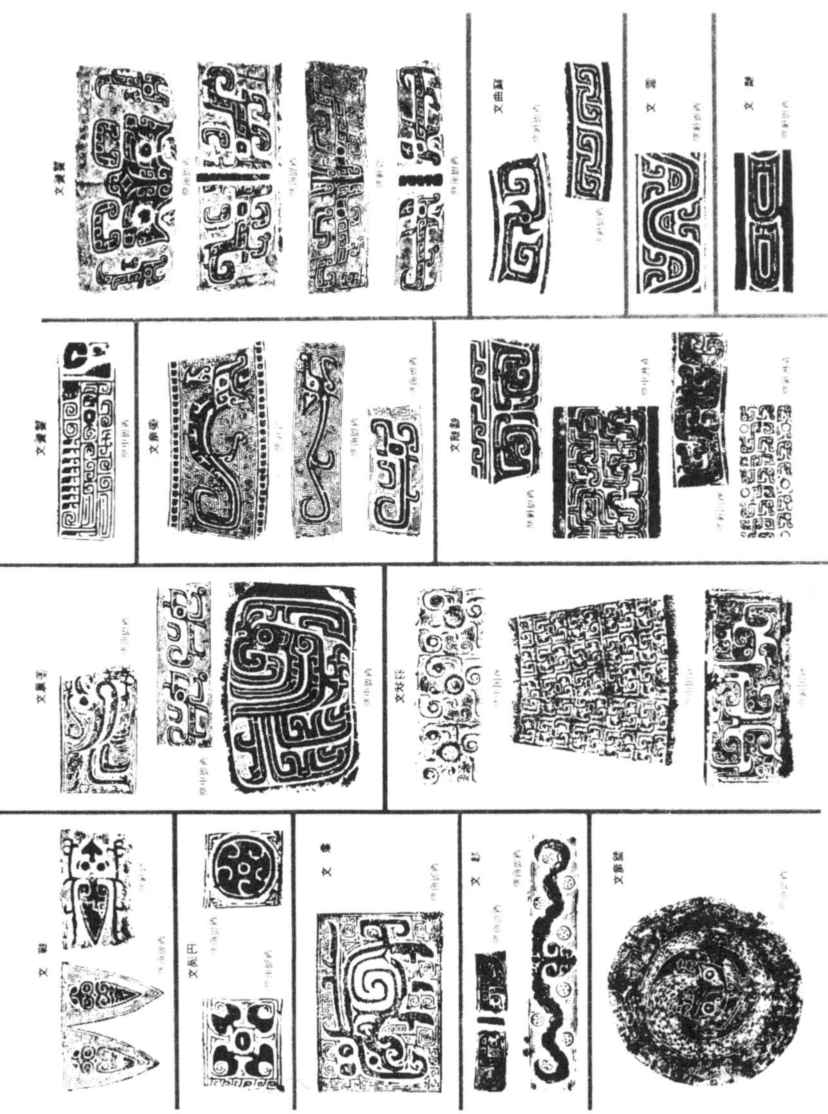

Figure 16. Some Common Decorative Motifs of Shang and Chou Bronzes

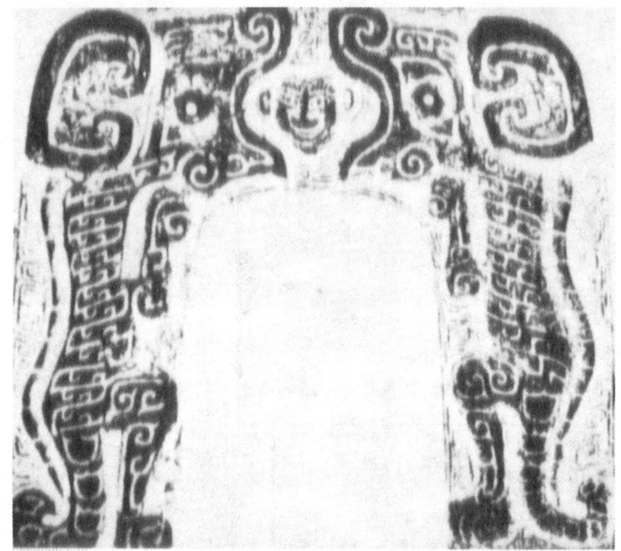

Figure 17. Animals and Men in Archaic Bronze Art

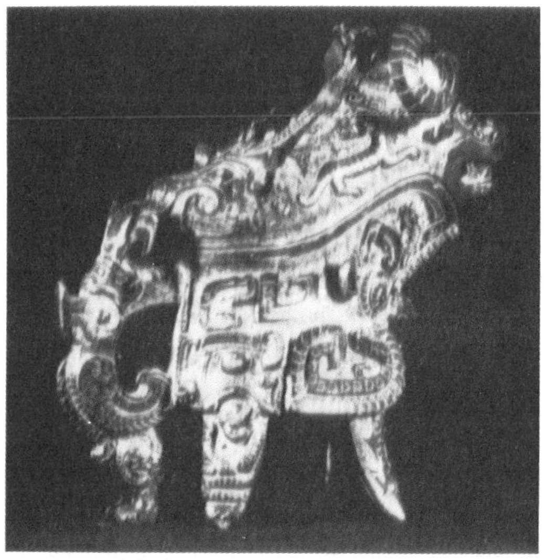

Figure 18. Animals and Men in Archaic Bronze Art

the period of the Huai style witnessed the appearance of the so-called hunting scenes wherein the mythical animals were being subdued or even killed by human archers and warriors (Figs. 19, 20, 21). In short, from the earliest Archaic to the latest Huai style, there is a pronounced change in the decorative animals in two respects. First, the *t'ao-tieh* and other mythical animals appeared vigorous and possessed of a mythological influence and dominating power during the earlier period, whereas they became conventionalized and seem to have been deprived of their supernatural force and attributes during the latter stages. Second, the Shang Dynasty vessel decorations depicted men as subordinate and submissive, whereas men became masters or at least challengers of the animals during the Eastern Chou period. In other words, man's relationship with the mythological animals in art underwent drastic changes from the Shang through the Eastern Chou periods, accomplished by conventionalizing old *t'ao-t'ieh* motifs and naturalizing new animal elements—both indicative of a new attitude toward these mythical animals that can no longer be characterized as reverence or awe.

What is more, similar changes are discernible in the myths of the Shang and Chou periods. Here we cannot concern ourselves with the troublesome problems of the chronology of the various mythological types and motifs, because this would lead to a long discussion which would leave us precisely where we started. It is hoped that the reader will permit the assumption that myths of the ancestral birth of the Shang and Chou groups probably originated during an earlier phase of the Shang-Chou period, and that myths of cosmogonic origins and transformations and those of heroes as saviors of man from natural calamities did not appear until the latter part of the Chou Dynasty. If this is generally valid, we find that in earlier periods the animals, in myths, assumed the following roles: being instrumental in the birth of clan ancestors, such as the relationship between the bird and the Shang's clan; being agents and/or messengers of the deities, such as the phoenix; being divine guardians or protectors of clan ancestors, such as the cattle, sheep, and birds in the poem "Sheng Min" in the *Book of Odes,* where the birth of Hou-chi, ancestor of Chou, was described; and being companions of ancestors in their ascent to the world of gods, such as the two dragons on which Ch'i or K'ai rode to meet the Supreme God in person. I think we are not far off if we say that in the earlier myths man's attitudes toward animals were those of affection, reverence, and awe. Such attitudes, however, were no longer in evi-

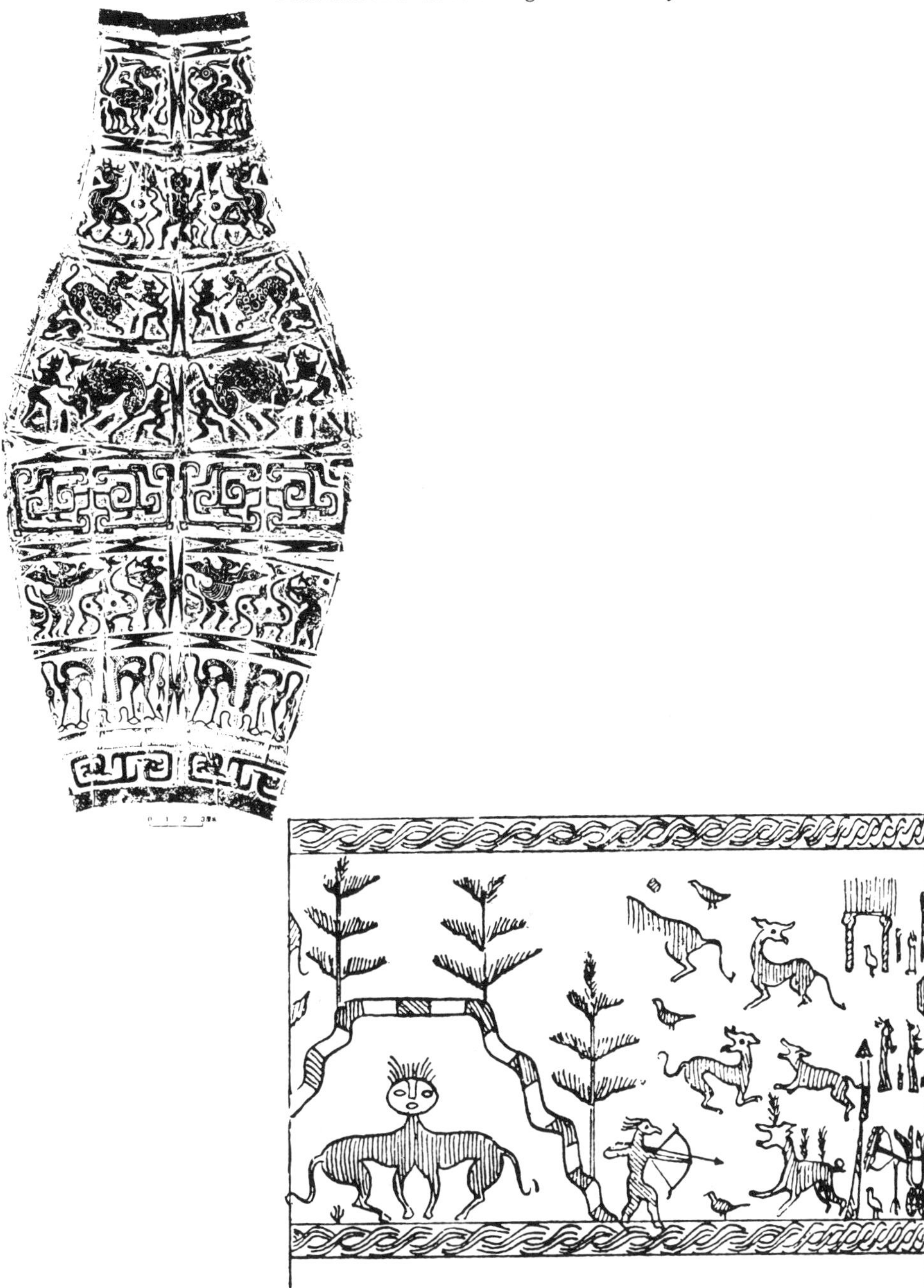

Figure 19. Scenes of Men Fighting Fantastic Animals in the Huai Style Art

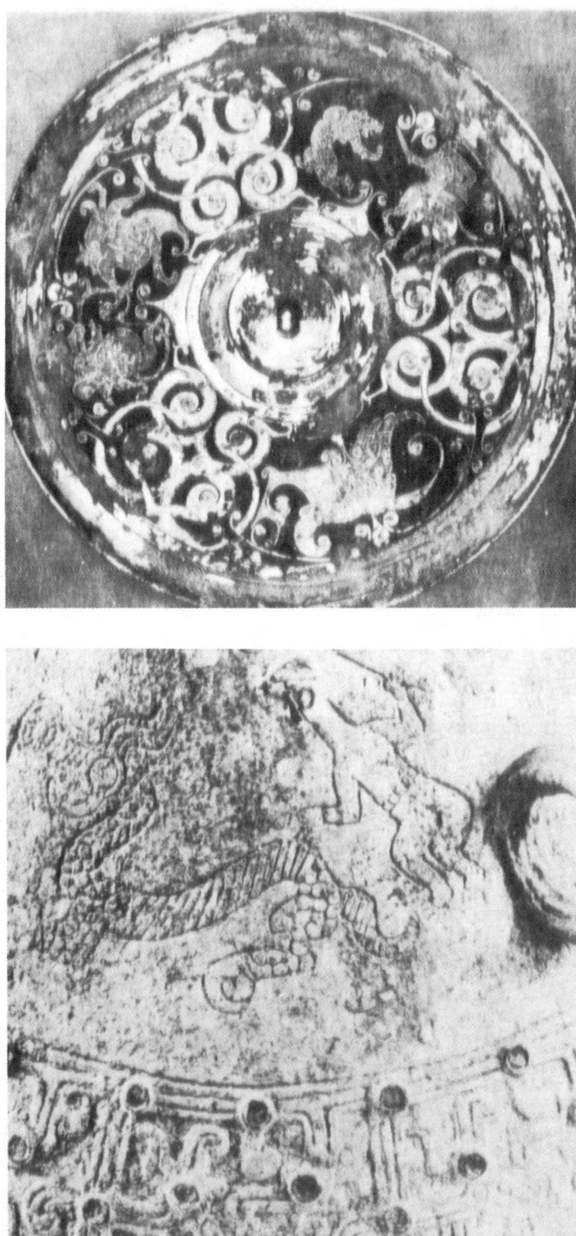

Figure 20. Scenes of Men Fighting Fantastic Animals in the Huai Style Art

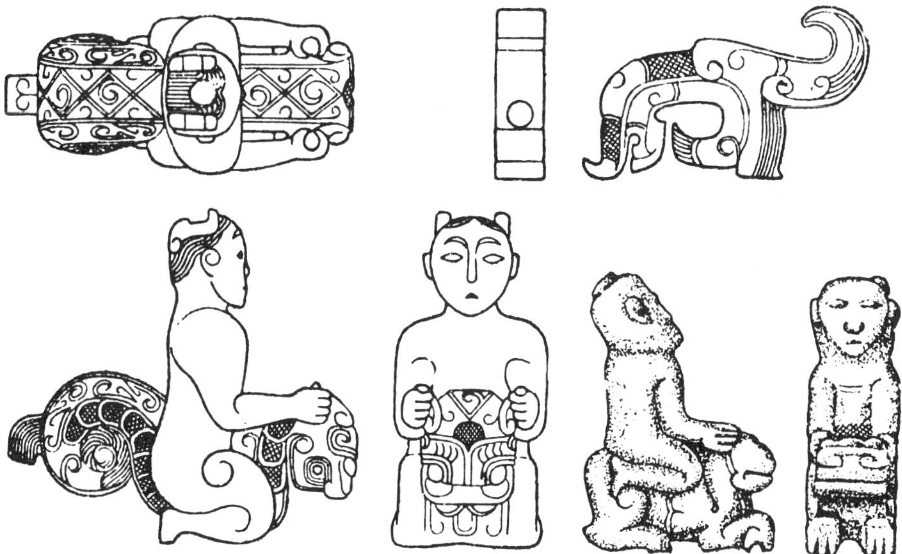

Figure 21. Men Riding Fantastic Animals in the Huai Style Art

dence in the Eastern Chou myths: instead of being protectors or instruments for ancestral birth, many animals became monstrous devils delivering suffering to the human world or enemies against which ancestral heroes fought and performed brave deeds. The best known of these heroes is, of course, Yi the Archer, and he shot down not only roaming man-eating beasts and snakes on earth, but also the symbolic birds of suns which were held responsible for a drought during the period of the so-called Emperor Yao.

Such changes in man's attitudes toward animals are also manifest in other archaeological and historical facts. Of these, I have only to mention the history of scapulimancy. Beginning with the Lung-shan stage of the Chinese Neolithic, the shoulder blades of oxen, deer, sheep, and pigs were scraped, polished, and burned, and their cracks were interpreted to foretell events. This practice was at a peak during the Shang Dynasty when turtle shells were also used for this purpose, and writing was often inscribed on bone to record questions and sometimes also the answers. From these writings we know that the divination was achieved by communication with ancestors through the medium of animal bones. After the downfall of the Shang, scapulimancy suffered a sharp decline, and it became totally negligible toward the end of the Eastern Chou, as indicated by archaeological evidence. The history of scapulimancy, therefore, indicates that in earlier periods the living communicated with the dead through the medium of diviners aided by the substance of animals, but that in later periods animal bones no longer possessed the quality essential for such communications and that divination took other means.

I consider that all these facts combined make a strong case for a changing attitude of man toward animals. In the Shang and the early part of the Chou Dynasties, the mythical animals had a good deal of potency and domination over men, who played subordinate and submissive roles. In the latter part of the Chou Dynasty, man emancipated himself from the mythological dominance of the animal and, at times, became the challenger or even the victor. And, of course, we would like to ask why. Many scholars have provided answers. The most commonly accepted answer is that during the latter part of the Chou Dynasty there was an awakening of intellect and a humanistic movement which was represented and consolidated by the Confucian disciples (K. Yang 1941; Bodde 1961: 372-376; Maspéro 1924: 1-2; 1950: 179-180). I think this answer is quite correct, but I don't think it is sufficient. Its insufficiency lies in the main in its failure to specify the parts of the Shang-Chou cultural and social context that have the most to do with man's change of attitude toward the mythological animal.

An effective and efficient interpretation of the mythological and artistic animals of the Shang and Chou Dynasties must be made, I think, in the light of the total Shang and Chou civilizational development, as reconstructed not only on the basis of archaeology but also on history, and not only on art and ideology but also on the total cultural and social configuration. More specifically, I submit the following hypothesis. The Shang-Chou mythological and artistic animals, in their salient features and their evolutionary sequence of change, must be interpreted according to the changing relationship of gods, ancestors, and animals in the Shang and Chou conceptions of the world.

Attributes of Shang and Chou Kin Groups

In order to make clear the relationship between ancestors and gods in the sacred world, we must first make clear the relationship between ancestors and men in the world of the profane. A brief description must therefore be given to the kinship groups of the Shang and Chou periods.

The Shang and Chou Chinese were organized into a certain number of unilinear kin groups—clans. Ting Shan (1956: 32) was confident that he was able to identify no less than two hundred names of "totemic clans" from the oracle-bone inscriptions of the Shang Dynasty. *Yi Chou Shu* recorded as many as 751 at the time of Chou's conquest of Shang. There is little question that the leading clans of the Shang and Chou were all patrilineal groups (that is, they reckoned their descent along the lines of fathers and sons)[1] or that these clans were tightly organized corporate social groups. Each patriclan had a name—in most cases that of its founding ancestor—carried from one generation to the next by patrilineal descent. Members of the same patriclan with a common name, *hsing,* were normatively forbidden to intermarry, and there is evidence to show that this norm was strictly enforced.[2] *Kuo Yü* explains why there was this marriage taboo:

People having different clan names are also different in virtue, and people of different virtues belong to different categories. Persons of opposite sexes and of different categories intermarry in order to propagate, even if they may be very close. People of the same clan name also have the same virtue, and people of the same virtue converge in mind, and people who converge in mind have the same goal. Persons of opposite sexes but having the same goal do not intermarry, even if they may be very distant from each other, for fear of committing incest.

The author of this passage was apparently an odd sort of geneticist, but some of the concepts expressed here are of crucial importance to our interpretation, as we shall see. Marriage rules clearly distinguished membership within the patriclans, which was further indicated by the kinship terminology (bifurcate merging for uncle-aunt terms and possibly the Omaha type for cousin terms [See Ruey 1954, 1958], to use some of the social anthropologist's

1. Several Eastern Chou and early Han texts, such as *Chuang Tzu* ("Tao Ch'uo"), *Lü Shih Ch'un Ch'iu* ("Shih Chün Lan"), and *Shang Chün Shu* ("K'ai Se"), mention an archaic stage of society, in which "the people knew about their mother but not their father." Some scholars (e.g., H. P. Li 1954: 74-77) treat this as evidence for a matrilinear or matriarchal society in Chinese history. This controversy is not pertinent in the present context; there can be no question that both the Shang and the Chou were both patrilineal and patriarchal. See, also, K. C. Chang (1960), for a possible matrilineal stage during the Neolithic period.

2. *Tso Chuan,* 23rd Year of Hsi Kung: "Union between the same *hsing* will not result in fertile propagation." See also *Tso Chuan* (First Year of Chao Kung), *Lun Yü* ("Shu Erh"), *Li Chi* ("Ch'ü Li"), and *Kuo Yü* ("Chin Yü" and "Cheng Yü").

jargon) as well as by definite privileges and obligations in terms of corporate property, both symbolic and substantive. The latter included such things as titles to land and specialized technological knowledge, which was probably kept secret within the patriclans and patrilineages.[3]

In this connection, we are more interested in the ritual obligations of lineage and clan members. Members of the same patriclan derived their common descent from male ancestors, which fact was symbolized by and crystallized in the ancestor cult. We know from archaeology and history not only some of the procedures and details of some of the related rituals but also a few tangible aspects of these cults, such as the ancestral temple (S. S. Ling 1959a), the ancestral tablet which was apparently a phallic image (M. J. Kuo 1952; S. S. Ling 1959b), and the ceremonial vessels of bronze, pottery, and other materials. In *Li Chi* we find:

In the lord's construction of palaces, the *tsung*-temple is the first thing to consider [to be built], the treasury the next, and the residential quarters the last. In building a house [for home] of a gentleman, the ceremonial vessels come first, storage for wealth next, and utensils for the living, last.

The importance of the ancestral temples and their paraphernalia reflects the importance of ancestral rituals in the Chou institution. *Li Chi* again makes this clear by saying:

The most urgent of the ways to govern is the *li,* or the social rules. The *li* consist of five elements, the most important being the *chi,* or rituals. Rituals are not imposed upon from without, but grow from within.

To reinforce such rules that were supposed to "grow from within," authorities made periodic inspections among the lords to see whether ancestral cults were properly performed.

If the rituals and their tangible associations—the temples, tablets, and treasures—provided the sanction, the reminder, and the symbols for the solidarity of the clans and the lineages, then myths

3. The names of the Shang *tsu* or lineages, as recorded in *Tso Chuan* (Fourth Year of Ting Kung), include Ch'ang Shao (Long Ladle), Wei Shao (Small or Terminal Ladle), and T'ao (Pottery). Near the bronze and pottery workshop remains uncovered in Cheng-chou, archaeologists found clusters of houses in apparent association with the workshops, suggesting ties of lineages or large families with specific handicrafts.

provided the charter, giving the *raison d'être* for such groups. Again in *Li Chi* and *Kuo Yü,* we find the following statement:

> For the progeny who maintains the ancestral temple and the state, it is deceitful to enumerate the deeds of ancestors when these did not exist; imbecile not to know the deeds when these existed; unkind not to publicize the deeds when these were known.

Under such circumstances it is a matter of course that each of these patriclans was associated with a number of myths whereby the ancestors' good deeds were publicized (Karlgren 1946). There are many kinds of such deeds, and they varied with time, as we shall see presently.

This description of the kinship system of the Shang and Chou Chinese is far from complete, but I have tried to make clear the place of myths in this system. There is another significant feature of that system that has not yet been mentioned, but that is particularly relevant to the subsequent discussion—namely, that in both Shang and Chou Dynasties kinship affiliation was a determinant of political status.

To simplify matters, let me say that there were three different situations concerning the relative political status among different patriclans and patrilineages.

(1) The first is the relation between rulers and ruled within the same state. It is commonly known that these groups often belonged to different patriclans. For instance, the ruling lords of the states of Wu, Chin, and Yü were all members of the clan of Chi (the clan of the royal Chou). The common people of Wu were so-called barbarians, those of Chin were descendants of the ancient kingdom of T'ang, and those of Yü were descendants of Yu Yü (S.N. Fu 1930b).

(2) The second is the relation between the ruling groups of different states who had the same clan names, such as the royal Chou and the ruling lords of the states of Lu, Chin, Wei, Yü, and many others. Their relative political status, it is well known, was determined by the so-called *tsung-fa* system, at least in a normative sense. The *tsung-fa* system of Chou is characterized by the fact that the eldest son of each generation formed the main line of descent and political authority, whereas the younger brothers were moved out to establish new lineages of lesser authority. The farther removed, the lesser was the political authority (A. C. Li 1931; H. Li 1957; Y. Sun 1931). There is evidence that such a system existed in

the Shang Dynasty as well (H. H. Hu 1944; S. T. Yang 1954: 48-51; M. C. Ch'en 1956).

(3) The third is the relation between the ruling groups of different states who also have different clan names, such as that between the Chi clan of Lu and the Chiang clan of Ch'i. The relative political status difference among such groups has very often been taken for granted, and the exact and precise mechanism whereby their relative political status was maintained or changed has yet to be characterized. A lengthy discussion of the subject is not pertinent here, but I wish to point out that in this connection kinship and marriage regulations played important roles. These regulations centered principally around the so-called matrilateral cross-cousin marriage. That is, between the ruling groups of different states and of different clans there appears to have been a preferred male marriage with mother's brother's daughters but not with father's sister's daughters. According to his findings among the Kachin group of Upper Burma, E. R. Leach (1951) argues convincingly that whenever and wherever matrilateral cross-cousin marriage regulations occur, they are a part of the political structure. Under such a system, the exchange of women between different clans cannot always be symmetrical, and therefore there must be unbalanced obligations and related prestiges. I think I can demonstrate that in the Eastern Chou period at least, such marriage regulations occurred, and that these regulations were accompanied by a relative difference in political status for the intermarrying parties.[4]

I hope that this discussion lends credence to the following assumptions: (1) that in Shang and Chou Dynasties the social stratification was to a large extent based upon kinship, by means of the varying proximity of the different kin groups to the main line of descent and their varying accessibility to land, other scarce goods, and the means and sources for subsistence; (2) that within the ruling class the various segments differed in political status, and that such segments were again founded upon kinship; and (3) that the competition for power and even dominance was from this point of view a competition among various kin groups. In this connection it must be remembered that the "kin groups" in question were not always at the "clan" level, but included lineages and sub-clans belonging to the same mythological clans. Let us now start from this basis.

4. See the discussions in pp. 89-92.

History of Shang and Chou Kingship and the Changing Concepts of Man, Ancestors, and Gods

This feature, the political orientation of kin groups, or the kinship orientation of political status, is distinctively, though not exclusively, a Chinese social feature. Under what circumstances and by what forces it came into being is a question beyond the scope of the present paper, but there is good reason to speculate that it started as early as the Neolithic period. Elsewhere I have made the inference that the Lung-shan farmers in north China had already developed a strongly organized system of patrilineage groups and that the social stratification during this stage was to a large extent grounded upon their membership in such groups (K. C. Chang 1960).

Out of the Lung-shan basis grew the historic Shang civilization, the available archaeological evidence being too ample and conclusive to be interpreted otherwise. Cultural continuities from the Lung-shan to the Shang abound, not only in the domain of cultural style but also in the realm of society and economy. Social stratification, metallurgy, specialization of handicrafts, and warfare and raiding, which developed in the Shang, all had a Lung-shan basis. If my inference about the Lung-shan religious features is valid in full or in appreciable part, we can further say that the Shang inherited from their Lung-shan forebears their ancestor worship and the political orientation of kinship groups.

The Shang was, nevertheless, a stage in ancient Chinese culture and social history that was drastically new and qualitatively revolutionary. For one thing, Shang achieved the status of a civilization, with writing, cities, sophisticated political institutions and administrative hierarchy, regional specialization of economy, and highly developed bronze metallurgy—all of which were lacking previously. For another, Shang was a dynasty, a hereditary political power generated from within a small number of local groups but ruling over a vast territory and a large number of communities. In other words, whereas the Lung-shan Neolithic period was barbarous, the Shang was civilized; while the Neolithic Lung-shan functioned at the village level, the Shang was a state.

We are therefore quite confident that the Shang religion acquired the following characteristic features which must have been hitherto insignificant or even totally absent: the concept of the Supreme Being and the identification of the Supreme Being with the ancestor of the ruling clan, the clan of Tzu.

The Shang Dynasty, is, in one sense, a dynastic rule of one city state over other city states, but it is also, in another sense, a dynastic rule of one clan over other clans. In the Shang Dynasty domain, there were several city centers, each consisting of an administrative and ceremonial center together with a small number of farming and technologically specialized hamlets. These city centers constituted a political hierarchy, with the ruling capital at the top. Most of the ruling members of each of these city centers belonged to the Tzu clan, which was the ruling clan of China, the nucleus of the total power of the king.

Leading authorities on the Shang religion and oracle bone inscriptions agree without exception that the concept of *Shang Ti* or Supreme Being was now well developed, and that the supremacy of the Shang and its ruling clan over the rest of China must have decisively facilitated the development of such a Supreme Being. Shang Ti was the ultimate authority of the human as well as the natural world, possessing the final say over such vital matters as drought and rain and the king's good or ill health, and presiding over a court composed of natural deities, deputies, and messengers.

On the other hand, there is something about this Shang Ti that is most peculiar. He was not given a specific location, he was not to be sacrificed to, and his relations with the early, legendary ancestors of the Tzu clan were not very clearly defined. Some of these early ancestors appear to be the personification of gods or even The God, and all the ancestors of kings had easy and free access to the world of gods and The God. Commenting on these facts, Kuo Mo-jo (1945:9) concludes that the Shang Ti of Shang is Ti K'u, at once the Supreme God and the Ancestor of the Clan. I would further suggest that the concept of Shang Ti was an abstraction, whereas the ancestor deities represented substance. In other words, in the Shang conception of the worlds of gods and of ancestors, the distinction between these two worlds was so narrow as to be practically negligible.

The Shang Dynasty was taken over by the Chou in 1122 BC or thereabouts. Traditional scholars considered this event—the downfall of the Shang Dynasty and the rise of the Chou—as a crucial event in the political history of the ancient Chinese, and a number of ethnohistorians read into it a replacement of one major ethnic division by another as the dominant power of China.

The conflict between Shang and Chou in ancient Chinese history may remind one of the problems concerning the relations between the Sumerians and the Semites in the early history of Babylonia.

Thorkild Jacobsen, in a monumental article, "The Assumed Conflict Between Sumerians and Semites in Early Mesopotamia History," has convincingly demonstrated that the conflict between the different human groups in early Mesopotamia was based not on "racial" factors, as previously assumed, but on purely political and territorial factors (Jacobsen 1939). I would like to stress that the conflicts between the Shang and the Chou were based upon essentially similar factors. Rather than marking ethnic conflicts, the Chou conquest of Shang was basically a triumph of one political segment over another within one and the same sphere of civilization. Insofar as the ancient Chinese political segments were to a considerable extent kinship oriented, we can further say that the conquest of Chou was the victory of one kin group (Chi clan) over another (Tzu clan). We say this because we find in the archaeological manifestations of the Shang and Chou civilizations a continuous development and propagation, but no evidence whatsoever for any discontinuity, implicit or explicit.

In religion, the essential religious forms of the Shang were also inherited by the Chou after the conquest. Ancestor worship in an elaborate form and the concept of Shang Ti were among the traditions that the Western Chou carried on from the Shang base (cf. M. C. Ch'en 1936a, 1956). Exerting a dynastic rule of a single clan, the Chi, it was apparently to the Chou's advantage to continue both the dominant status of Shang Ti and the close relation between Shang Ti and the ruler's ancestors. Chiang Yüan, the mother of the founding ancestor of the clan of Chi, was conceived as a result of "treading in God's footprint," and the Western Chou poem of *Wen Wang* says that Wen Wang is "at Ti's left and right."

We must nevertheless remember that the Chou rulers belonged to a different kin group from that of the Shang rulers. Whatever cultural legacy the Chou inherited from the Shang, it could not have included the Shang conception of identifying Shang Ti with the ancestors of the Tzu clan. Two courses were apparently open to the Chou lords—namely, to sever the connection between Shang Ti and the Shang ancestors, and to identify Shang Ti with their own ancestors, or to sever that connection, period. The origin myth of the Chi clan testifies to the fact that the former course was not entirely untried, but the subsequent development in religious concepts of the Chou shows that the latter course had its way, and that the worlds of gods and of ancestors became separated for the first time and, historically, forever.

First of all, the Western Chou developed the concept of *t'ien*, or

Heaven, and located Shang Ti in this heaven. Heaven and its Shang Ti were still regarded with great reverence and awe. Chou's ancestors were still very close to the heaven and to the world of gods in general. But, unlike the Shang, the Western Chou ancestors were not gods in themselves. The kings ruled the world of man, because they were *t'ien tzu,* or sons of Heaven, and because they were vested with and trusted upon the Order of Heaven, *t'ien-ming.*[5] But on the other hand, Heaven's order, or mandate, did not *have* to be vested in the Chou automatically; recall that it was the same Shang Ti on whose mandate both the Shang and the Chou ruled. Why was the Order now vested in the Chou? Because, in the first place, Heaven's Order was not absolute or unchangeable (*t'ien-ming wu ch'ang*) (see S. N. Fu 1940), and in the second place, Shang Ti vested the power to rule only in those who had virtue and merit, which concept, the concept of *te,* was now also developed for the first time in the Western Chou.[6]

Let me recapitulate at this point: the Western Chou seizure of China from the Shang marks the replacement of one clan by another as the paramount ruler of the land. The Shang concept of the Supreme God and its dominance, power, and high influence was taken over by the Chou. The Chou's ancestors were close to The God, had His favor, and ruled the land on His Order. The

---

5. Poem "Yün Han" (in "Ta Ya," *Shih Ching*) contrasts "Shang Ti" and "Hsien Tsu," or "God" and "ancestors." The word *t'ien* in this context first appeared in "Chou Shu" and "Chou Sung," and, also, in bronze texts dated to Ch'eng Wang and K'ang Wang (e.g., *Ta Yü Ting*). In most bronze texts after Ch'eng Wang and K'ang Wang the word "t'ien" was gradually replaced by the term, "T'ien Tzu." See M. C. Ch'en 1956: 98.

6. Even though the Royal House of the Weston Chou was in possession of *t'ien ming,* and the king *t'ien's* son, the reason that God gave the mandate to the Chou house was nonetheless because of their *te.* Both Hou-chi, Chou's ancestor, and Ch'i, Shang's ancestor, were mythologically given birth to, but their legends show an interesting difference. Ch'i founded Shang by virtue of his birth, but Hou-chi suffered hardships and made meritorious deeds before *he* founded the Chou house. Poem "Huang Yi" (in "Ta Ya," *Shih Ching*):

God on high in sovereign might
Looked down majestically,
Gazed down upon the four quarters,
Examining the ills of the people.
Already in two kingdoms
The governance had been all awry;
Then every land
He tested and surveyed.
God on high examined them
And hated the laxity of their rule.
So he turned his gaze to the west
And here made his dwelling-place. (translated, Waley 1960).

origin myth of the Chi clan replaced the origin myth of the Tzu clan as the official sanction for the Chou monarchy. On the other hand, Shang Ti now became divorced from any identification with the Shang ancestors, and the world of gods and the world of ancestors became two distinctly different worlds. The world of Chou ancestors dominated the world of profane men, just as The God dominated the world of gods and natural deities. But their relation was not absolute, and The God's Order was not permanent. Whoever had virtue and merit merited the role of dominance and, needless to say, it was the Chou who had the virtue and merit and who deserved the mandate.

All of this was drastically changed after the beginning of the Eastern Chou period. The change under King P'ing of the royal capital from the neighborhood of Sian in the west to that of Loyang in the east (hence the appellation of Eastern Chou) owing to the pressures of the nomadic tribes in Shensi, was not an isolated political event, but symbolic of a series of profound changes in the entire Chinese society and culture. First and foremost, the royal Chou's political, military, and religious power diminished greatly in reverse proportion to the growth of the local states, which were ruled either by the lesser lineages of the Chi clan or by other clans. The Chinese civilization, of which the royal Chou and its representatives had hitherto been the sole guardians, expanded in space and penetrated in depth. Technology, writing, and knowledge in science and in political philosophy were no longer the monopoly of the Chou rulers, but spread to formerly barbarous countries on the Chou's peripheries and to the lower classes. From the middle of the Spring-and-Autumn period onward, iron metallurgy began to develop at an accelerated pace, and cities grew in number and in size, incorporating not only the rulers and the priests but also craftsmen and merchants, a fact that accounts to a considerable extent for the rise of the local powers. Historians now speak of a renaissance movement and a humanistic current of thinking as taking place at this time.

The immediate consequences of such total and intensive changes in society and culture in the realm of religion and mythology are a further separation of the world of gods from the world of ancestors and, moreover, a frontal attack upon Heaven's ultimate authority. In a number of aspects of Eastern Chou culture, this period is one of diversification and competition. In terms of kin groups, this is a period in which the lesser lineages of the Chi clan and the hitherto politically subordinate clans, vested with newly acquired powers, competed for dominance. Up to this time, political and mythological supremacy had been held by the royal Chou by virtue of their close relationship to the world of gods and The God. The immediate manifestation of the competition, then, was to challenge this close relationship on the one hand, and to emphasize individual virtue and merit, on the other.

The ultimate outcome of this competition certainly depended upon political and military might, as the unification of China under the Ch'in Dynasty finally and historically attested, and it was accompanied by a fierce ideological struggle. In the realm of mythology, we find the following indications.

In the first place, the close relationship, let alone total identification, between the world of ancestors and the world of gods was severed once and for all. The God, the gods, and the rest of the deities belonged to a world that became increasingly inaccessible to man. Insofar as no single clan or lineage, including that of the royal Chou, could claim identification or exclusive linkage with The God, the world of God did not belong to anybody, which put the competition on a fair religious basis.

Furthermore, the Eastern Chou myths show plainly that the world of gods not only lacked the ultimate authority but that its activities were also very often against human interests. In political thought the lesser lords challenged each other's authority and the ultimate authority of the royal Chou rulers as well; in the mythological charter, they challenged the ultimate authority of Heaven, the Supreme Being, and the world of gods and nature in general.

Thus we see that during the Eastern Chou period the Western Chou concept of *t'ien-ming wu ch'ang* was intensified. In *Meng Tzu, Shang Chün Shu,* and the Han text of *Huai Nan Tzu,* the concept of *shih pien,* or the change or trend of the time, played a significant role.[7] Heaven gave no absolute orders, and the world had no absolute monarch. But who received the mandate and who deserved to rule the world? He who had virtue and merit, of course, following the Western Chou concept of *te.* Recall that *Kuo Yü* says, as quoted before, that "people of the same *hsing* have the same virtues." The clan or lineage whose ancestors had virtues and merits was as a group considered virtuous and meritorious, and their members thus deserved the position of orthodoxy.

---

7. *Meng Tzu* ("Kung Sun Ch'ou," Part 2): "The people of Ch'i have a saying, You may be clever, But it is better to make use of circumstances; You may have a plough, But it is better to wait for the right season" (translated Lau 1970: 75). See, also, *Shang Chün Shu* ("Hua Tz'e") and *Huai Nan Tzu* ("Fan Lun").

A study of myths and religion in relation to the political history of kin groups thus shows that the Shang and Chou Dynasties are divisible into three segments: Shang, Early Chou, and Late Chou. It was during the Western Chou period that the world of gods and the world of ancestors were first significantly separated and the concept of *te* first introduced as the link between the two worlds. The lords of the late Eastern Chou period made use of both of these concepts to the utmost, providing a totally new picture of the mythological structure. After the conquest, the Chi clan's elders probably thought that by the introduction of these two concepts their rule of China in place of the Tzu clansmen was rational, fully justified, and sanctioned. They undoubtedly did not foresee that, ironically, a new and intensified application of these same concepts caused their own descendants on the Eastern Chou throne to lose their mythological supremacy.[8]

Role of the Animal

At this point we can return to the problem of the changing roles played by animals in Shang and Chou myths and art. It is now clear that in the earlier period, the mythological animal served as a link between the world of man and the world of the ancestors and the gods, and that in later periods when the worlds of the ancestors and the gods were forcibly separated, the animal was identified with the world of the gods and became a symbol against which men struggled as though they were struggling against the gods.

The myth of Ch'ung and Li and the practice of bone divination indicate that in earlier periods the communication between the world of man and the world of ancestors and gods was probably accomplished through the medium of priests and shamans. In *Shan Hai Ching,* we find that Ch'i ascended to Heaven riding two dragons, and many witches described in this same text had animals as standard equipment. It is a fair inference to say that the priests and shamans made use of mythological animals in their communication functions. A study by Mircea Eliade (1951: 99-102) has shown that among many peoples of the world shamans were the mediums between the worlds of the living and the dead, and that they accomplished their missions with the assistance of animals. Joseph Campbell (1959: 257) says:

8. In his review of Karlgren (1946), W. Eberhard (1946) expressed views in many ways similar to the above.

As Eliade has pointed out, the shaman's power rests in his ability to throw himself into a trance at will. . . . The drum and dance simultaneously elevate his spirit and conjure to him his familiars—the beasts and birds, invisible to others, that have supplied him with his power and assist him in his flight. And it is while in his trance of rapture that he performs his miraculous deeds. While in his trance he is flying as a bird to the upper world, or descending as a reindeer, bull, or bear to the world beneath.

Divination in ancient China—that is, communication with ancestors—was made through the bones of animals. Ritual bronzes were used in connection with ancestor rites and buried with dead lords who went to join their ancestors. It is then completely fitting that these objects were decorated with mythological animals, which served as agents between the world of man and the world of gods and ancestors.

The relations between ancestors and gods underwent a drastic and basic change during a later period of ancient Chinese history when these two worlds were rearranged into a new framework. Gods no longer monopolized human affairs, and in art we find that potent animals had lost their influence in the composition of motifs, and that divination made more use of other mediums than the bones of animals. God's world was to be challenged, and its ultimate authority badly shaken. In art and in myths we find that the powerful animals, long identified with the world of gods either as mediums or as messengers, were being fought and even conquered by human heroes. In the myths, monster beasts were said to roam about, making men suffer, as a part of the natural calamity descending upon the human world by the gods' evil will, and we find that a human hero, Yi the Archer, shot them to death. When the Sun God made drought, it was at the sun birds that Yi the Archer aimed his arrows. It is both interesting and instructive to note that the word *t'ao-t'ieh* first appeared in *Tso Chuan* to designate one of the *Ssu Hsiung,* or Four Evil Creatures, that were conquered by heroes (J. H. Ch'ang 1940: 4-6). If Eastern Chou had a humanistic movement that euhemerized deities into ancestral heroes and transformed mythical and potent animals into human subjects, it is, I believe, in these profane realms that we must look for the specific mechanisms whereby such results were being achieved.

Bibliography

Glossary

Index

Bibliography

Ackerman, Phyllis
1945 *Ritual Bronzes of Ancient China.* New York: Dryden Press.

Allchin, F. R.
1969 Early cultivated plants in India and Pakistan, in *The Domestication and Exploitation of Plants and Animals,* eds. Ucko and Dimbleby, pp. 323-329. London: G. Duckworth.

Amano, Motonosuke
1959 Chugaku kodai nōgyo no tenkai, *The Tōhōgakuhō* (Kyoto) 30:67-166.

An, Chih-min
1959 Shih lun Huang-ho Liu-yü hsin-shih-ch'i shih-tai wen-hua, *K'ao-ku* 1959 (10):559-565.
1961 Kuan-yü Cheng-chou Shang ch'eng ti chi-ko wen-t'i, *K'ao-ku* 1961(8):448-450.
1972a Kuan-yü wo-kuo jo-kan yüan-shih wen-hua nien-tai ti t'ao-lun, *K'ao-ku* 1972(1):57-59.
1972b Lüeh lun wo-kuo hsin-shih-ch'i shih-tai wen-hua ti nien-tai wen-t'i, *K'ao-ku* 1972(6):35-44.

An, Chin-huai
1961 Shih lun Cheng-chou Shang-tai ch'eng chih—Ao tu, *Wen-wu* 1961(4/5):73-80.

Anderson, E. N., Jr.
1970 Réflexions dur la cusine, *L'Homme* 9(2):122-124.

Andersson, J. G.
1943 Researches into the Prehistory of the Chinese, *Bulletin of the Museum of Far Eastern Antiquities,* no. 15.
1947 Prehistoric sites in Honan, *Bulletin of the Museum of Far Eastern Antiquities,* no. 19.

Anonymous
1958 Shan-hsi Shih-lou hsien Erh-lang-p'o ch'u-t'u Shang Chou t'ung-ch'i, *Wen-wu Ts'an-k'ao Tzu-liao* 1958(1):36.

Bachhofer, L.
1946 *A Short History of Chinese Art.* New York: Pantheon Books.

Bain, Read
1947 Man, the myth-maker, *The Scientific Monthly* 65(1):61-69.

Barrau, Jacque
1970 La Région Indo-Pacifique comme centre de mise en culture et de domestication des végétaux, *Journal l'Agriculture Tropicale et de Botanique Appliquée* 17(12):487-503.

Bayard, Donn T.
1971 *Non Nok Tha: The 1968 Excavation.* University of Otago: Studies in Prehistoric Anthropology 4.

1972 Early Thai bronzes: Analysis and new dates, *Science* 176: 1411-1412.

Beyer, H. Otley

1956 Preliminary note on eight papers on Chinese archaeology and early history, *Proceedings of the 4th Far Eastern Prehistory Congress and the 8th Pacific Science Congress Combined* 1(1): 86.

Bidney, David

1953 *Theoretical Anthropology.* New York: Columbia University Press.

Bodde, Derk

1942 Dominant ideas in the formation of Chinese culture, *Journal of American Oriental Society* 62(4):293-299.

1961 The myths of ancient China, in *Mythologies of the Ancient World,* ed. S. Kramer. New York: Doubleday & Co.

Boule, M., H. Breuil, E. Licent, and P. Teilhard de Chardin

1928 *Le Paléolithique de la Chine.* Paris: Institut Paléontologie Humain.

Boyd, Andrew

1962 *Chinese Architecture and Town Planning, 1500 B.C.-A.D. 1911.* Chicago: University of Chicago Press.

Braidwood, Robert J.

1952 *The Near East and the Foundation for Civilization.* Eugene, Oregon: Oregon State System of Higher Education.

Brothwell, D., and P. Brothwell

1969 *Food in Antiquity.* London: Thames and Hudson.

Burkill, I. H.

1953 Habits of man and the origins of the cultivated plants of the Old World, *Proc. Linnaean Soc. London* (*Botany*) 164:12-42.

Campbell, Joseph

1959 *The Masks of God: Primitive Mythology.* New York: Viking.

Candolle, A. de

1883 *Origine des plantes cultivées,* Paris. (English translation: *Origins of Cultivated Plants,* London: Hafner, 1967).

Ch'ang, Jen-hsia

1940 T'ao-t'ieh chung-k'uei shen-t'u yü-lei shih-kan-tang k'ao, *Shuo-wen* 2(9):4-6.

Chang, Kwang-chih

1958 New light on early man in China, *Asian Perspectives* 2:41-61.

1959a Chung-kuo hsin-shih-ch'i shih-tai wen-hua tuan-tai, *Bulletin of the Institute of History and Philology,* Academia Sinica, 30:259-309.

1959b A working hypothesis for the early cultural history of South China, *Bulletin of the Institute of Ethnology,* Academia Sinica, no. 7:43-103.

1960 Chung-kuo yüan ku shih-tai yi-shih sheng-huo ti jo-kan tzu-liao, *Bulletin of the Institute of Ethnology,* Academia Sinica, 9:253-270.

1962 Major problems in the culture history of Southeast Asia, *Bulletin of the Institute of Ethnology,* Academia Sinica, 13: 1-26.

1963a Shang wang miao hao hsin k'ao, *Bulletin of the Institute of Ethnology,* Academia Sinica, 15:65-95.

1963b Shang Chou shen-hua chung suo chien jen yü t'ung-wu kuan-hsi chih yen-pien, *Bulletin of the Institute of Ethnology,* Academia Sinica, 16:115-146.

1963c *Kingship, the Ancestors, and the Gods: The Politics of Mythology in Ancient China.* Mimeographed. New Haven: Yale University.

1964 Some dualistic phenomena in Shang society, *Journal of Asian Studies,* 24:45-61.

1966 Relative chronologies of China to the end of Chou, in *Chronologies in Old World Archaeology,* ed. R. Ehrich, pp. 503-526. Chicago: University of Chicago Press.

1967 The Yale expedition to Taiwan and the Southeast Asian horticultural evolution, *Discovery* 2(2):3-10.

1968 *The Archaeology of Ancient China,* Revised and enlarged edition. New Haven and London: Yale University Press.

1972 Shang Chou ch'ing-t'ung-ch'i ch'i-hsing chuang-shih hua-wen yü ming-wen tsung-ho yen-chiu ch'u-pu pao-kao, *Bulletin of the Institute of Ethnology,* Academia Sinica, 30:253-330.

ms. Ancient farmers in the Asian tropics: Major problems for archaeological and palaeoenvironmental investigations of Southeast Asia at the earliest neolithic level.

Chang, K. C., and Minze Stuiver

1966 Recent advances in the prehistoric archaeology of Formosa, *Proceedings of the National Academy of Sciences* 55:539-543.

Chang, K. C., C. C. Lin, M. Stuiver, H. Y. Tu, M. Tsukada, R. J. Pearson, T. M. Hsü

1969 *Fengpitou, Tapenkeng, and the Prehistory of Taiwan.* Yale University Publications in Anthropology, no. 73.

Chang, K. C., K. C. Li, H. Li, C. H. Chang Frankel

1973 *Shang Chou Ch'ing-t'ung-ch'i yü Ming-wen ti Tsung-ho Yen-chiu (Inscribed Bronzes of the Shang and Chou: A Comprehensive Study).* Institute of History and Philology, Academia Sinica, Special Publications no. 62.

Chang, Ping-ch'üan

1967 Chia ku wen suo chien jen ti t'ung ming k'ao, *Papers in Honor of Professor Li Chi on His Seventieth Birthday,* vol. 2: 657-776. The Ch'ing-hua Journal.

Chao, Buwei Yang

1972 *How to Cook and Eat in Chinese.* New York: Vintage Books.

Chao, Ch'üan-ku, W. C. Han, M. H. Pei, C. H. An
1957 Cheng-chou Shang tai yi-chih ti fa-chüeh, *K'ao-ku Hsüeh Pao* 1957(1):53-73.
Chao, T'ieh-han
1954 Yü yü hung shui, *Mainland Magazine* 9(6).
Chekiang Provincial Commission for the Preservation of Cultural Objects
1960 Wu-hsing Ch'ien-shan-yang yi-chih ti yi erh ts'e fa-chüeh pao-kao, *K'ao-ku Hsüeh Pao* 1960(2):73-90.
Ch'en, Chiu-heng
1959 Lo-yang hsi chiao yi-ko Chan-kuo mu chih fa-chüeh, *K'ao-ku* 1959(12).
Ch'en, Meng-chia
1936a Ku wen-tzu chung chih Shang Chou chi-ssu, *Yenching Journal of Chinese Studies* 19:91-155.
1936b Shang tai ti shen-hua yü wu-shu, *Yenching Journal of Chinese Studies* 20:485-576.
1956 *Yin-hsü P'u Tz'u Tsung Shu*. Peking: Science Press.
Ch'en, P'an
1953a Hsien Ch'in Liang Han chien tu k'ao, *Hsüeh-shu Chi K'an* 1(4):1-13.
1953b Hsien Ch'in Liang Han po shu k'ao, *Bulletin of the Institute of History and Philology,* Academia Sinica, 24:185-196.
Chen, T. S., and J. K. Shryock
1932 Chinese relationship terms, *American Anthropologist* 34:623-669.
Cheng, Nai-wu, and Tuan-chü Hsieh
1960 Lin-hsia Ta-ho-chuang Ch'in-wei-chia liang ch'u Ch'i-chia wen-hua yi-chih fa-chüeh chien pao, *K'ao-ku* 1960(3): 9-12.
Cheng, Te-k'un
1932 Shan-hai-ching chi ch'i shen-hua, *Shih-hsüeh Nien Pao* 1(4).
1957 The origin and development of Shang culture, *Asia Major,* n.s., 6:80-98.
1959 *Archaeology in China, I: Prehistoric China*. Cambridge: W. Heffer & Sons.
Chin, Chao-tzu
1956 Feng yi pang kuo fang pien, *Li-shih Yen-chiu* 1956(2):79-88.
Chin, Hsiang-heng
1959 *Chia-ku-wen Hsü Pien*. Taipei: National Taiwan University.
Ch'in, Kuang-chieh, Ling Liu, and Shih-fan P'eng
1962 Chiang-hsi Hsiu-shui shan pei ti-ch'ü k'ao-ku tiao-ch'a yü shih chüeh, *K'ao-ku* 1962(7):353-367.
Ch'ü, Wan-li
1948 Shih fa lan-shang yü Yin tai lun, *Bulletin of the Institute of History and Philology,* Academia Sinica, No. 13:219-226.
Chung-kuo K'o-hsüeh Yüan K'ao-ku Yen-chiu Suo
1959 *Lo-yang Chung-chou-lu*. Peking: Science Press.
1962 *Feng-hsi Fa-chüeh*. Peking: Wenwu Press.

Chung-kuo K'o-hsüeh Yüan K'ao-ku Yen-chiu Suo and Hsi-an Pan-p'o Museum
1962 *Hsi-an Pan-p'o.* Peking: Science Press.
Chung-kuo K'o-hsüeh Yüan K'ao-ku Yen-chiu Suo Shih-yen Shih
1972a Fang-she-hsing t'an su ts'e-ting nien-tai pao-kao (1), *K'ao-ku* 1972(1):52-56.
1972b Fang-she-hsing t'an su ts'e-ting nien-tai pao-kao (2), *K'ao-ku* 1972(5):56-58.
Creel, H. G.
1937a *The Birth of China.* New York: F. Ungar.
1937b *Studies in Early Chinese Culture.* Baltimore: Waverly Press.
Darlington, C. D.
1963 *Chromosome Botany and the Origin of Cultivated Plants.* London: Allen & Unwin.
1969 The silent millennia in the agriculture of agriculture, in eds. Ucko and Dimbleby, pp. 67-72.
Douglas, Mary
1971 Deciphering a meal, *Daedalus*, Winter 1971:61-81.
Dunn, F. L.
1970 Cultural evolution in the late Pleistocene and Holocene of Southeast Asia, *American Anthropologist* 72:1041-1054.
Eberhard, Wolfram
1942 *Lokalkulturen im Alten China.* I (Leiden) and II (Peking).
1946 Review of *Bulletin of the Museum of Far Eastern Antiquities,* no. 18, *Artibus Asiae* 9:355-364.
Eliade, Mircea
1951 *Le Chamanisme et le Techniques Archaïques de l'Extase.* Paris: Payot.
Erkes, Eduard
1926 Chinesisch-amerikanische Mythenparallelen, *T'oung Pao*, n.s. 24:32-54.
Eyde, David, and Paul Postal
1961 Avunculocality and incest: The development of unilateral cross-cousin marriage and Crow-Omaha kinship systems, *American Anthropologist* 63:747-771.
Fairbank, Wilma
1972 *Adventures in Retrieval.* Harvard-Yenching Institute Studies 28.
Fei, Hsiao-t'ung
1953 *China's Gentry.* Chicago: University of Chicago Press.
Feng, Ch'eng-chün
1929 Chung-kuo ku-tai shen-hua chih yen-chiu, *Kuo-wen Chou Pao* (Tien tsin) 6:9-17.
Feng, Han-yi
1948 *The Chinese Kinship System.* Cambridge: Harvard University Press.
Ferguson, John C.
1928 *Chinese Mythology.* Boston.

Firth, Raymond

1939 *Primitive Polynesian Economy*. London: G. Routledge & Sons.

Frake, Charles

1961 The diagnosis of disease among the Subanun of Mindanao, *American Anthropologist* 63:113-132.

Frankfort, Henri

1948 *Kingship and the Gods*. Chicago: University of Chicago Press.

Fu, Ssu-nien

1930a Ta Tung Hsiao Tung shuo, *Bulletin of the Institute of History and Philology,* Academia Sinica, 2:101-107.

1930b Chiang yüan, *Bulletin of the Institute of History and Philology,* Academia Sinica, 2:130-135.

1935 Yi Hsia tung hsi shuo, *Papers Presented to Mr. Ts'ai Yüan P'ei on His 65th Birthday,* pp. 1093-1134.

1940 *Hsing Ming Ku Hsün Pien Cheng*. Institute of History and Philology, Academia Sinica.

Gernet, Jacques

1962 *Daily Life in China on the Eve of the Mongol Invasion 1250-1276*. Stanford: Stanford University Press.

Goody, Jack (ed.)

1966 *Succession to High Office*. Cambridge University Press.

Gorman, Chester

1969a Hoabinhian: A pebble-tool complex with early plant associations in Southeast Asia, *Science* 163:671-673.

1969b Hoabinhian transformations in early Southeast Asia: A cultural-chronological sequence *c*. 10,000 to 5500 BC, ms.

1972 Excavations at Spirit Cave, North Thailand: Some interim interpretations, *Asian Perspectives* 13:109-143.

Granet, Marcel

1926 *Dances et Légendes de la Chine Ancienne,* 2 vols. Travaux de l'Année Sociologique. Paris: Librairie Félix Alcan.

1930 *Chinese Civilization*. London: K. Paul, Trench, Trübner.

1939 Categories matrimoniales et relations de proximité dans la Chine ancienne, *Annales Sociologiques,* S.B. Fs. 1-3.

1953 La polygynie sororale et le sororat dans la Chine feodale, *Études Sociologiques sur la Chine*. Paris: Univ. de France.

Grist, D. H.

1955 *Rice*. London and New York.

Harris, D. R.

1967 New light on plant domestication and the origins of agriculture: A review, *Geographical Review* 57:90-107.

1969 Agricultural systems, ecosystems and the origins of agriculture, in eds. Ucko and Dimbleby, pp. 3-15.

Haudricourt, A. G.

1962 Domestication des animaux, cultures des plantes, et civilisation d'autui, *L'Homme* 2:40-50.

1964 Nature et culture dans la civilisation de l'igname, origine des clones et des clans, *L'Homme* 4:93-104.

Hawkes, David (translator)

1959 *Ch'u Tz'u, The Songs of the South.* Oxford: Clarendon Press.

Hayashi, Minao

1961/62 Sengoku Jidai no Gazōmōn, *Kokogaku Zasshi* 47:190-212, 264-292;48:1-22.

1964 In Shū seidō hiki no meishō to yōto, *Tōhōgakuhō* 34 (Kyoto): 199-297.

Ho, Ping-ti

1969 *Huang-t'u yü Chung-kuo Nung-yeh ti ch'i-yüan.* Hong Kong: The Chinese University.

Hou, Wai-lu

1955 *Chung-kuo Ku-tai She-hui Shih Lun.* Peking: Jenmin Press.

Hsia, Nai

1957 Our neolithic ancestors, *Archaeology* 10:181-187.

Hsü, Francis L. K.

1945 Observations on cross-cousin marriage in China, *American Anthropologist* 47(1):83-103.

Hsü, Ping-ch'ang

1946 *Chung-kuo Ku Shih ti Ch'uan-shuo Shih-tai.* Shanghai: China Culture Service. Second edition.

Hsüan, Chu

1928 *Chung-kuo Shen-hua Yen-chiu A B C.* Shanghai: World Book Co.

Hu, Hou-hsüan

1944 *Chia Ku Hsüeh Shang Shih Lun Ts'ung,* vol. I. Chinan: Ch'i-lu University.

1959 Yin p'u-ts'e chung ti shang ti ho wang ti, *Li-shih Yen-chiu* 9 & 10.

Huang, Hsüan-p'ei

1962 Shang-hai shih Ch'ing-p'u hsien Sung-tse yi-chih ti shih chüeh, *K'ao-ku Hsüeh Pao* 1962(2):1-28.

Izushi, Yoshihiko

1943 *Shina Shinwa Densetsu no Kenkyū.* Tokyo: Central Tribune.

Jacobsen, Thorkild

1939 The assumed conflict between Sumerians and Semites in early Mesopotamia history, *Journal of the American Oriental Society* 59:485-495.

Jao, Tsung-yi

1959 *Yin Tai Chen-p'u Jen-wu K'ao.* Hong Kong University Press.

Jung, Keng

1941 *Shang Chou Yi Ch'i T'ung K'ao.* Peking: Harvard-Yenching Institute.

1959 *Chin Wen Pien.* Peking: Science Press.

Kaizuka, Ishigeda

1947 Kiboku to miko, *Tōhōgakuhō* (Kyoto) 19.

1956 *Confucius.* Translated by G. Bownas. London: G. Allen & Unwin.

Kaizuka, Ishigeda, and Michiharu Ito

1953 Kōkotsubun dandai kenkyūhō no sai kentō, *Tōhōgakuhō* (Kyoto) 23:1-78.

Kamaki, Yoshimasa (ed.)

1965 *Nihōn no Kokōgaku, II: Jomon Jidai.* Tokyo: Kawade.

Kao, Chih-hsi

1963 Hu-nan Ning-hsiang Huang-ts'ai Shang Yin t'ung-ch'i yü yi-chih, *K'ao-ku* 1963(12):646-648.

Kao, Ch'ü-hsün

1959 The royal cemetery of the Yin dynasty at An-yang, *Bulletin of the Department of Archaeology and Anthropology, National Taiwan University,* nos. 13/14:1-9.

Kao, Ming

1963 *Li Hsüeh Hsin Yen.* Hong Kong: The Chinese University and the Union College.

Karlgren, Bernhard

1936 Yin and Chou in Chinese bronzes, *Bulletin of the Museum of Far Eastern Antiquities,* no. 8.

1937 New studies of Chinese bronzes, *Bulletin of the Museum of Far Eastern Antiquities,* no. 9.

1946 Legends and cults in ancient China, *Bulletin of the Museum of Far Eastern Antiquities,* no. 18.

1959 Marginalia on some bronze albums, *Bulletin of the Museum of Far Eastern Antiquities,* no. 31:289-331.

1960 Marginalia on some bronze albums II, *Bulletin of the Museum of Far Eastern Antiquities,* no. 32:321-324.

1962 Some characteristics of the Yin art, *Bulletin of the Museum of Far Eastern Antiquities,* no. 34:1-28.

Kimura, Masao

1965 *Chūgoku Kodai Teikoku no Keisei.* Tokyo: Fubido.

Kotani, Y.

1969 Upper Pleistocene and Holocene environmental conditions in Japan, *Arctic Anthropology* 5(2):133-158.

Ku, Chieh-kang

1923 Yü Ch'ien Hsüan-t'ung hsien-sheng lun ku shih shu, *Tu-shu Tsa-chih* (supplement to *Nu-li Tsa-chih,* Peking), no. 9.

1926 *Ku Shih Pien.* Peking: P'u-she.

1930 Hung shui chih ch'uan-shuo chi chih shui teng chih ch'uan-shuo, *Shih-hsüeh Nien Pao* 2:61-67.

1935 Chan-kuo Ch'in Han chien jen ti tsao wei yü pien wei, *Shih-hsüeh Nien Pao* 2(2):209-248.

Kuo, Mo-jo
1930 *Chung-kuo Ku-tai She-huei Yen-chiu.* Shanghai: Shen-chou Kuo-kuang She.
1945 *Ch'ing-t'ung Shih-tai.* Chungking: Wen-chih.
1952 *Chia Ku Wen-tzu Yen-chiu.* Peking: Wen-wu Press.

Kuo, Pao-chün
1959 *Shan-piao-chen yü Liu-li-ko.* Peking: Science Press.

Kuo, Pao-chün, and Nai Hsia
1956 *Hui Hsien.* Peking: Science Press.

Lattimore, Owen
1951 *Inner Asian Frontiers of China.* American Geographic Society, Res. Ser. 21, New York.

Lau, D. C. (translator)
1970 *Mencius.* Middlesex: Penguin Books.

Leach, E. R.
1951 The structural implications of matrilateral cross-cousin marriage, *Journal of the Royal Anthropological Institute,* vol. LXXXI.

Legge, James
1872 *The Ch'un Ts'ew, with the Tso Chuen,* vol. V of *The Chinese Classics.* Oxford: Clarendon Press.
1885 *The Li Ki,* vols XXVII and XXVIII of *The Sacred Books of the East,* ed., F. Max Müller. Oxford: Clarendon Press.
1893 *Confucian Analects,* vol. I of *The Chinese Classics.* Oxford: Clarendon Press.
1895 *The Works of Mencius,* vol. II of *The Chinese Classics.* London: Henry Frowde (second edition). Reprinted in 1960 by Hong Kong University Press.

Lévi-Strauss, Claude
1958 *Anthropologie Structuralle.* Paris: Plon.
1964 *Mythologiques I: Le cru et le cruit.* Paris: Plon. (English translation, *The Raw and the Cooked,* New York, 1969.)
1965 Le triangle culinaire, *L'Arc* (*Aix-en-Provence*), no. 26:19-29. (English translation in *New Society,* Dec. 22, 1966, pp. 937-940, London.)
1966 *Mythologiques II: Du miel aux cendres,* Paris: Plon. (English translation, *From Honey to Ashes,* New York, 1973.)
1968 *Mythologiques III: L'origine des manières de table.* Paris: Plon.

Li, An-che
1931 *Yi Li yü Li Chi chih She-hui-hsüeh ti Yen-chiu.* Shanghai: Commercial.

Li, Chi
1928 *The Formation of the Chinese People.* Cambridge: Harvard University Press.
1948 Chi Hsiao-t'un ch'u-t'u ti ch'ing-t'ung-ch'i, I, *Chung-kuo K'ao-ku Hsüeh Pao* 3:1-99.

1951 Yin-hsü yu-jen shih-ch'i t'u shuo, *Bulletin of the Institute of History and Philology,* Academia Sinica, no. 23:523-619.

1956 *Hsiao-t'un T'ao Ch'i.* Inst. Hist. Phil., Academia Sinica.

1957a *The Beginnings of Chinese Civilization.* Seattle: University of Washington Press.

1957b Yin-hsü pai t'ao fa-chan chih ch'eng-hsü, *Bulletin of the Institute of History and Philology,* Academia Sinica, 23:853-882.

1957c Hunting record, faunistic remains and decorative patterns from the archaeological site of An-yang, *Bulletin of the Department of Archaeology and Anthropology, National Taiwan University,* nos. 9/10:10-20.

1958 Yu pien hsing yen-pien suo k'an-chien ti Hsiao-t'un yi-chih ho Hou-chia-chuang mu-tsang chih shih-tai kuan-hsi, *Bulletin of the Institute of History and Philology,* Academia Sinica, no. 29:809-816.

1959 Pien hsing pa lei chi ch'i wen-shih chih yen-pien, *Bulletin of the Institute of History and Philology,* Academia Sinica, no. 30:1-69.

Li, Chi, S. Y. Liang, T. P. Tung, S. N. Fu, C. T. Wu, P. C. Kuo, Y. H. Liu

1934 *Ch'eng-tzu-yai.* Nanking: Institute of History and Philology, Academia Sinica.

Li, Han-san

1967 *Hsien Ch'in Liang Han Yin Yang yü Wu Hsing Hsüeh-shuo.* Taipei: Chung-ting.

Li, Hsüan-po

1939 *Chung-kuo Ku-tai She-hui Hsin Yen.* Shanghai: Kaiming.

1944 Chung-kuo ku-tai hun-yen chih-tu ti chi chung hsien-hsiang, *Shih-hsüeh Chi K'an* 4:1-19.

1954 *Chung-kuo Ku-tai She-hui Shih.* Taipei: Commission for Chinese Culture Publication Affairs.

Li, Hsüeh-ch'in

1957 P'ing Ch'en Meng-chia Yin-hsü P'u Tz'u Tsung Shu, *K'ao-ku Hsüeh Pao* 1957(3):119-130.

Li, Hui-lin

1966 *Tung-nan Ya Tsai-p'ei Chih-wu chih Ch'i-yüan.* Hong Kong: The Chinese University.

1969 The vegetables of ancient China, *Economic Botany* 23:253-260.

Li, Hwei

1957 Chung-kuo yü Polynesia ti chih tsu chih, *Bulletin of the Institute of Ethnology,* Academia Sinica, 4:123-134.

Li, Shu-hua

1954 Chih wei fa-ming yi-ch'ien Chung-kuo wen-tzu liu-ch'uan kung-chü, *Mainland Magazine* 9(6):165-173, Taipei.

Li, Yü

1730 *Li-weng Ou Chi.* In ed. Chieh-tzu-yüan, *Li-weng Yi-chia-yen Ch'üan-chi.*

Liang, Ssu-yüng

1939 The Lungshan Culture: A prehistoric phase of Chinese civilization, *Proceedings of the 6th Pacific Science Congress* 4:69-79.

Liang, Ssu-yung, and Ch'ü-hsün Kao

1962 *Hsi-pei-kang 1001 Ta Mu.* Taipei: Institute of History and Philology, Academia Sinica.

Lin, Hsiang Ju, and Tsuifeng Lin

1969 *Chinese Gastronomy.* New York: Hastings House.

Lin, Nai-hsin

1957 Chung-kuo ku-tai ti p'eng-t'iao ho yin-shih, *Bulletin of Peking University* (*Humanities Section*) 1957(2):131-144.

Lin, Yutang

1935 *My Country and My People.* New York: John Day.

Ling, Shun-sheng

1959a Chung-kuo tsu miao ti ch'i-yüan, *Bulletin of the Institute of Ethnology,* Academia Sinica 7:141-184.

1959b Chung-kuo ku-tai shen chu yü yin yang hsing ch'i ch'ung-pai, *Bulletin of the Institute of Ethnology,* Academia Sinica, 8:1-46.

Liu, Ch'i-yi

1961 Ao tu chih yi, *Wen-wu* 1961(10):39-40.

Liu, Hsiao-ch'un

1961 Honan Meng hsien Chien-hsi yi-chih fa-chüeh, *K'ao-ku* 1961 (1):33-39.

Liu, Pin-hsiung

1965 Yin Shang wang-shih shih fen tsu chih shih lun, *Bulletin of the Institute of Ethnology,* Academia Sinica, 19:89-112.

Ma, Ch'eng-yüan

1961 Man t'an Chan-kuo ch'ing-t'ung-ch'i shang ti hua-hsiang, *Wen-wu* 1961(10):26-29.

Mao, Hsieh-chüin, and Yen Yin

1959 Dental condition of the Shang dynasty skulls excavated from Anyang and Huii-Xian, *Vertebrata Palasiatica* 3(2):79-80.

Maspéro, Henri

1924 Légendes mythologiques dans le *Chou King, Journal Asiatique* 204:1-100.

1950 Les religions chinoises, *Mélanges posthumes sur les religions et l'histoire de la Chine I.* Paris: Musée Guimet.

Matthews, J. M.

1968 A review of the 'Hoabinhian' in Indo-China, *Asian Perspectives* 9:86-95.

Mei, Yi-pao

1929 *The Ethical and Political Works of Motse.* London: A. Probsthain.

Meng, Wen-t'ung

1933 *Ku Shih Chen Wei.* Shanghai: Commercial.

Middleton, John, and David Tait

1958 *Tribes without Rulers.* London: Routledge and Kegan Paul.

Mishina, Shōei

1948 *Shinwa to Bunka Kyōiki.* Kyoto.

Miyazaki, Ichisada

1957 Chugoku jyōkaku no kigen ruisetsu, *Asiatica: Studies in Oriental History 1*: 50-65, Kyoto University, Tōhōshi Kenkyūkai.

Mori, Mikisakuro

1944 *Shina Kodai Shinwa.* Kyoto.

Movius, Hallam L., Jr.

1944 Early man and Pleistocene stratigraphy in southern and eastern Asia, *Papers of the Peabody Museum, Harvard University,* no. 19.

1955 Palaeolithic archaeology in southern and eastern Asia, exclusive of India, *Cahiers d'Histoire Mondiale* 2:257-282, 520-553.

Mumford, Lewis

1961 *The City in History.* New York: Harcourt, Brace, and World.

Ōshima, Riichi

1959 Chugoku kodai no shiro ni tsuite, *Tōhōgakuhō* (Kyoto): 30:39-66.

P'ei, Wen-chung

1939 An attempted correlation of Quaternary geology, palaeontology and prehistory in Europe and China, *Institute of Archaeology, University of London, Occasional Papers,* no. 2.

Rooth, Anna B.

1957 The creation myths of the North American Indians, *Anthropos* 52(3/4).

Rubin, V. A.

1965 Tzu-ch'an and the city-state of ancient China, *T'oung Pao* LII: 8-34.

Ruey, Yih-fu

1938 Miao tsu hung-shui ku-shih yü Fu-hsi Nü-wa ti ch'uan-shuo, *Jen-lei-hsüeh Chi-kan* 1.

1947 Shih sheng, *Bulletin of the Institute of History and Philology,* Academia Sinica, 16.

1949 Po shu yi chiu ku k'ao, *Bulletin of the Institute of History and Philology,* Academia Sinica, 14.

1950a Erh Ya Shih Ch'in pu cheng, *Bulletin of the College of Arts, National Taiwan University,* no. 1.

1950b Chiu tsu chih yü Erh Ya Shih Ch'in, *Bulletin of the Institute*

of History and Philology, Academia Sinica, 22:209-231.
1954 Lun ku chin ch'in-shu ch'eng-wei chih yi chih, *Annals of Academia Sinica* 1:53-67.
1958 The similarity of the ancient Chinese kinship terminology to the Omaha type, *Bulletin of the Department of Archaeology and Anthropology, National Taiwan University,* 12:1-19.
1959 Lun sheng chiu chih kuo, *Bulletin of the Institute of History and Philology,* Academia Sinica 30:237-258.

Sauer, Carl O.
1948 Environment and culture during the last deglaciation, *Proceedings of the American Philosophical Society* 92:65-77.
1952 *Agricultural Origins and Dispersals.* New York: American Geographic Society.

Shang, Ping-ho
1938 *Li Tai She-hui Feng-ssu Shih-wu K'ao.* Shanghai: Commercial.

Shen, Yen-ping
1925 Chung-kuo shen-hua yen-chiu, *Hsiao-shuo Yüeh Pao* 16(1): 1-26.

Shih, Chang-ju
1933 Ti ch'i ts'e Yin-hsü fa-chüeh: E ch'ü kung-tso pao-kao, *An-yang Fa-chüeh Pao-kao* 4:709-728. Shanghai.
1945 Honan An-yang Hou-kang ti Yin mu, *Liu-t'ung Pieh Lu* 1(3).
1950 Ts'ung pien tou k'an Tai-wan yü ta-lu, *Mainland Magazine* 1(4):7-10; 1(5):16-17.
1959 *Yin-hsü Chien-chu Yi-ts'un.* Institute of History and Philology, Academia Sinica.
1969 Yin tai ti tou, *Bulletin of the Institute of History and Philology,* Academia Sinica, 39:51-82.
1970a *Pei tsu Mu-tsang.* Institute of History and Philology, Academia Sinica.
1970b Yin tai ti-shang chien-chu ti yu yi li, *Bulletin of the Institute of Ethnology,* Academia Sinica, no. 29:321-341.
1971 *Chung-tsu Mu-tsang.* Institute of History and Philology, Academia Sinica.

Shinoda, Isamu
1959 Kodai Shina ni okeru kakkyō, *Tōhōgakuhō* 30:253-274.

Sirén, Osvald
1929 Histoire des arts anciens de la Chine, I: La période préhistorique, l'époque Tcheou, l'époque Tch'ou et T'sin, *Annales du Musée Guimet, Bibliothèque d'art,* n.s. 3, Paris and Bruxelles.

Smith, M. G.
1956 On segmentary lineage systems, *Journal of the Royal Anthropological Institute* 86 (2).

Solheim, Wilhelm G., II

1964 Pottery and Malayo-Polynesians, *Current Anthropology* 5:360, 376-384.

1969 Reworking southeast Asian Prehistory, *Paideuma* 15:125-139.

1972 Northern Thailand, Southeast Asia, and world prehistory, *Asian Perspectives* 13:145-162.

Solomon, Richard H.

1971 *Mao's Revolution and the Chinese Political Culture.* Berkeley: University of California Press.

Steele, John

1917 *The I-Li, or Book of Etiquette and Ceremonial.* London: Probsthain.

Stuiver, Minze

1969 Yale natural radiocarbon measurements IX, *Radiocarbon* 11: 545-658.

Suess, Hans E.

1970 Bristlecone-pine calibration of the radiocarbon time-scale 5200 B.C. to the present, in *Radiocarbon Variations and Absolute Chronology,* ed. I. U. Olsson, pp. 303-311. Stockholm: Almquist and Wiksell.

Sugimoto, Katsutaro, and Mitarai Masaru

1950 Chugaku kodai ni okeru taiyō setsuwa ni tsuite, *Japanese Journal of Ethnology* 15:304-327.

Sun, Hai-p'o

1934 *Chia Ku Wen Pien.* Peking: Harvard-Yenching Institute.

1965 *Chia Ku Wen Pien.* New Edition. Peking: Science Press.

Sun, Tso-yün

1941 Ch'ih Yu k'ao, *Chung-ho Yüeh K'an* 2(4):27-50; 2(5):36-57. Peking.

1943 Fei lien k'ao, *Hua Pei Pien-chi-kuan Kuan K'an* 2(3):6-1—6-29; 2(4):7-1—7-22.

1944a Hou Yi ch'uan-shuo ts'ung k'ao, *Chung-kuo Hsüeh Pao* 1 (3): 19-29; 1(4):67-80; 1(5):49-66. Peking.

1944b T'ao-t'ieh k'ao, *Chung-ho Yüeh K'an,* 5(1):2-19; 5(2):13-25; 5(3):12-26. Peking.

1945 Chung-kuo ku tai niao shih-tsu chu ch'iu-chang k'ao, *Chung-kuo Hsüeh Pao* 3(3):18-36.

1946 Shuo Tan Chu, *Li-shih yü K'ao-ku* 1:76-95, Shenyang.

1947 Shuo yü jen, *Bull. National Shenyang Museum* 1.

Sun, Yao

1931 *Ch'un-ch'iu Shih-tai Chih Shih Tsu.* Shanghai: Chung-hua.

T'ang, Lan

1962 Hsi Chou t'ung-ch'i tuan-tai chung ti K'ang Kung wen-t'i, *K'ao-ku Hsüeh Pao* 1962(2):15-48.

Teilhard de Chardin, Pierre

1941 *Early Man in China.* Inst. Géo-Biol., Peking, Publication 7.

Teilhard de Chardin, P., and P'ei Wen-chung

1944 *Le Néolithique de la Chine.* Inst. Géo-Biol., Peking, Publication 10.

Ting, Shan

1956 *Chia Ku Wen Suo Chien Shih-tsu chi ch'i Chih-tu.* Peking: Science Press.

Trewartha, Glenn T.

1952 Chinese cities: Origins and functions, *Annals of the Association of American Geographers* 42:69-93.

Tsien, T. H.

1962 *Written on Bamboo and Silk: The Beginnings of Chinese Books and Inscriptions.* Chicago: University of Chicago Press.

Tsukada, Matsuo

1966 Late Pleistocene vegetation and climate in Taiwan (Formosa), *Proc. Nat. Acad. Sci.* 55:543-548.

1967 Vegetation in subtropical Formosa during the Pleistocene glaciations and the Holocene, *Palaeogeography, Palaeoclimatology, Palaeoecology* 3:49-64.

Tung, Tso-pin

1945 *Yin Li P'u.* Li-chuan: Institute of History and Philology, Academia Sinica.

1951 Lun Shang jen yi shih jih wei ming, *Mainland Magazine* 2(3): 6-10.

1953 Yin tai: li chih ti hsin chiu liang p'ai, *Mainland Magazine* 6(3): 1-6.

Ucko, P. J., and G. W. Dimbleby

1969a (eds.) *The Domestication and Exploitation of Plants and Animals.* London: G. Duckworth.

1969b Introduction: Context and development of studies of domestication, in eds. Ucko and Dimbleby, pp. xvii-xxi.

Umehara, Sueji

1940 *Kanan Anyō Ihō.* Kyoto.

1944 *Rakuyō Kinson Kobo Shōei.* Kyoto.

van Heusden, William

1952 *Ancient Chinese Bronzes of the Shang and Chou Dynasties.* Tokyo: Privately printed

Vavilov, N. I.

1949/51 *The Origin, Variation, Immunity, and Breeding of Cultivated Plants.* Translated by K. S. Chester. Chronica Botanica 13.

Verdier, Yvonne

1969 Pour une Ethnologie culinaire, *L'Homme* 9(1):49-57.

Waley, Arthur (translator)

1960 *The Book of Songs.* New York: Grove (Evergreen Edition).

Waltham, Clae (translator)

1971 *Shu Ching.* Chicago: H. Regnery.

Wang, Chia-yu

1961 Chi Ssu-ch'uan P'eng hsien Chu-wa-chieh ch'u-t'u ti t'ung-ch'i, *Wen-wu* 1961(11):28-31.

Wang, Kuo-wei

1956 *Kuan T'ang Chi Lin.* Taipei: Yi-wen (reprint).

Ward, Lauriston

1954 The relative chronology of China through the Han period, in *Relative Chronologies in Old World Archaeology,* ed. R. W. Ehrich. Chicago: University of Chicago Press.

Waterbury, Florance

1942 *Early Chinese Symbols and Literature: Vestiges and Speculations.* New York: E. Weyhe.

Weber, Charles D.

1969 *Chinese Pictorial Bronze Vessels of the Late Chou Period.* Ascona: Artibus Asiae.

Wen, Yi-to

1956 *Shen-hua yü Shih.* Shanghai: Ku-tien Wen-hsüeh Press.

Wheatley, Paul

1971 *The Pivot of the Four Quarters.* Chicago: Aldine.

Williamson, Robert W.

1924 *The Social and Political Systems of Central Polynesia.* Cambridge University Press.

Wright, Arthur F.

1965 Symbolism and function: Reflections on Changan and other great cities, *Journal of Asian Studies* 24:667-679.

Wu, Ch'i-ch'ang

1936 *Chin Wen Shih-tsu P'u.* Institute of History and Philology, Academia Sinica, Memoirs 12, Shanghai.

Wu, G. D.

1938 *Prehistoric Pottery in China.* London: Kegan Paul.

Wu, Ju-tso

1963 Ch'ing-hai Tu-lan hsien No-mu-hung Ta-li-t'a-li-ha yi-chih tiao-ch'a yü shih chüeh, *K'ao-ku Hsüeh Pao* 1963(1):17-44.

Wu, Nelson I.

1963 *Chinese and Indian Architecture.* New York: George Braziller.

Wu, Tse

1953 *Chung-kuo Li-shih Ta Hsi Ku-tai Shih.* Shanghai: T'ang-ti.

Yang, Hsi-mei

1970 Honan An-yang Yin-hsü mu-tsang chung jen-t'i ku-ko ti cheng-li ho yen-chiu, *Ancient History of China Preprint,* Institute of History and Philology, Academia Sinica.

Yang, K'uan

1941 *Chung-kuo Shang Ku Shih Tao Lun.* Ku Shih Pien, vol. 7.

1957 *Chung-kuo Li Tai Ch'ih Tu K'ao.* Shanghai: Commercial.

Yang, Shang-k'uei

1962 *Chung-kuo Ku-tai She-huei yü Ku-tai Ssu-hsiang Yen-chiu.* Shanghai: Jenmin Press.

Yang, Shu-ta

1954 *Chi Wei Chü Chia Wen Shuo*. Peking: Science Press.

Yü, Hsing-wu

1959 Lüeh shuo t'u-t'eng yü tsung-chiao ch'i-yüan ho Hsia Shang t'u-t'eng, *Li-shih Yen-chiu* 11:60-69.

Yüan, K'o

1960 *Chung-kuo Ku-tai Shen-hua*. Shanghai: Chung-hua.

Yunnan Museum

1958 Chien-ch'uan Hai-men-k'ou ku wen-hua yi-chih ch'ing-li chien pao, *K'ao-ku T'ung-hsün* 1958(6):5-12.

Glossary

Listed here are Chinese characters whose romanized versions have appeared in the text in italized form. All characters are romanized according to their modern Mandarin pronunciation.

chang 丈
Ch'ang Hsi 常羲
chao 昭
ch'eng 城
chi 己
chi 祭
chia 甲
chia 斝
chiang 漿
chiao 郊
chih 雉
ch'ih 尺
ch'in t'ung hsing 親同姓
chiu 舅
chiu ko 九歌
chiu pien 九辯
chiung 坰
Chu Lung 燭龍
Chu Yin 燭陰
chüeh 爵
fan 飯
fu 釜
fu 簠
hai 醢
hang-t'u 夯土
ho 禾
Hsi Ho 羲和
Hsi Mu 西母
Hsi pi 西鄙
hsiao tsung 小宗
hsien 甗
hsin 辛
hsing 姓
hsü 盨

hsüan niao 玄鳥
hsün 旬
hu 鑊
hu 壺
jen 壬
jen 荏
keng 庚
keng 羹
ko p'eng 割烹
ku 姑
ku 觚
kuan 鑵
kuei 癸
kuei 𣪘
kuo 國
kuo 郭
k'uo 槨
lei-wen 雷文
li 鬲
li 里
li 禮
lin 林
mu 木
mu 穆
ni 臡
Nü Wa 女媧
pan 板
p'an 盤
pang 邦
p'ei 配
pi 鄙
pien 籩
pin 賓
ping 丙
p'o 瓿
shan 膳
shan-hsiu 膳羞
shang 上
Shang Ti 上帝
sheng 生
sheng 甥
shih 食
shih 示
shih pien 時變

shui 水

ssu fang 四方

ssu hsiung 四凶

ssu t'u 四土

ta tsung 大宗

Ta yi 大邑

Ta yi Shang 大邑商

t'ao-t'ieh 饕餮

Ti Chün 帝俊

t'ien 天

t'ien 田

t'ien ming 天命

t'ien ming wu ch'ang 天命無常

t'ien tzu 天子

ting 丁

ting 鼎

tou 豆

ts'ai 菜

tsao 灶

ts'ao 草

tseng 甑

tsu 俎

tsu 族

tsu hsiung ti 族兄弟

tsun 尊

tsung 宗

tsung fa 宗法

tsung fu 宗婦

tsung shih 宗室

tsung tzu 宗子

tsung yi 宗邑

tu 都

tu 堵

tui (*tuei*) 敦

Tung pi 東鄙

tzu tzu sun sun yüng pao yüng 子子孫孫永寶用

wu 戊

yang 陽

yen-chiu fan-wei 研究範圍

yi 邑

yi 彝

yi 乙

yieh 野

yin 陰

yin 飲

yin-shih 飲食

yu 卣

Index

Affines, 77-78

Agriculture, 25-29; slash and burn cultivation, 12, 28; irrigation, 13, 30, 56, 60; rice cultivation, 14; implements, 27, 30, 60; Lungshanoid, 30, 32-33; fallowing of fields, 30; fertilizer, 30, 56; distribution of produce, 34; Shang dynasty, 34, 35, 55, 56-57, 59; tilling by team and plow, 35, 56; farming communities, 36; collective farming, 55, 59. *See also* Animals, Plant Domestication, Villages

Almond (*Prunus*), 10

Amaranth (*Amaranthus mangostanus*), 18

Ancestral cult, 35, 57, 71, 74, 75, 80, 102, 140, 186-187, 196; ancestral temples, 54, 83, 84, 107; Chou dynasty, 88; Shang dynasty, 95-96, 105, 191; ancestors and gods, 156-157, 160, 161, 163, 165, 166-170, 171, 190, 191-192, 193, 194, 195; mythical origins of ancestors, 168, 170, 171, 180, 190, 194, 195; and divination, 183; Lungshanoid, 189. *See also* Kinship

Andersson, J. G., 22

Angelica kiusiana, 18

Animals: remains, 23, 44; wild, 24; husbandry, 26, 27, 29, 30, 33, 35, 122; as decorative motifs, 143-144, 174-184; mythological, 143-144, 175, 195-196; as familiars, 196

Anthropophagy, 126

Anyang, 34, 47, 48-49, 63, 66; excavations, 73, 79, 86, 93-95, 102-103, 105, 109-112, 147

Ape (*Alocasia macrorrhiza*), 17

Apricot: *Prunus armeniaca*, 19, 122; Japanese (*P. mume*), 19

Archaeology, Chinese, 22-23, 39, 94; and radiocarbon dating, 40-41

Architecture: construction techniques, 14, 15, 33, 48, 49, 51, 67; Mesolithic. 26; Neolithic, 26, 35; Yang-shao, 27; non-monumental, 47, 48, 49, 54, 71. *See also* Palace, Temples

Arrowhead (*Sagittaria sinensis*), 17

Artichoke, Chinese (*Stachys sieboldii*), 17

Artisans: craft materials, 30, 35; craft specialization, 31, 34, 36, 189; Shang, 51, 55, 56; and kinship, 186; Eastern Chou, 193

Arts, decorative, 35, 47; Yang-shao, 28; materials, 30, 49; theocratic, 31; Lungshanoid, 33; Shang, 34, 49, 51; bronzes, 106-113; feasting and cooking motifs, 115-116; animal motifs, 174-180, 181, 182. *See also* Bronzes, Pottery

Babylonia, 49, 190-191

Ballace, 122

Balsam pear (*Memordica charantia*), 18

Bamboo (*Dendrocalamus asper*, *Phyllostacy* spp.), 7, 9, 121; bamboo books, 152

Bamboo Annals, The, see *Chi Nien*

Banana (*Musa paradisiaca*, *M. sapientum*), 8, 20

Barrau, Jacques, 14, 15

Basket wares: Hoabinhian, 4

Bean: broad (*Vicia faba*, *Phaseolus*), 7, 10, 15-16, 45; velvet (*Stizolobium hassjoo*), 7; adsuki (*Phaseolus angularis*), 17

Betel: nut (*Areca catechu*), 10, 20; leaf (*Piper betle*), 20

Birds: as food, 122; decorative motifs, 144, 175; mythological, 167, 168, 180, 183

Bodde, Derk, 162, 172

Bone: inventories, 15, 55; ornaments, 174; and divination, 183, 184, 195, 196. *See also* Oracle bones

Book of History, The, see *Shu Ching*

Book of Odes, 180. See also *Shih Ching*

Book of Poetry, see *Shih Ching*

Books, 149-150, 152

Borneo, 2, 6

Bottle gourd (*Lagenaria vulgaris*, *L. siceraria*), 7, 9, 10, 121

Boyd, Andrew, 68

Braidwood, Robert, 25

Breadfruit (*Artocarpus incisa*), 19

Bronze: metallurgy, 46, 49, 55, 56; ritual bronzes, 51, 71, 150, 196; decorative styles, 106-113, 143-144, 174, 176-180; domestic vessels, 115-116, 126-128, 141-144, 146; bronze inscriptions, 150, 151

Bronze Age, 22, 34, 35, 149, 153
Buckwheat (*Fagopyrum esculentum*), 7
Burials, 35; Lungshanoid, 31; chamber, 35; sacrificial, 48; royal tombs, 49, 52-53, 56, 93, 94-95, 102-103, 109-111, 196; and vessels, 115-116; mortuary taboos, 137; food offerings, 139-140, 146; of books, 150. *See also* Cemeteries
Butternut (*Madhuca*), 10

Cabbage: Chinese (*Brassica* spp., *B. chinensis*), 13, 19, 45; oil (*B. chinensis* var. *oleifera*), 18; celery (*B. pekinensis*), 19
Calendar, 34, 79, 80
Cambias (*Averrhoa bilimbi*), 19
Campbell, Joseph, 195-196
Candlenut (*Aleurites*), 10
Carambola (*Averrhoa carambola*), 19
Cassia (*Cinnamomum cassia*), 20
Celebes, Paleolithic culture, 2
Cemeteries: Yang-shao, 28; Anyang, 48, 93, 94-95, 102-103, 109-110; Shang, 51, 68
Ceramic complexes, 4, 6, 12, 42-43, 46
Cereal crops, 7, 9, 13, 15, 17, 121
Chan Kuo period, cities, 65
Chan Kuo Ts'e, 135
Ch'ang-sha (Hunan) site, 41, 150
Chao, B.Y., 122, 135-136
Chao-mu system, 87-88, 90, 94, 95-103
Chariot, horse-drawn, 34, 35, 57, 59, 174
Chekiang site, plant remains, 7
Ch'en Meng-chia, 101
Cheng-chou (Honan) site, 34, 47, 49, 66, 186n
Ch'eng-tzu-yai (Shantung) site, 31
Cherry, Chinese (*Prunus pseudocerasus*), 19
Ch'i, 170
Chi clan, 167, 168, 170, 187, 188, 191, 193, 195
Chi Hsien (Honan) site, 152
Chi Nien, 79, 86, 149, 150, 152, 160, 165
Chiang clan, 188
Chian-yüan, myth of, 168, 170, 191
Chiao ("suburbs"), 62
Chien-hsi, Meng Hsien (Honan) site, 112
Ch'ien-shan-yang, Wu-hsing (Chekiang) site, 15, 41, 45
Chien Ti, myth of, 167
Childe, V. Gordon, 25
Ch'in dynasty, 33, 194
China, 2-6, 38, 60
China, north, 4, 5; agriculture, 2, 12-15, 17-21; nuclear area, 25-26, 27, 32, 42
China, south, 15, 17-21
Chinese Academy of Sciences, 39
Ch'ing-lien-kang (Kiangsu) culture, 6, 41, 43
Chiu Chang, 161
Chopsticks, 128
Chou dynasty, 47, 59-60; cities, 61-71; kinship system, 72-92, 149, 184-195; genealogies, 102; decorative arts, 106-108, 175-180; culinary arts, 117-118; mythology, 149-173, 174-184, 195-196; Shang conquest, 192, 195
Chou, Eastern, 169, 172, 193-195, 196; mythology, 151-154, 167, 183; literature, 171
Chou, Western, 191-193; mythology, 151, 152, 153-154; literature, 171
Chou Li, 116, 135, 151, 155
Chou Shu, 152
Choukoutien, 23, 24
Ch'ü-chia-ling (Hupei) culture, 6, 15, 41, 43
Chu-jung clan, 170
Ch'u Tz'u, 116, 124-125, 151, 158, 160, 167
Chu-wa-chieh, P'eng Hsien (Szechwan) site, 113
Chuan, 151
Chuang Tzu, 151
Chuang Tzu, 123n, 158, 161, 165, 185n
Ch'un Ch'iu, 61, 151
Chung-kuo shang-ku-shih tao-lun (*An Introduction to the Ancient History of China*), 169
Chrysanthemum (*Chrysanthemum coronarium*), 18-19
Cinnamon, 122
Cities: Shang, 47-49, 54, 61-71; layout, 48, 55, 60, 68; walled cities, 54, 64, 65, 66, 67, 71; changes of location, 62, 150-151; town-building, 64-65, 69-70; characteristics of, 67-68; measurements, 67n-68n; directional orientation, 68; Eastern Chou, 193
Civilization; 32, 34-38, 47, 169, 172, 189, 193
Clans, 27, 53-54; conical, 53; mythological origins, 166-167, 168, 188; ancestors, 181; rituals, 186-187; names, 187-188. *See also* Chi clan, Kinship, Lineage, Tzu clan
Clothing and fabrics: cotton, 21; Neolithic, 26; silk, 26, 35; weaving, 26, 28; fabric, 28; wool, 44
Clove (*Eugenia caryophylla*), 21

Cocklebur (*Xanthium strumarium*) 18
Coconut (*Cocos nucifera*), 19
Concubinage, 76, 78
Confucius, 144, 151, 172, 184. See also *Lun Yü*.
Conservatives, Shang, 103-106
Copper, 46
Cordage plants, 9, 11
Cotton (*Gossypium arboreum*, *G. herbaceum*), 21
Creel, Herrlee Glessner, 129
Cucumber (*Cucumis*), 10
Culinary arts, 51, 115-148; recipes, 124-126, 146-148; hierarchy of food, 134-143
Cultural Revolution, 39
Currency, 39

Darlington, C.D., 5, 10
Date, sour (*Spoudias auxilliaris*), 45, 122
Daylily (*Hemerocallis fulva*), 19
Divination, 105-106, 183, 195, 196. *See also* Scapulimancy
Douglas, Mary, 134
Dragons, 175, 180, 195
Drought, in myth, 164-165, 183, 196
Dualism: in kinship, 54; Shang society, 93-114; bronze art, 108-109; food preparation and meals, 141, 143. *See also* Chao-mu system, Yi-ting system, Yin and yang
Durian (*Durio zibethinus*), 20
Dynasty: definition, 189

Economy, 34, 35, 36, 51, 57, 189
Egyptian art, 175
Eight Delicacies, 126, 146-148
Eliade, Mircea, 195-196
Ellice Islands, 84n, 99-100
Endogamy, 99. *See also* Marriage
Erh-lang-p'o, Shih-lou (Shansi) site, 112
Etiquette, 132-134, 144
Euhemerisis, 166, 172, 174, 196
Eyde, D., and Postal, P., 92

Fagara, 122
Far East, definition, 1
Fecundity cult, 28
Fei Hsiao-t'ung, 54, 71
Feng-pi-t'ou (Taiwan) culture, 6
Feng Su T'ung, 159
Fertility ritual, 28
Fibrous plants, 11, 21
Firth, R., 119
Fish: fishing, 8-9, 11, 25, 28, 30, 122; as decorative motif, 144, 145, 175
"Five Elements," 142
Flake and blade technology, 2, 4, 23, 26
Flood: in myth, 164, 165
Food: preparation and serving, 115-148; importance in China, 118-121, 128
Formosa: excavations, 6, 10-11, 33. *See also* Taiwan
Frake, Charles, 119
Frankfort, Henri, 175
Fruits, 8, 9, 13, 19-20, 33, 121-122
Fu Hsi myth, 158, 169
Fu Ssu-nien, 168
Funafuti society, Ellice Islands, 84n, 99-100

Garlic (*Allium sativum*), 18, 121
Genealogy: Shang, 73, 79-89, 95-103; Chou, 88; Hsia, 101; of heroes, 170
Geology of North China, 23, 24
Gernet, Jacques, 118, 120
Ginger (*Zingibera officinale*), 20, 121
Ginkgo (*Ginkgo biloba*), 7
Glacial periods, 2-3, 23; postglacial era, 4, 5
Gods: Shang, 57; nature gods, 155, 157, 159, 169; and ancestors, 156-157, 160, 161, 163, 165, 166-170, 171, 190, 191-192, 193, 194, 195; and men, 159-163; contests of men against, 163-165; Eastern Chou, 193-194, 196; and animals, 195. *See also* Heaven, Shang Ti
Gorman, Chester, 10, 11, 46
Gourd: White (*Benincasa cerifera*), 18; serpent (*Trichosanthes anguina*), 18
Grain dishes, 134-142
Granet, Marcel, 89, 98
Greece: architecture, 49
Groundnut (*Arachis hypogaea*), 7, 15-16

Hai-men-k'ou, Chien-ch'uan (Yunnan) site, 40, 46
Han dynasty, 33, 117-118; art, 131; food vessels, 141, 142; literary texts, 152, 153, 161, 164, 165, 194; mythology, 158, 159; scholars, 172
Haudricourt, A.G., 13-14
Haw, 122
Hawthorn, Chinese (*Crataegus pinnatifida*), 19
Hazelnut, 122
Heaven: concept of, 156, 157, 158, 191-192
Hemp (*Canabis sativa*), 13, 21, 26, 28, 35
Herbs, 9, 122

Heroes: origin myths, 165-170, 171, 180; Eastern Chou, 183; and gods, 196
Historians, Chinese, 50, 51
Ho Ping-ti, 13
Hoabinhian culture, 3-4, 6, 33; stone assemblages, 10; pottery, 11
Hou-chi myth, 180
Hou-kang (Honan) site, 31
Hovenia dulcis, 122
Hsia dynasty, 47, 64, 86-87, 101, 160
Hsiao-t'un (Anyang) site, 93-94, 95, 110-112
Hsing (mythological clan), 75-76, 77
Hsing T'ien myth, 163-164
Hsi-pei-kang (Anyang) site, 93, 94-95, 102-103, 109-110, 111
Hsiu-shui culture, 43
Hsü Cheng, 158n, 159
Hsüan Chu, 157
Hu-shu (lower Yangtze) culture, 15
Hua Hsien (Shensi) sites, 28
Huai Nan Tzu, 142, 161, 164, 165, 194
Huai style, bronzes, 180, 181, 182, 183
Huang Shih-ch'iang, 39
Huang Ti (Yellow Emperor), 169, 170
Huang ts'ai, Ning-hsiang (Hunan) site, 112-113
Huangho (Yellow River) Basin: excavations, 4, 27; agriculture, 12, 25-34; emergence of civilization, 22, 34-38
Humanist movement: Eastern Chou, 172, 184, 193, 196
Hunting: cultures, 23, 24, 28, 30, 122; as sport, 51; decorative motifs of, 180

Implements. *See* Tools, Weapons
India, plant domestication, 6, 13, 15, 16
Indochina, 3, 11, 33. *See also* Southeast Asia
Industrial crops, 8, 9, 21
Industrial development, 59
Insects: as food, 122; as decorative motif, 175
Institute of Archaeology, Peking, 39
Iron: tools, 30, 60, 149

Jack-fruit (*Artocarpus integrifolia*), 19
Jacobsen, Thorkild, 191
Jade artifacts, 26, 31, 35
Jambu (*Eugenia javanica*), 20
Japan, 2, 4-5, 12
Java, Paleolithic culture, 2
Jen (*Perilla frutescens*), 121
Job's-tears (*Coix lachryma-jobi*), 9, 17
Jomon (Japan) culture, 4-5, 10
Jujube, Chinese (*Zizyphus vulgaris*), 20, 122
Jute: Chinese (*Abutilon avicinnae*), 21; *Corchorus capsularis*, 21

Ka fruit, 122
Kachin group of Upper Burma, 188
Kalanay ceramic complex, 6
Kale, Chinese (*Brassica alboglabra*), 18
Karlgren, Bernhard, 106-108, 109, 111, 176
Kao Ch'ü-hsün, 94
Kaoliang plant, 13, 26, 35
Keng soup, 123, 125, 135
Kingship: Shang, 51-53, 59, 96-97; royal succession, 53, 84, 99; identity of alternate generations, 79-89, 97-98, 99, 101; posthumous naming, 79, 80, 83, 87-88, 97-98, 101-102; feasts and food preparation, 116-117; ancestor cult, 156-157; Eastern Chou, 193, 194
Kinship groups, 184-195; Lungshanoid, 31, and political power, 59, 72-92; and mythology, 173. *See also* Clans, Kingship, Lineage system, Marriage
Knotweed (*Polygonum hydropiper*), 18
Kotamba (*Terminalia catappa*), 10, 20
Ku Chieh-kang, 150n, 166, 169
K'ua-fu myth, 163
Kuan Tzu, 132
Kudzu vine (*Pueroria thungbergiana*), 21
Kumquat (*Fortunella japonica*), 19
Kun myth, 47, 64, 165
Kung-kung myth, 164, 165
Kuo (state), 62, 63
Kuo Mo-jo, 167, 190
Kuo P'u, 160
Kuo Yü, 151, 162, 170, 185, 187, 194

Lactuca denticulata, 18
Land tenure, 70, 78, 186, 188
Language, 26-27, 35. *See also* Books, Writing
Lansoné (*Lansium domesticum*), 20
Lao Tzu, 151
Laos, ceramic complex, 6
Lard, 122
Leach, E.R., 188
Leek, Chinese (*Allium ramosum*), 19, 121
Legume crops, 7, 17
Lemon (*Citrus lemon*), 19
Lévi-Strauss, Claude, 115, 120, 149
Li Chi: on towns and cities, 69; on lineage system, 76, 78, 87, 89; on dualistic phenomena, 95n, 103, 110,

111; on meals and food preparation, 116, 117, 125, 126, 131-133, 135, 136-137, 139-140, 142-143; on mythology, 151, 156, 186, 187
Li Hsuan-po, 89. *See also* Li Tsung-t'ung
Li Hui-lin, 7-8, 12, 16, 121
Li Tsung-t'ung, 96, 98
Li Yün, 140
Liang-ch'eng-chen, Jih-chao (Shantung) site, 31
Liang-chu (Chekiang) culture, 6, 15, 43
Licent, Père Emile, 22
Lieh-tzu, 161
Lily (*Lilium tigrinium*), 18
Lime (*Citrus aurantifolia*), 19
Lin Hsiang Ju, 123
Lin Tsuifeng, 123
Lin Yutang, 119-120, 123
Lineage system: Yang-shao, 27; segmentation, 47, 53-54, 74, 78, 79-89, 95; royalty, 53-55; and political power, 54-55, 72-92; definition of, 70-71, 74-75; Shang, 98-99; rituals, 186-187. *See also* Clans, Kingship, Kinship, Marriage
Litchi (*Litchi chinensis*), 19
Literacy, 149. *See also* Books, Writing
Literature: Eastern Chou, 151-152, 161, 169, 171; Shang, 152, 170-171; Western Chou, 171. *See also* Mythology
Lithic technology, 2
Liu-li-ko, Huei Hsien (northern Honan) site, 112
Liu Pin-hsiung, 142
Longan (*Euphoria longana*), 20
Loquat (*Eriobotrya japonica*), 19
Loyang, 67, 149, 193
Lü Kuei, 101
Lü Shih Ch'un Ch'iu, 185n
Luffa (*Luffa acutangula*), 18
Lun Yü (*Confucian Analects*), 116, 133, 135, 136, 185
Lungshanoid cultures, 5, 6, 34, 56; agriculture, 7, 12, 14, 15, 16; traits of, 29-30, 189; Lungshanoid horizon, 29-34, 44; expansion of, 32-33; pottery, 37-38; radiocarbon dating, 43, 44, 46; walled villages, 66; ancestor cult, 75; scapulimancy, 183; kinship system, 189

Magicians, 163
Malaya, 2, 3, 6
Mallow (*Malva verticillata*), 18, 121
Malus prunifolia, 19
Manchuria, Pleistocene sites, 24
Manogosteen (*Garcinia mangostana*), 19
Marriage, 53, 54, 113; taboos, 76, 84, 185; royal, 83, 84, 85-86, 89, 96, 98, 99; cross-cousin, 89-92, 188
Masticatory crops, 20
Matriarchy, 75, 185n
Meat dishes, 125-126, 134-142
Melon (*Cucumis melo*), 15, 45, 121
Mencius, 58-59, 151
Meng Tzu, 57, 59, 116, 135, 160, 165, 194
Mesolithic cultures, 24, 25, 26, 33
Mesopotamian art, 175
Metallurgy, 46, 189; Lungshanoid, 30, 31, 33; bronze, 34, 35, 49; iron, 193. *See also* Bronze, Copper, Iron
Miao-ti-kou (Honan) culture, 5, 40, 43, 44, 169
Microblade tradition, 24
Microlithic technology, 2, 24n
Middleton, John, and Tait, David, 70, 74
Migration, 14, 15
Military establishment, 34, 51, 55, 193. *See also* Warfare
Millet, 9, 35; foxtail (*Setaria italica*), 12, 13, 15, 17, 27, 45, 121; broom-corn (*Panicum miliaceum*), 12, 13, 17, 27, 121; Japanese (*Echinochloa frumentacea*), 17; Neolithic, 26; Lungshanoid, 30, 33; *P. miliglutinosa*, 121; in meals, 135
Mo Tzu, 116, 118, 142, 144
Mongolia: Pleistocene sites, 24
Moon deities, 155, 156, 157, 160
Mounds, 32, 68
"Mousterian" flakes, 23
Mu T'ien Tzu Chuan, 152, 157, 160, 161
Mulberry (*Morus alba*), 8, 13, 21
Mumford, Lewis, 49
Mustard: water (*Brassica japonica*), 18, 45; leaf, 121
Myrica rubra, 19
Mythology, 149-173; and lineage system, 71, 75, 77; animals in, 143-144, 174-175, 180-183, 195-196; nature myths, 155-159, 172; Separation thesis, 157, 158; Transformation thesis, 157-158, 158-159; genesis myths, 157-158, 171, 180; paradisial world, 161; and natural calamities, 164-165; Shang and Chou, 180. *See also* Gods, Heroes

Nasturtium indicum, 18
National Taiwan Universtiy, excavation, 11
Neolithic cultures, 12, 13, 15, 34, 37-38, 56, 183, 189; excavations, 22, 25-26, 46, 75; "neolithic revolution," 25; traits of, 26-27, 35; subneolithic culture, 33; walled villages, 66
Non Nok Tha (Thailand) site, 46
Nü Wa myth, 158, 159
Nut crops, 10
Nutmeg (*Myristica fragrans*), 21

Oil crops, edible, 7, 10, 18
Olive, Chinese (*Canarium pimela*), 10, 20
Omaha system of cousin terminology, 92, 185
Onion, spring or Welsh (*Allium fistulosum*), 19, 121
Oracle: bones, 48, 75, 79, 80, 82, 86, 150, 155, 156, 157, 160, 164, 167-168, 185, 190; takers, 51; records, 54, 56, 57, 60, 100, 103-106. *See also* Divination, Scapulimancy
Oral tradition, 149, 153, 155, 161
Orange: mandarin (*Citrus reticulata*), 19; sour (*C. aurantium*), 19; sweet (*C. sinensis*), 19
Ōshima Riichi, 65

Palace, Shang, 34, 48, 49, 51, 52, 67, 116-117
Palawan: Paleolithic culture, 2
Paleolithic cultures, 2, 5, 23; excavations, 22, 23-24
P'an Ku myth, 158, 159n-160n
P'an-keng, Shang king, 49, 50, 52, 102, 103
Pan-shan culture, 28, 40
Pang (state), 62
Pao-chi Hsien site, 25
Patriarchy, 75, 76; patrilineal groups, 73, 185; patrisibs, 76, 84; patriclans, 185, 186, 187
Pea (*Pisum* or *Raphia*), 10
Peach (*Prunus persica*), 13, 15, 19, 45, 122
Peanut (*Arachis hypogaea*), 45. *See also* Groundnut
Pear, 122; sand (*Pyrus pyrifolia*), 13, 19
Pepper (*Piper nigrum*), 10, 21
Persimmon (*Diospyros kaki*), 20, 122
Phallic imagery, 75, 167, 186
Philippines, ceramic complex, 6
Philosophers, Chinese, 151
Phoenix, 167, 175, 180
Pi, 63-64
Pickling, 126
Pivot of the Four Quarters, The (Wheatley), 61n
Plants: domestication of, 1-2, 6-16, 17-21, 121; radiocarbon dating of, 44, 45
Pleistocene age, 24
Plum, Chinese (*Prunus salicina*), 19, 122
Poisons, 9
Political structure: Lungshanoid, 31; Shang, 34, 47, 51, 56, 57; centralization of, 34, 35, 36; and kinship system, 59, 70-71, 78, 173, 187, 188, 189, 191, 194, 195; and marriage regulations, 90-92, 188; and civilization, 189, 190; Eastern Chou, 193. *See also* Kingship
Pollen profile; Taiwan, 2, 3, 11, 15
Polynesia, 99-100
Population growth, 29, 31, 32, 35
Pottery: cord-marked, 3, 4, 5, 6, 11, 12, 15, 26, 27, 28, 33, 44; painted, 4, 5, 27, 28, 29, 37-38; paddy-husk imprinted, 15; tripods, 26, 27, 29; steamers, 26; forms, 27, 35; coiled, 28; molded, 28; domestic, 28, 126-128, 141, 142, 143, 144, 146; Yang-shao, 28; Lungshanoid, 29-30, 31, 33 35; use of pottery wheel, 31; "black pottery," 37-38; decoration of vessels, 143-144, 145; texts on, 150; animal motifs, 174
Priests, 31, 51, 163, 195
Progressives, Shang, 103-106
Public works, Lungshanoid, 30
Pummelo (*Citrus grandis*), 19

Radiocarbon dating, 23, 38-46
Radish (*Raphanus sativus*), 7
Ramage, 53
Rambutan (*Nephelium lappaceum*), 19
Ramie (*Boehmeria nivea*), 21
Recent period, 24
Religious system, 47; Yang-shao, 28; Lungshanoid, 31, 189; Shang, 34, 51, 57, 150, 189, 190, 191; Eastern Chou, 193-194. *See also* Gods, Mythology, Shang Ti
Renaissance movement: Eastern Chou, 172, 193
Reptiles: as food, 122; decorative motifs, 175
Rice: *Oryza sativa*, 9, 13-15, 17, 121;

remains, 14-15, 30, 46; cultivation and harvesting, 15, 26, 33, 35; Manchurian water rice (*Zizania latifolia*), 18; radiocarbon dating, 45; in meals, 133n-134n, 135-136
Ritual, 29, 31, 35, 36, 80, 97, 155, 160; vessels and objects, 26, 31, 35, 56, 107, 115, 142, 150, 186; Shang, 34, 105; ancestral, 100, 186; food and feasts, 116, 119, 130, 131, 132, 137, 139-140; animals, 143-144. *See also* Sacrifice
Root crops, 7, 9, 13, 14, 17, 33
Rosaceae family, 8
Royen, P. van, 10

Sa-Huynh (Vietnam and Laos) ceramic complex, 6
Sacrifice, 80, 88, 105, 140; human, 35, 48, 52-53, 55, 69, 94; and burials, 109; and food, 143; nature deities, 155
Salt, 122
San Li, 151
San Wu Li Chi, 158n
Sauces, 122, 126
Sauer, Carl, 9, 25
Scallion (*Allium bakeri*), 19
Scapulimancy, 26, 29, 31, 35, 183-184, 195-196
Science, 34, 47, 193
Sculpture: stone, 49; animal, 174, 175
Sesame (*Sesamum indicum orientale*), 15-16, 45
Sha-yüan assemblages, 24, 25
Shallot, Chinese (*Allium bakeri*), 121
Shamans, 31, 162-163, 195-196
Shan Hai Ching, 151, 157, 158-159, 160, 161, 162, 163, 165
Shang dynasty, 5, 47, 49, 189-190; conception of world, 51; cities, 61-71; kinship system, 72-92, 167, 184-195; dualism, 93-114; genealogy, 95-103; art, 106-108, 175-180; mythology, 149-173, 174-184, 195-196; oracle bones, 150, 151; literature, 150-151, 170-171; conflicts with Chou, 190-191; religion, 190, 191
Shang Chün Shu, 186, 194
Shang Sung, 167
Shang Ti (Supreme Being), 155, 156-157, 160, 163, 164, 165, 167, 169, 171, 189, 190, 191, 192, 193
Shellfish, 9, 122
Sheng Min, 140
Shengwen horizon, 27, 35
Shih Chang-ju, 93, 95, 111, 141-142
Shih Chi, 50, 86, 116, 142, 152, 164
Shih Ching, 54, 62, 65, 70, 87, 95n, 116, 121n-122n, 128-129, 131, 133, 137, 151, 155, 156n, 167, 168, 192n
Shih Pen, 79, 151-152, 170
Shih pien concept, 194
Shu Ching, 58, 62, 87, 95n, 151, 160, 162
Shui-tung-kou, Ordos (Ninghsia) site, 23
Shuo Wen, 159
Sian, 149, 193
Siberia; Paleolithic culture, 2
Sibs, mythological, 166
Silk, 13, 26, 28, 35, 150, 175
Sjara-osso-gol (Suiyuan) site, 23
Slavery, 35, 55
Smartweed (*Polygonum hydropiper*), 121
Social structure: status and role differentiation, 28, 29, 30; class differentiation, 34, 35; economic exploitation, 47, 57; stratification, 51, 53, 188, 189; life quality, 51-52, 55, 56-57; dualism in, 104; and power, 193
Sorghum, 9
Southeast Asia: plant domestication, 2, 6, 7, 8, 9, 13, 14, 17-21; ceramic tradition, 46
Soybean (*Glycine max*), 13, 17, 18, 26, 121
Specialization: Lungshanoid, 31; community, 34, 35-36; technical and industrial, 35, 47; Shang, 48, 59; cities, 68
Spices, 10, 21
Spinach, water (*Ipomoea aquatica*), 18
Ssu-ma Ch'ien, 50, 79, 80, 101, 152, 164
Stimulants, crops, 10
Stone: inventories, 3, 4, 5, 11, 15, 27, 56; Stone Age, 22; implements, 30, 33, 35; sculptures and carvings, 35, 49. *See also* Tools
Stuckenrath, Robert, 39
Subsistence patterns, 4, 8-9, 26
Sugarcane (*Saccharum offininarum*), 8, 20
Sui cities, 71
Sun: deities, 155, 156, 157; worship, 165
Sun Tso-yün, 169, 174
Sung period, 129, 144
Suo Yü, 152

Ta-ch'eng-shan (Hopei) site, 31

Ta Tai Li, 170
Ta-wen-k'ou (Shantung) culture, 5-6
Ta Yi, 101
Taboos, 76, 84, 137, 185
Taiwan: pollen profile, 2, 3, 11, 15; excavations, 5; radiocarbon dating, 38, 39, 42-43
Tallow tree, Chinese (*Sapium sebiferum*), 21
T'ang: Shang king, 49, 58, 116; cities, 71
T'ao-t'ieh mask motif, 176, 180
Taoism, 123n; and food, 139
Taro (*Colocasia antiquorum*), 9, 14, 17, 121
Taxation, 60
Te, concept of, 192, 194, 195
Tea: *Thea sinensis*, 20; oil (*Camellia oleifera*), 21
Technology, development of, 35, 47, 172, 186, 193
Teilhard de Chardin, Pierre, 23
Temples, 63, 64, 67, 68, 69-70, 71; ancestral, 87; arrangement of, 94, 95-96
Ten Heavenly Stems, 79, 81-83, 86, 87-88, 97, 101
Ten Suns, myth of, 164-165
Thailand, 3, 5, 6, 10, 16
Three Books of Rites (*Li Chi*, *Chou Li*, and *Yi Li*), 116, 117-118
Ti Hsin, Shang king, 102-103
T'ien (concept of Heaven), 191-192, 194
T'ien (farming fields), 61
T'ien Wen, 161, 164, 165
Tikopia society, 119
Ting Shan, 166, 185
Tools: lithic, 2; chopping, 2; pebble, 2, 3; ground and edge ground, 3; stone, 3, 4, 15, 26, 27, 30, 35; Hoabinhian, 4; carpenter, 11; knives, 15, 26, 27; Paleolithic, 23-24; composite, 24; Mesolithic, 26; axes, 27, 28; Yang-shao, 27; fishing, 28; Lungshanoid, 30; polished, 33. *See also* Flake and blade technology, Weapons
Totemic: ancestors, 174; clans, 185
Trade, 33, 34, 35
Traditions, regional, 33-34
Transformation thesis, 157-159, 180
Tso Chuan, 76, 87, 90, 95n, 118, 123n, 144, 185n, 186, 196
Tsu (lineage segment), 70, 72-74, 75, 76, 77
Tsukada Matsuo, 11
Tsung (lineage grade), 70, 74-75, 76, 77, 78
Tsung-fa system, 53-54, 187-188
Tu (state capital), 63-64
Tuber crops, 7, 9, 13, 14
Tung oil tree (*Aleurites cordata, A. fordii*), 21
Tung Tso-pin, 104-105
Turmeric (*Curcuma domestica*), 21
Turnip (*Brassica rapa*), 121
Turtles, 122, 183
Tze-yang Man, 42
Tzu clan, 53-54, 84, 98, 167, 170, 189, 190, 191, 195; mythic origins, 168, 193
Tzu Lu, 126

Urbanism, 23, 47, 60; characteristics and criteria, 34, 35, 36; urban revolution, 57, 59, 60; Shang, 59; and civilization, 189, 190. *See also* Cities
Utensils: for food, 126-128; decorative elements, 174

Varnish tree (*Rhus verniciflua*), 8, 21
Vavilov, N.I., 6-7, 121
Vegetable crops, 7-8, 18-19, 121
Vessels, 115-116, 141, 144, 186. *See also* Bronze, Culinary Arts, Pottery
Vietnam, ceramic complex, 6
Villages: patterns of settlement, 27, 29; Yang-shao, 28; expansion of in Huangho Basin, 29-34; walled, 30, 31-32; Lungshanoid, 30, 31, 35, 189; community specialization, 34, 35-36; Shang, 48
Vinegar, 122
Violet (*Viola verucunda)*, 18

Wampi (*Clausanea lansium*), 19
Warfare, development of, 29, 189; Yang-shao, 28; Lungshanoid, 32, 34, 35; Shang, 51, 55, 56, 57, 58; Chou, 59
Warring States period, 67, 142, 151, 152
Water caltrop or chestnut (*Trapa natans*), 7, 10, 15-16, 45; water chestnut (*Eleocharis tuberosa*), 17, 122
Water dropwort (*Oenanthe stolonifera*), 18
Water-shield (*Brasenia schreberi*), 18
Weapons, 35; Lungshanoid, 32; bronze, 55, 56, 57; Shang, 59; decorative elements, 174
Weaving, 26, 28
Weishui River: pottery remains, 4
Wen Wu Ting, king of Shang, 104
Wheat, 12, 13, 35, 121
Wheatley, Paul, 61n
Whitehead, Alfred, 37

Williamson, Robert W., 84, 99-100
Woodworking complex, 26, 30; food vessels, 141, 142; books, 149, 150; animal motifs in carving, 174-175
Wool, 144
Wright, Arthur F., 71
Writing, 34, 35, 47, 49, 152-153, 154, 189, 193
Wu, king of Chou, 95
Wu, Nelson, 68
Wu Ting, king of Shang, 100, 104, 105
Würm glacial, 23

Yale University, Taiwan excavation, 11
Yam, 9, 14; Chinese (*Dioscorea batatas*), 17; greater (*D. alata*), 17; *D. esculenta*, 17; yam bean (*Pachyrrhizus erosus*), 17
Yang K'uan, 169-170, 174
Yang-shao culture, 6, 12, 25-26, 40; pottery, 5, 29, 37-38, 44, 145; traits of, 27-29; settlements, 30; transition to Lungshanoid, 32; radiocarbon dating, 43, 44, 46
Yang-shao-ts'un, Mien-ch'ih Hsien (Honan) site, 22, 32, 75
Yangtze Valley: spread of civilization, 6, 46
Yayoi (Japan) culture, 5
Yellow River. *See* Huangho
Yen, Douglas, 10
Yen Tzu, 123n
Yen-shih (Honan) excavations, 47, 49, 66
Yi (settlement), 60-63, 64
Yi Chou Shu, 65, 185
Yi Li, 116, 117, 151
Yi Shih, 159n
Yi-ting system, 87-88, 89, 97-98, 98-99, 101, 102-103, 105
Yi the Archer, myth of, 165, 183, 196
Yin and *yang*, 114; in meals and food, 141, 142, 143; in mythology, 158. *See also* Dualism
Yin dynasty: bronze art, 106; tombs, 111
Yin-Shang dynasty, 34; burial, 31
Ying Shao, 159
Ying-p'u (Taiwan) culture, 15
Yü myth, 165, 169
Yü Yü, 187